WebAssembly:
The Definitive Guide
Safe, Fast, and Portable Code

Brian Sletten

Beijing · Boston · Farnham · Sebastopol · Tokyo

WebAssembly: The Definitive Guide

by Brian Sletten

Copyright © 2022 Bosatsu Consulting, Inc. All rights reserved.

Published by O'Reilly Media, Inc., 1005 Gravenstein Highway North, Sebastopol, CA 95472.

O'Reilly books may be purchased for educational, business, or sales promotional use. Online editions are also available for most titles (*http://oreilly.com*). For more information, contact our corporate/institutional sales department: 800-998-9938 or *corporate@oreilly.com*.

Acquisitions Editor: Suzanne McQuade
Development Editor: Angela Rufino
Production Editor: Kate Galloway
Copyeditor: Piper Editorial Consulting, LLC
Proofreader: JM Olejarz

Indexer: nSight, Inc.
Interior Designer: David Futato
Cover Designer: Karen Montgomery
Illustrator: Kate Dullea

December 2021:   First Edition

Revision History for the First Edition
2021-12-01:   First Release

See *http://oreilly.com/catalog/errata.csp?isbn=9781492089841* for release details.

978-1-492-08984-1

[LSI]

This book was born on a mountain of privilege during a period when many people didn't have the luxury of working from home. It is therefore dedicated to the frontline and essential workers who kept the lights on during a dark time.

Table of Contents

Preface

I believe WebAssembly is an ascendant technology that has the potential to transform the entire software development industry in one form or another. I do not believe WebAssembly is going to be transformative because I am writing a book on the topic. I'm writing a book on it because I believe it will be transformative.

Presumably you are interested in the technology as well. The problem is, I think I have less of an idea of who you are as a reader than many authors do. If this were a book about a particular programming language or a specific topic, there would be a self-selecting aspect to the audience and I could proceed apace. But WebAssembly is a much larger topic than most people realize, and I am trying to paint a very large picture with this book. Most of the other books that have been published have focused on a single aspect of it, and I can understand why.

Some of you might think WebAssembly is a technology for killing JavaScript. It isn't. Some of you may think it is about bringing applications to the browser. It is that, but it is also so much more. It is useful on the server side, in the video game world, as a plug-in mechanism, in support of serverless functions and edge computing, in embedded systems, for the blockchain, and in many other topics we will investigate together. This is the first attempt I know of to be this comprehensive with the topic, and I felt it was important to tell this more complete version.

In the lead-up to the publication of this book, I have mostly gotten positive support and excitement from people I have spoken to about the project. One limited form of pushback I have gotten is with respect to the title. Some folks felt it was premature to have "The Definitive Guide" for this new of a technology. That is a fair position to take, but because I am trying to describe an extremely big and encompassing technical landscape, I thought it was reasonable. I hope by the end of the book you agree.

All I ask is that you have an open mind and a bit of patience. WebAssembly touches a lot of languages, runtimes, and operational environments. In addition to teaching you about the low-level details, we will look at integrations with the dominant programming languages in this space and several different use cases. I have tried not to make too many assumptions about your background, so I have heavily annotated the text with breadcrumbs for further exploration and discovery via footnotes. If you are a more advanced developer just seeking details about WebAssembly, feel free to ignore these and don't take offense. I expect a rather wide audience will be at least perusing this book, and I want them to feel welcome, too.

If you are on the junior side development-wise, this will be a challenging book. But I have tried to make it possible for you to at least see what is going on. Consider the various links and references as a personal guide into a more sophisticated development reality. Don't get overwhelmed, just tackle things one at a time in whatever order interests you or makes sense. There is no single way into this industry, and however you get there is legitimate.

At the end of the day, WebAssembly is going to allow us to basically choose our programming languages and run them securely in just about any computational surface area. We have been promised this before, but I think this time it is more likely to come to fruition. Thank you for giving me the opportunity to explain why.

Conventions Used in This Book

The following typographical conventions are used in this book:

Italic
: Indicates new terms, URLs, email addresses, filenames, and file extensions.

`Constant width`
: Used for program listings, as well as within paragraphs to refer to program elements such as variable or function names, databases, data types, environment variables, statements, and keywords.

`Constant width bold`
: Shows commands or other text that should be typed literally by the user.

`Constant width italic`
: Shows text that should be replaced with user-supplied values or by values determined by context.

 This element signifies a tip or suggestion.

This element signifies a general note.

Using Code Examples

Supplemental material (code examples, exercises, etc.) is available for download at *https://github.com/bsletten/wasm_tdg*.

If you have a technical question or a problem using the code examples, please send email to *bookquestions@oreilly.com*.

This book is here to help you get your job done. In general, if example code is offered with this book, you may use it in your programs and documentation. You do not need to contact us for permission unless you're reproducing a significant portion of the code. For example, writing a program that uses several chunks of code from this book does not require permission. Selling or distributing examples from O'Reilly books does require permission. Answering a question by citing this book and quoting example code does not require permission. Incorporating a significant amount of example code from this book into your product's documentation does require permission.

We appreciate, but generally do not require, attribution. An attribution usually includes the title, author, publisher, and ISBN. For example: *"WebAssembly: The Definitive Guide* by Brian Sletten (O'Reilly). Copyright 2022 Bosatsu Consulting, Inc., 978-1-492-08984-1."

If you feel your use of code examples falls outside fair use or the permission given above, feel free to contact us at *permissions@oreilly.com*.

O'Reilly Online Learning

 For more than 40 years, *O'Reilly Media* has provided technology and business training, knowledge, and insight to help companies succeed.

Our unique network of experts and innovators share their knowledge and expertise through books, articles, and our online learning platform. O'Reilly's online learning platform gives you on-demand access to live training courses, in-depth learning paths, interactive coding environments, and a vast collection of text and video from O'Reilly and 200+ other publishers. For more information, visit *http://oreilly.com*.

How to Contact Us

Please address comments and questions concerning this book to the publisher:

O'Reilly Media, Inc.
1005 Gravenstein Highway North
Sebastopol, CA 95472
800-998-9938 (in the United States or Canada)
707-829-0515 (international or local)
707-829-0104 (fax)

We have a web page for this book, where we list errata, examples, and any additional information. You can access this page at *https://oreil.ly/webassemblyTDG*.

Email *bookquestions@oreilly.com* to comment or ask technical questions about this book.

For news and information about our books and courses, visit *http://oreilly.com*.

Find us on Facebook: *http://facebook.com/oreilly*

Follow us on Twitter: *http://twitter.com/oreillymedia*

Watch us on YouTube: *http://youtube.com/oreillymedia*

Acknowledgments

> At times, our own light goes out and is rekindled by a spark from another person. Each of us has cause to think with deep gratitude of those who have lighted the flame within us.
>
> —Albert Schweitzer

The myth of the sole author is persistent. I have huge communities of people to thank for the production of this book and their assistance to me along the way. On the other hand, I alone am responsible for any errors, inaccuracies, and problems.

I would like to start with the larger WebAssembly community. They have done a remarkable job in designing this platform without overdesigning it. It is a moving target, and they are busy juggling and balancing a surplus of competing issues. Along the way, they have left breadcrumbs to explain decisions and lay the foundations for the future. I would like to call special attention to the contributions of Lin Clark, who has emerged as one of my favorite technical communicators. Not only is she generous with her time, but her cartoon introductions to complex topics are also among the most effective forms of technical communication I have encountered.

The O'Reilly community is a top-notch organization. Everyone I have encountered there, current and past, has been a solid representative of the brand. I would like to thank Mike Loukides for his time in discussing my much larger views and suggesting we start with WebAssembly. My editors, Zan McQuade and Angela Rufino, have been stalwart champions of the project with the absolute patience of Job. Kate Galloway and her team helped me get it across the finish line. I would like to issue a special thank you to Karen Montgomery for the beautiful cover. My dogs' groomer is especially fond of it, as you caught the essence of this ridiculously lovable breed of Norwich terriers. For those who have questioned the relevance, they are the smallest working dog and—as I pitched it—small, fast, and portable, just like WebAssembly.

For insight into the various WebAssembly use cases, I interviewed several members of the projects and companies I mention throughout. In no particular order, I would like to express my gratitude to Tim McCallum, Aaron Turner, Connor Hicks, Liam Randall, Kevin Hoffman, Sasha Krsmanovic, Jérôme Laban, and Francois Tanguay.

The technical reviewers have honored me with the gift of their time and feedback. I would like to thank Dr. Sam Bail, Taylor Poindexter, Hannah Thoreson, Brooks Townsend, Jay Phelps, David Sletten, and the incomparable Dr. Venkat Subramaniam.

I was given a venue to begin speaking professionally about WebAssembly by Jay Zimmerman of the No Fluff Just Stuff conference series back in 2017. He and I knew it was too soon, but we wanted to start the conversation and I appreciate the opportunity. The rest of the speakers and attendees of this remarkable technical carnival have given me no end of inspiration and feedback, for which I am so much the richer.

My friends and family have encouraged and supported me in all things, a debt I will never be able to repay. No one has done more than my wife and friend, Kristin. She and our dogs, Loki and Freyja, have made this time at home during the pandemic not just bearable, but richer than my life on the road.

Thank you, all.

## CHAPTER 1

Introduction

Extraordinary claims require extraordinary evidence.
—Dr. Carl Sagan

This chapter will introduce WebAssembly and provide context for its expansive reach. In some sense it is a culmination of the evolution of the web over the last several decades. There is quite a bit of history to cover to make sense of it all. If you are not a fan of history and exposition, you can skip this chapter and go to directly to Chapter 2, but I hope you don't. I think it is important to understand why this technology is so important and where it came from.

What WebAssembly Offers

One of the greatest skills an engineer can develop is the ability to assess what a new technology brings to the table. As Dr. Fred Brooks of the University of North Carolina reminds us, there are no "silver bullets" (*https://oreil.ly/7isP5*); everything has trade-offs. Complexity is often not eliminated with a new technology, but is simply moved somewhere else. So when something does actually change what is possible or how we do our work in a positive direction, it deserves our attention and we should figure out why.

When trying to understand the implications of something new, I usually start by trying to determine the motivation of those behind it. Another good source of insight is where an alternative has fallen short. What has come before, and how does it influence this new technology we are trying to decipher? As in art and music, we are constantly borrowing good ideas from multiple sources, so to truly understand why WebAssembly deserves our attention and what it provides, we must first look at what has preceded it and how it makes a difference.

In the paper that formally introduced the world to WebAssembly, the authors indicate that the motivation was about rising to meet the needs of modern, web-delivered software in ways that JavaScript alone could not.[1] Ultimately, it was a quest to provide software that is:

- Safe
- Fast
- Portable
- Compact

In this vision, WebAssembly is centered at the intersection of software development, the web, its history, and how it delivers functionality in a geographically distributed space. Over time, the idea has expanded dramatically beyond this starting point to imagine a ubiquitous, safe, performant computational platform that touches just about every aspect of our professional lives as technologists. WebAssembly will impact the worlds of client-side web development, desktop and enterprise applications, server-side functionality, legacy modernization, games, education, cloud computing, mobile platforms, Internet of Things (IoT) ecosystems, serverless and microservices initiatives, and more. I hope to convince you of this over the course of this book.

Our deployment platforms are more varied than ever, so we need portability at both the code and application levels. A common instruction set or byte code target can make algorithms work across various environments because we just need to map logical steps to how they can be expressed on a particular machine architecture. Programmers use application programming interfaces (APIs) such as OpenGL,[2] POSIX,[3] or Win32[4] because they provide the functionality to open files, spawn subprocesses, or draw things to the screen. They are convenient and reduce the amount of code a developer needs to write, but they create a dependency on the presence of libraries to provide the functionality. If the API is not available in a target environment, the application will not run. This was one of the ways Microsoft was able to use its

---

1 Andreas Haas et al., "Bringing the Web Up to Speed with WebAssembly," presented at the 38th ACM SIG-PLAN Conference on Programming Language Design and Implementation, June 2017, *http://dx.doi.org/ 10.1145/3062341.3062363*.

2 For many years, OpenGL was the defining standard for portable 3D graphics applications. These days it is being supplanted by more modern APIs such as Vulkan and Metal, but you can learn more about the standards on the OpenGL website (*https://www.opengl.org*).

3 The Portable Operating System Interface (POSIX) (*https://oreil.ly/H5l9c*) is a collection of IEEE standards for defining common application functionality so that it works across multiple operating systems.

4 Win32 (*https://oreil.ly/YACjw*) is one part of a larger collection of APIs that provide developers with access to common functionality available from the Windows operating systems.

strength in the operating system marketplace to dominate in the application suite space as well. On the other hand, open standards can make it easier to port software into different environments.

Another issue with the runtime side of the software we are building is that different hosts have different hardware capabilities (number of cores, presence of GPUs) or security restrictions (whether files can be opened or network traffic can be sent or received). Software often adapts to what is available by using features-testing approaches to determine what resources an application can take advantage of, but this often complicates the business functionality. We simply cannot afford the time and money needed to rewrite software for multiple platforms constantly. Instead, we need better strategies for reuse. We also need this flexibility without the complexity of modifying the code to support the platform on which it will run. Making the code different for different host environments increases its complexity and complicates testing and deployment strategies.

After several decades, the value proposition of open source software is clear. We gravitate toward valuable, reusable components written by other developers as a means of satisfying our own needs.[5] However, not all available code is trustworthy, and we open ourselves up to software supply chain attacks when we execute untrusted bits we have downloaded from the internet. We become vulnerable to the risks, business impacts, and personal costs of insecure software systems through phishing attacks, data breaches, malware, and ransomware.

Until now, JavaScript has been the only way to solve some of these problems. When it is run in a sandboxed environment, it gives us some manner of security. It is ubiquitous and portable. The engines have gotten faster. The ecosystem has exploded into an avalanche of productivity. Once you leave the confines of browser-based protections, however, we still have security concerns. There is a difference between JavaScript code running as a client and JavaScript running on the server. The single-threaded design complicates long-running or highly concurrent tasks. Due to its origins as a dynamic language, there are several classes of optimizations that are available to other programming languages that are, and will remain, unavailable as options to even the fastest and most modern JavaScript runtimes.

Additionally, it is too easy to add JavaScript dependencies and not realize how much baggage and risk are being pulled in transitively. Developers who do not take the time to consider these decisions carefully end up encumbering every aspect of upstream software testing, deployment, and use. Each of these scripts has to be loaded and validated once it is transferred over the network. This slows down the time to use and

---

5 This technique allows a decision-maker to establish minimum criteria for deciding when their needs are being met. The goal of satisficing (*https://oreil.ly/KgXx6*) is not to find a perfect solution, but one that is acceptable given the situation at hand.

makes everything feel sluggish. When a dependent package is modified or removed, it has the potential to disrupt enormous amounts of deployed software.[6]

There is a perception among casual observers that WebAssembly is an assault on JavaScript, but that simply is not the case. Sure, you will be able to avoid JavaScript if you want to, but it is mostly about giving you options to solve problems in the language of your choice without requiring a separate runtime or having to care what language another piece of software is written in. It is already possible to use a WebAssembly module without knowing how it was built. This is going to increase the lifetime of business value we get out of our software and yet simultaneously allow us to innovate in adopting new languages without impacting everything else.

We have experienced several tools, languages, platforms, and frameworks over the course of the past several decades that have attempted to solve these problems, but WebAssembly represents one of the first times we are getting it right. Its designers are not attempting to overspecify anything. They are learning from the past, embracing the web, and applying problem-space thinking to what is ultimately a hard and multi-dimensional problem. Let's look at the formative influences on this exciting new technology before we dive into it further.

History of the Web

There is a running joke in the WebAssembly community that WebAssembly is "neither web nor assembly."[7] While this is true on some levels, the name is suggestive enough of what it provides. It is a target platform with a series of instructions that are vaguely assemblyesque.[8] The fact that WebAssembly modules are frequently going to be delivered over the web as another type of URL-addressable resource justifies the inclusion of the word *Web* in the name.

One of the main distinctions between "conventional software development" and "web development" is that there is effectively no installation required with the latter once you have a browser available. This is a game-changer in terms of costs to deliver and the ability to quickly turn new releases around in the face of bugs and feature requests. When couched in other cross-platform technology ecosystems such as the internet and the web, it makes supporting multiple hardware and software environments much easier too.

---

6 The Wikipedia page on npm (*https://oreil.ly/RRTC9*) highlights several cases where broken dependencies have had large impacts.

7 Best anyone can tell it was J.F. Bastien (*https://oreil.ly/l5ATA*) who first said it, but even he is not sure.

8 Assembly language (*https://oreil.ly/Ymw8q*) is a low-level programming language usually associated with a particular machine's processor architecture and instruction set.

Sir Tim Berners-Lee, the inventor of the World Wide Web, worked at the European Organization for Nuclear Research (CERN), where he submitted a proposal for interlinking documents, images, and data in the pursuance of CERN's larger research goals.[9] Even though the impact is clear in hindsight, he had to advertise his ideas internally several times before he was asked to act on them.[10] As an organization, CERN was represented by dozens of research facilities around the world, which sent scientists with their own computers, applications, and data. There was no real capacity to force everyone to use the same operating systems or platforms, so he recognized the need for a technical solution to solve the problem.

Prior to the web, there were services such as Archie,[11] Gopher,[12] and WAIS,[13] but he imagined a more user-friendly platform that was ultimately engendered as an application-level innovation at the top of the internet's layered architecture. He also took ideas from the Standard Generalized Markup Language (SGML) and made them the basis of the HyperText Markup Language (HTML).[14]

The result of these designs quickly became the major mechanism for delivering information, documentation, and eventually application functionality to the world. It did so without requiring the various stakeholders to agree on specific technologies or platforms by defining the exchange of standards, and included both how requests were made and what was returned in response. Any piece of software that understood the standards could communicate with any other piece of software that did as well. This gives us freedom of choice and the ability to evolve either side independent of the other.

Origins of JavaScript

The web's interaction model is called Hypertext Transfer Protocol (HTTP). It is based upon a constrained set of verbs for exchanging text-based messages. While it was a simple and effective model that was easy to implement, it was quickly seen to be inadequate for the task of interactive, modern applications because of inherent latencies in returning to the server constantly. The idea of being able to send code down to the

---

9 The name CERN comes from the French *Conseil Européen pour la Recherche Nucléaire*. Its many exciting projects are detailed on its homepage (*https://home.cern*).

10 On his own time!

11 Archie (*https://oreil.ly/kgQKI*) was an early search engine for helping people find files on FTP servers.

12 Gopher (*https://oreil.ly/OgxGb*) was an exciting precursor to the HTTP-based web we have become dependent upon.

13 Wide Area Information Server (WAIS) (*https://oreil.ly/n8XCt*) was another early system for searching for and requesting text information in distributed systems.

14 SGML (*https://oreil.ly/Q665x*) is an ISO standard for defining structured, declarative documents that served as the basis of HTML, DocBook, and LinuxDoc.

browser has always been compelling. If it ran on the user's side of the interaction, not every activity would require a return to the server. This would make web applications dramatically more interactive, responsive, and enjoyable to use. How to achieve this was not entirely clear, though. Which programming language would make the most sense? How would we balance expressive power with shallow learning curves so more individuals could participate in the development process? Which languages performed better than others, and how would we protect sensitive resources on the client side from malicious software?

Most of the innovation in the browser space was originally driven by Netscape Communications Corp. Believe it or not, Netscape Navigator was originally a paid piece of software, but the company's larger interest was in selling server-side software.[15] By extending what was possible on the client, it could create and sell more powerful and lucrative server functionality.

At the time, Java was emerging from its beginnings as an embedded language for consumer devices, but it did not yet have much of a track record of success. It was a compelling idea as a simplified version of C++ that ran on a virtual platform and was therefore inherently cross-platform. As an environment designed to run software downloaded over the network, it had security built in via language design, sandboxed containers, and fine-grained permission models.

Porting applications between various operating systems was tricky business, and the prospect of not needing to do so created a frenzy around what the future of software development would be. Sun Microsystems found itself in the enviable position of having a solution to a perfect storm of problems and opportunities. Given this potential, discussions were underway to bring Java to the browser, but it was not clear what that deal would look like or when it would land.

As an object-oriented programming (OOP) language, Java contained sophisticated language features such as threads and inheritance. There was concern at Netscape that this might prove too difficult for nonprofessional software developers to master, so the company hired Brendan Eich to create a "Scheme[16] for the browser," imagining an easier, lightweight scripting language.[17] Brendan had the freedom to make some decisions about what he wanted to include in the language, but he was also under pressure to get it done as quickly as possible. A language for interactive applications was seen as a crucial step forward for this emerging platform, and everyone wanted it

---

15 I bought a license for Netscape 1.0 Silicon Graphics IRIX at the time. I still have the CD floating around someplace for…historical reasons.

16 Scheme (*https://oreil.ly/4NmPN*) is a fairly lightweight version of Lisp.

17 There is a nice summary of the early history of JavaScript online (*https://oreil.ly/HxiNS*).

yesterday. As Sebastián Peyrott notes in the blog post, "A Brief History of JavaScript," what emerged was "a premature lovechild of Scheme and Self, with Java looks."[18]

Initially JavaScript in the browser was limited to simple interactions such as dynamic menus, pop-up dialogs, and responding to button clicks. These were significant advances over roundtrips to the server for every action, but they were still toys compared to what was possible on desktop and workstation machines at the time.

The company I worked for during the early days of the web created the first whole-earth visualization environment, involving terabytes of terrain information, hyperspectral imagery, and pulling video frames from drone videos.[19] This required Silicon Graphics workstations initially, of course, but it was able to run on PCs with consumer-grade graphics processing units (GPUs) within a couple of years. Nothing like that was remotely possible on the web back then, although, thanks to WebAssembly, that is no longer true.[20]

There was simply no confusing real software development with web development. As we have noted, though, one of the nice things about the separation of concerns between the client and the server was that the client could evolve independently of the server. While Java and the Java Enterprise model came to dominate the backend, JavaScript evolved in the browser and eventually became the dominant force that it is.

Evolution of the Web Platform

As Java applets and JavaScript became available in the Netscape browser, developers began to experiment with dynamic pages, animations, and more sophisticated user interface components. For years these were still just toy applications, but the vision had appeal and it was not difficult to imagine where it could eventually lead.

Microsoft felt the need to keep up but was not overly interested in directly supporting its competitors' technologies. It (rightly) felt that this web development might eventually upend its operating system dominance. When Microsoft released Internet Explorer with scripting support, the company called it JScript to avoid legal issues and reverse-engineered Netscape's interpreter. Microsoft's version supported interaction with Windows-based Component Object Model (COM) elements and had other twists that made it easy to write incompatible scripts between the browsers. Its initial support of the efforts to standardize JavaScript as ECMAScript waned for a while and

---

18 Self (*https://oreil.ly/hSGMo*) is an object-oriented programming language that influenced JavaScript's prototype-based inheritance.

19 Autometric (*https://oreil.ly/ff3sc*) had a wild background involving Paramount Pictures, the Trinitron tube, and helping NASA decide where to land on the moon! It has since been purchased by Boeing.

20 Google Earth (*https://oreil.ly/sIlwP*) now runs in the browser.

eventually the Browser Wars began.[21] This was a frustrating time for developers and ultimately involved anticompetitive lawsuits against Microsoft by the US government.

As Netscape's fortunes waned, Internet Explorer began to dominate the browser space and cross-platform innovation subsided for a while even as JavaScript went through the standardization process. Java applets became widely used in some circles, but they ran in a sandboxed environment, so it was trickier to use them as the basis for driving dynamic web page activity. You could certainly use Sun's graphics and user interface APIs to do productive and fun things, but they ran in a separate memory space than the HTML Document Object Model (DOM).[22] They were incompatible and had different programming and event models. User interfaces did not look the same between the sandboxed elements and the web elements. It was overall a wholly unsuitable development experience.

Other nonportable technologies such as ActiveX became popular in the Microsoft web development space. Macromedia's Flash became Adobe's Flash and had a short but active period of popularity for about a decade. The problems remained with all of these secondary options, however. The memory spaces were walled off from each other and the security models were less robust than anyone had hoped. The engines were new and under constant development, so bugs were common. ActiveX provided code-signing protections but no sandboxing, so rather terrifying attacks became possible if certificates could be forged.

Firefox emerged from Mozilla as a viable competitor from the ashes of Netscape. It and Google's Chrome eventually became suitable alternatives to Internet Explorer. Each camp had its adherents, but there was a growing interest in solving the incompatibilities between them. The introduction of choice in the browser space forced each of the vendors to work harder and do better to outshine each other as a means of achieving technical dominance and attracting market share.

As a result, JavaScript engines got significantly faster. Even though HTML 4 was still "quirky" and painful to use across browsers and platforms, it was starting to be possible to isolate those differences. The combination of these developments and a desire to work within the structures of the standards-based environments encouraged Jesse James Garrett (*https://oreil.ly/L0DCk*) to imagine a different approach to web development. He introduced the term *Ajax*, which stood for the combination of a set of standards: asynchronous JavaScript and XML. The idea was to let data from backend systems flow into the frontend applications, which would respond dynamically to the

---

21 While browser vendors tend to work together more closely on standards these days, for a while they competed fiercely. This time period is discussed on Wikipedia (*https://oreil.ly/Rmg9i*).

22 The DOM (*https://oreil.ly/OpTD5*) is the tree structure of a web page or application that is rendered by the browser. It is often sent in a declarative textual form from server to client as HTML, but JavaScript is able to manipulate it in the browser.

new inputs. By working at the level of manipulating the DOM rather than having a separate, sandboxed user interface space, browsers could become universal application consumers in web-based client-server architectures.

The long-suffering HTML 5 standardization process had begun during this period as well in an attempt to improve consistency across browsers, introduce new input elements and metadata models, and provide hardware-accelerated 2D graphics and video elements, among other features. The convergence of the Ajax style, the standardization and maturation of ECMAScript as a language, easier cross-browser support, and an increasingly feature-rich web-based environment caused an explosion of activity and innovation. We have seen innumerable JavaScript-based application frameworks come and go, but there was a steady forward momentum in terms of what was possible. As developers pushed the envelope, the browser vendors improved their engines to allow the envelope to be pushed further still. It was a virtuous cycle that ushered in new visions of the potential for safe, portable, zero-installation software systems.

As other obstacles and limitations were removed, this strange little language at the heart of it all became an increasingly high-inertia drag on forward motion. The engines were becoming world-class development environments with better tools for debugging and performance analysis. New programming paradigms such as the Promise-based style allowed better modularized and asynchronous-friendly application code to achieve powerful results in JavaScript's notoriously single-threaded environment.[23] But the language itself was incapable of the kinds of optimizations that were possible in other languages such as C or C++. There were simply limits on what was going to be possible from a language-performance perspective.

The web platform standards continued to advance with the development and adoption of technologies such as WebGL[24] and WebRTC.[25] Unfortunately, JavaScript's performance limitations made it ill suited to extend the browsers with features involving low-level networking, multithreaded code, and graphics and streaming video codecs.

The platform's evolution required the painful slog of the W3C member organizations to decide what was important to design and build and then roll it out in the various browser implementations. As people became ever more interested in using the web as a platform for heavier-weight, interactive applications, this process was seen as increasingly untenable. Everything either had to be written (or rewritten) in

---

23 Promises (*https://oreil.ly/lcozC*) (or futures) allow developers relatively simple programming models while still providing concurrent-enabled applications.

24 WebGL (*https://oreil.ly/pM90T*) brought a similar model of 3D graphics from the OpenGL world to the web.

25 WebRTC (*https://oreil.ly/7JRIc*) provides mechanisms for establishing permissioned access to cameras and microphones as well as encrypted peer-to-peer connections.

JavaScript or the browsers had to standardize the behavior and interfaces, which could mean it would take years to realize new advancements.

It was for these and other reasons that Google began to consider an alternative approach to safe, fast, and portable client-side web development.

Native Client (NaCl)

In 2011, Google released a new open source project called Native Client (NaCl). The idea was to provide near-native speed execution of code in the browser while running in a limited privilege sandbox for safety reasons. You can think of it as a bit like ActiveX with a real security model behind it. The technology was a good fit for some of Google's larger goals such as supporting ChromeOS and moving things away from desktop applications and into web applications. It was not initially meant to extend the capabilities of the open web for everyone.

The use cases were mainly to support browser-based delivery of computationally intensive software such as:

- Games
- Audio and video editing systems
- Scientific computing and CAD systems
- Simulations

The initial focus was on C and C++ as source languages, but because it was based upon the LLVM compiler toolchain,[26] it would be possible to support additional languages that could generate the LLVM Intermediate Representation (IR).[27] This will be a recurring theme in our transition to WebAssembly, as you will see.

There were two forms of distributable code here. The first was the eponymous NaCl, which resulted in "nexe" modules that would target a specific hardware architecture (e.g., ARM or x86-64) and could only be distributed through the Google Play store. The other was a portable form called PNaCl[28] that would be expressed in LLVM's Bitcode format, making it target independent. These were called "pexe" modules and would need to be transformed into a native architecture in the client's host environment.

---

26 LLVM (*https://llvm.org*) does not stand for anything, but it is an extremely influential toolchain you should know more about. We will mention it frequently in this book.

27 Normally, software is compiled to a binary, executable form. The IR allows it to exist in a parsed, structured form for the purposes of optimization, among other reasons.

28 Pronounced "pinnacle."

The technology was successful in the sense that the performance demonstrated in the browser was only minimally off of native execution speeds. By using software fault isolation (SFI) techniques, it was possible to download high-performance, secure code from the web and run it in browsers. Several popular games such as *Quake* and *Doom* were compiled to this format to show what was ultimately possible. The problem was that the NaCl binaries would need to be generated and maintained for each target platform and would only run in Chrome. They also ran in an out-of-process space, so they could not directly interact with other Web APIs or JavaScript code.

While running in limited-privilege sandboxes was achievable, it did require static validation of the binary files to ensure that they did not attempt to invoke operating system services directly. The generated code had to follow certain address boundary-alignment patterns to make sure it did not violate allocated memory spaces.

As indicated above, the PNaCl modules were more portable. The LLVM infrastructure could generate either the NaCl-native code or the portable Bitcode without modifying the original source. This was a nice outcome, but there is a difference between code portability and application portability. Applications require the APIs that they rely upon to be available in order to work. Google provided an application binary interface (ABI) called the Pepper APIs[29] for low-level services such as 3D graphics libraries, audio playback, file access (emulated over IndexedDB or LocalStorage), and more. While PNaCl modules could run in Chrome on different platforms because of LLVM, they could only run in browsers that provided suitable implementations of the Pepper APIs. While Mozilla had originally expressed interest in doing so, they eventually decided they wanted to try a different approach that came to be known as asm.js. NaCl deserves a tremendous amount of credit for moving the industry in this direction, but it was ultimately too fiddly and too Chrome-specific to carry the open web forward. Mozilla's attempt was more successful on that front even if it did not provide the same level of performance that the native client approach did.

asm.js

The asm.js project (*https://asmjs.org*) was at least partially motivated by an attempt to bring a better gaming story to the web. This soon expanded to include a desire to allow arbitrary applications to be delivered securely to browser sandboxes without having to substantively modify the existing code.

As we have previously discussed, the browser ecosystem was already advancing to make 2D and 3D graphics, audio handling, hardware-accelerated video, and more available in standards-based, cross-platform ways. The idea was that operating within that environment would allow applications to use any of those features that were

---

29 Because, NaCl...get it?

defined to be invoked from JavaScript. The JavaScript engines were efficient and had robust sandboxed environments that had undergone significant security audits, so no one felt like starting from scratch there. The real issue remained the inability to optimize JavaScript ahead-of-time (AOT) so runtime performance could be improved even further.

Because of its dynamic nature and lack of proper integer support, there were several performance obstacles that could not meaningfully be managed until the code was loaded into the browser. Once that happened, just-in-time (JIT) optimizing compilers were able to speed things up nicely, but there were still inherent issues like slow bounds-checked array references. While JavaScript in its entirety could not be optimized ahead-of-time, a subset of it could be.

The exact details of what that means are not super relevant to our historical narrative, but the end result is. asm.js also used the LLVM-based clang[30] frontend parser via the Emscripten toolchain.[31] Compiled C and C++ code is very optimizable ahead-of-time, so the generated instructions can be made very fast through existing optimization passes. LLVM represents a clean, modular architecture, so pieces of it can be replaced, including the backend generation of machine code. In essence, the Emscripten team could reuse the first two stages (parsing and optimization) and then emit this subset of JavaScript as a custom backend. Because the output was all "just JavaScript," it would be much more portable than the NaCl/PNaCl approach. The trade-off, unfortunately, was in performance. It represented a significant improvement over straight JavaScript but was not nearly as performant as Google's approach. It was good enough to amaze developers, though. Beyond the modest performance improvements, however, the mere fact that you could deploy existing C and C++ applications into a browser with reasonable performance and virtually no code changes was compelling. While there were extremely compelling demos involving the Unity engine,[32] let's look at a simple example. "Hello, World!" seems like a good place to start:

```
#include <stdio.h>
int main() {
  printf("Hello, world!\n");
  return 0;
}
```

Notice there is nothing unusual about this version of the classic program. If you stored it in a file called *hello.c*, the Emscripten toolchain would allow you to emit a

---

30 Clang (*https://clang.llvm.org*) is an LLVM compiler toolsuite for C, C++, and Objective-C.

31 We will learn more about Emscripten (*https://emscripten.org*) over the course of the book, but if you are curious.

32 Getting a zero-installation gaming experience in the browser is driving much of this innovation. You can see an example of the Unity engine using WebGL in the browser (*https://oreil.ly/qoDTv*).

file called *a.out.js*,[33] which can be run directly in Node.js or, via some scaffolding, in a browser:

```
brian@tweezer ~/s/w/ch01> emcc hello.c
brian@tweezer ~/s/w/ch01> node a.out.js
Hello, world!
```

Pretty cool, no?

There's only one problem:

```
brian@tweezer ~/s/w/ch01> ls -lah a.out.js
-rw-r--r--  1 brian  staff    119K Aug 17 19:08 a.out.js
```

At 119 kilobytes, that is an awfully large "Hello, World" program! A quick look at the native executable might give you a sense of what is going on:

```
brian@tweezer ~/s/w/ch01> clang hello.c
brian@tweezer ~/s/w/ch01> ls -lah a.out
-rwxr-xr-x 1 brian  staff    48K Aug 17 19:11 a.out
```

Why is our supposedly optimized JavaScript program close to three times bigger than the native version? It is not just because as a text-based file, JavaScript is more verbose. Look at the program again:

```
#include <stdio.h>  ❶
int main() {
  printf("Hello, world!\n");  ❷
  return 0;
}
```

❶ The header identifies the source for standard IO-related function definitions.

❷ The reference to the `printf()` function will be satisfied by a dynamic library loaded at runtime.

If we look at the symbols defined in the compiled executable using nm, we will see that the definition of the `printf()` function is not contained in the binary.[34] It is marked "U" for "undefined":

```
brian@tweezer ~/s/w/ch01> nm -a a.out
0000000100002008 d __dyld_private
0000000100000000 T __mh_execute_header
0000000100000f50 T _main
                 U _printf
                 U dyld_stub_binder
```

---

33 Node.js is an extremely popular server-side JavaScript environment that we will discuss more in Chapter 8.

34 nm is a Unix command to display the symbol table of an executable file.

When Clang generated the executable, it left a placeholder reference to the function that it expects to be provided by the operating system. There is no standard library available in this way for a browser, at least not in the dynamically loadable sense, so the library function and anything it needs have to be provided. Additionally, this version cannot talk directly to the console in a browser, so it will need to be given hooks to call into a function such as the browser's `console.log()` functionality. In order to work in the browser, the functionality has to be shipped with the application, which is why it ends up being so big.

This highlights nicely the difference between portable code and portable applications, another common theme in this book. For now, we can marvel that it works at all, but there is a reason this book is not called *asm.js: The Definitive Guide*. asm.js was a remarkable stepping-stone that demonstrated it was possible to generate reasonably performant sandboxed JavaScript code from various optimizable languages. The JavaScript itself could be optimized further as well in ways that the superset could not. By being able to generate this subset through LLVM-based toolchains and a custom backend, the level of effort was much smaller than it might otherwise have been.

asm.js represents a nice fallback position for browsers that do not support the WebAssembly standards, but it is now time to set the stage for the subject of the book.

Rise of WebAssembly

With NaCl, we found a solution that provided sandboxing and performance. With PNaCl, we found platform portability but not browser portability. With asm.js, we found browser portability and sandboxing, but not the same level of performance. We also were limited to dealing with JavaScript, which meant we could not extend the platform with new features (e.g., efficient 64-bit integers) without first changing the language itself. Given that this was governed by an international standards organization, this was unlikely to be an approach with quick turnarounds.

Additionally, JavaScript has certain issues with how browsers loaded and validated it from the web. The browser has to wait until it finishes downloading all of the referenced files before it starts to validate and optimize them (while further optimizations will require us to wait until the application is already running). Given what we have already said about how developers encumber their applications with ridiculously large amounts of transitive dependencies, the network transfer and load-time performance of JavaScript is another bottleneck to overcome beyond the established runtime issues.

After seeing what was possible with these partial solutions, there arose a strong appetite for high-performance, sandboxed, portable code. Various stakeholders in the browser, web standard, and JavaScript environments felt a need for a solution that worked within the confines of the existing ecosystem. There had been a tremendous amount of work done to get the browsers as far as they had gone. It was entirely possible to create dynamic, attractive, and interactive applications across operating system platforms and browser implementations. With just a bit more effort, it seemed possible to merge these visions together into a unifying, standards-based approach.

It was under these circumstances in 2015 that none other than Brendan Eich, the creator of JavaScript, announced that work had begun on WebAssembly.[35] He highlighted a few specific reasons for the effort and called it a "binary syntax for low-level safe code, initially co-expressive with asm.js, but in the long run able to diverge from JS's semantics, in order to best serve as common object-level format for multiple source-level programming languages."

He continued: "Examples of possible longer-term divergence: zero-cost exceptions, dynamic linking, call/cc. Yes, we are aiming to develop the Web's polyglot-programming-language object-file format."

As to why these various parties were interested in this, he offered this justification: "asm.js is great, but once engines optimize for it, the parser becomes the hot spot— very hot on mobile devices. Transport compression is required and saves bandwidth, but decompression before parsing hurts."

And finally, perhaps the most surprising part of the announcement was who was to be involved:

> A W3C Community Group, the WebAssembly CG, open to all. As you can see from the GitHub logs, WebAssembly has so far been a joint effort among Google, Microsoft, Mozilla, and a few other folks. I'm sorry the work was done via a private GitHub account at first, but that was a temporary measure to help the several big companies reach consensus and buy into the long-term cooperative game that must be played to pull this off.

In short order, other companies such as Apple, Adobe, AutoCAD, Unity, and Figma got behind the effort. This vision that had started decades before and had involved no end of conflict and self-interest was transforming into a unified initiative to finally bring us a safe, fast, portable, and *web-compatible* runtime environment.

There was no end to the potential confounding complexities involved in shepherding this platform into existence. It was not entirely clear exactly what should be specified up front. Not every language supports threads natively. Not every language uses exceptions. C/C++ and Rust were examples of languages that had runtimes that did not require garbage collection. The devil is always in the details, but the will to collaborate was there. And, as they say, where there is a will, there is a way.

---

35 Brendan Eich, "From ASM.JS to WebAssembly," June 17, 2015, *https://brendaneich.com/2015/06/from-asm-js-to-webassembly*.

Over the next year or so, the CG became a W3C Working Group (WG), which was tasked with defining actual standards. They made a series of decisions to define a Minimum Viable Product (MVP) WebAssembly platform that would be supported by all major browser vendors. Additionally, the Node.js community was excited as this could provide a solution to the drudgery of managing native libraries for the portions of Node applications that needed to be written in a lower-level language. Rather than having dependencies on Windows, Linux, and macOS libraries, a Node.js application could have a WebAssembly library that could be loaded into the V8 environment and converted to native assembly code on the fly. Suddenly, WebAssembly seemed poised to move beyond the goals of deploying code in browsers, but let's not get ahead of ourselves. We have the rest of this book to tell you that part of the story.

## CHAPTER 2

"Hello, World!" (Sort of)

How does it, um—how does it work?
 —King Arthur, *Monty Python and the Holy Grail*

Part of the difficulty in teaching people about WebAssembly is that there are many places to start. If they are a C/C++ developer, that might be a reasonable place to begin framing the discussion. If they are a Rust developer, that would be. But you can also talk about the mechanics of WebAssembly independent of the languages you use to generate it. In this chapter, I am going take that approach. We are going to learn low-level details incrementally over the next few chapters before we start to build up to the connection to higher-level languages. These details will seem simplistic and confounding initially, but we are looking at the basic mechanisms, which is ultimately not where you will be working. Let's begin by considering why we cannot start where most programming books do.

In Chapter 1, I introduced the first program most people write in a new programming language or technology when I discussed asm.js. We show it again in Example 2-1. We call this program a "Hello, World!" example in a nod to the first program used in Brian Kernighan and Dennis Ritchie's seminal book, *The C Programming Language* (Pearson). Many quality programming books[1] begin with that example because it gives the reader a taste of what is going on without delving too far down into the details. It is fun, empowering, and a good way to make sure the reader has their tools set up correctly.

---

1 And most WebAssembly tutorials!

Example 2-1. The typical "Hello, World!" program as expressed in C

```c
#include <stdio.h>

int main() {
  printf("Hello, World!\n");
  return 0;
}
```

Unfortunately, WebAssembly has no way of printing to the console, so we cannot start that way.

Wait, what?

I will give you a moment to digest that sentence, perhaps rereading it a few times to make sure it says what you think it says.

Convinced? Confused?

Yes, it is fair to say that there is no way for WebAssembly to print to the console, read a file, or open a network connection…unless you give it a way to do so.

If you examine Example 2-1, you will get a hint about what the issue is. For that program to work, it needs a working copy of the `printf()` function, which can be found in the standard library. Part of what makes C programs so portable is the existence of standard libraries such as this on a variety of platforms. So-called POSIX libraries extend these common features beyond printing to the console to include file manipulation, signal handling, message passing, and more. An application will write to an API such as POSIX, but the executable will need either a static or a dynamic library that provides the behavior of the invoked methods suitable for running in the target platform. This will be in the native executable format for the operating system you are planning to use.

This is why I say that WebAssembly makes code portable, but we will need something else to help us make applications portable. We will revisit this topic throughout the book, but for now it is enough for you to know that there is no direct way for WebAssembly to write to the console.

I promise you we will honor Kernighan and Ritchie in Chapter 5 by running that exact program. First, however, we are going to learn about a human-friendly format for WebAssembly and how the low-level instructions interact with the stack machine. I still want you to have a "Hello, World!" experience here, however, so we will pick something else to write and run that is not too challenging but still legitimate. It is "Hello, World!" (sort of).

WebAssembly Text Format (Wat)

We have mentioned that the binary format (Wasm) is designed to make it faster to transfer, load, and verify WebAssembly modules. We will introduce modules more formally in Chapter 3, but for now just think of them as units of deployment like libraries or Jar files in Java. There is also a text format that describes the behavior of a module that is easier for humans to read: Wat. While there is nothing stopping you from writing code in the text format by hand, you are unlikely to do so. This format is sometimes also referred to as "Wast" in writing, but that was the original name. Many tools support both flavors and people often confuse the two. We will stick with Wat and its suffix of *.wat*.

In Example 2-2, we see a fully formed, valid Wasm module expressed in Wat. This Lisp-like format has functions expressed via their signatures and a collection of stack machine instructions. The WebAssembly abstract machine is a virtual stack machine, a concept I will explain further in a moment. Most compiled software is turned into the executable format of a particular hardware architecture. If you are targeting an Intel x86 machine, the behavior will be converted from a high-level language into a series of instructions that will run on that chip. Without some kind of emulator, it will not run anywhere else. Platforms such as Java and .NET have an intermediate byte code representation that will be interpreted by a runtime environment that has been ported to various platforms. WebAssembly instructions are more like that, but involve the manipulation of a stack through a small set of instructions. Ultimately, these instructions will be mapped to a particular chip's instructions when it executes in a WebAssembly host.

Example 2-2. A simple WebAssembly text file

```
(module
    (func $how_old (param $year_now i32) (param $year_born i32) (result i32) ❶
        get_local $year_now
        get_local $year_born
        i32.sub)

    (export "how_old" (func $how_old)) ❷
)
```

❶ The internal function $how_old

❷ The exported function how_old

The function shown here is called $how_old, and it is not visible outside of this module until we explicitly export it. Note the name distinction. The internal name starts with a $. The exported version does not. It simply executes the inner function if someone calls it externally.

This module has one function defined that takes two integer parameters and returns another integer. As defined in the MVP, WebAssembly is a 32-bit environment.[2] That restriction is being relaxed over time, as you will see. By the time this book is available, it is likely that 64-bit Wasm environments will be available in some form. That being said, WebAssembly supports 32- and 64-bit integers (known as $i32$ and $i64$) and 32- and 64-bit floating point numbers (known as $f32$ and $f64$). That is it.

At this level, there are no strings, objects, dictionaries, or other data types you would expect. Please do not worry; we will address how to overcome these issues later, but this is among the reasons we are not doing a typical "Hello, World!" application. There are no strings! It is easier just to deal with numbers until we introduce some more ideas. So, in the *spirit* of this style of program, we are showing you enough to see it work without overwhelming you.

The purpose of this inner function is to calculate how old someone is based upon what year they were born and what year it currently is. At this point, you may not be surprised to hear that WebAssembly has no concept of dates nor any ability to request the current time by default. I am expecting that you are wondering what exactly WebAssembly *can* do! Happily, it can do math. If you give it the current year and the year someone was born, it can absolutely subtract the one from the other and produce a result. Please do not be underwhelmed; we are just isolating things to be clear about what is being provided by which part of the system.

As you may know, a stack is a convenient and widely used data structure in the software world. It is often described as being like a stack of trays in a cafeteria. The workers will place clean trays on top of any other trays. Customers will take one from the top.

Consider an empty stack as shown in Figure 2-1. We say we *push* something to the top of the stack and *pop* it off of the top of the stack. We only ever manipulate this location, so this is not an appropriate data structure if you need to traverse a list. At the same time, there is only one place to look for the things we are interested in, so we do not need to specify locations, indices, or keys. It is a fast and efficient structure to manipulate.

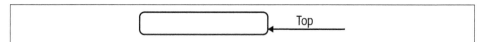

Figure 2-1. An empty stack

---

2 The details of the design decisions and their motivations for the basic WebAssembly functionality are documented on GitHub (*https://oreil.ly/YRYOG*).

Look back to the list of instructions in our function in Example 2-2. The first one is `get_local`. The WebAssembly host environment will retrieve the value of the parameter named `$year_now` and then push it to the stack. Assuming the current year is 2021, the result is shown in Figure 2-2.

Figure 2-2. A stack with one value

At this point, the WebAssembly host environment will advance to the second instruction. It is also a `get_local` instruction and will retrieve the value of the parameter named `$year_born` and push it to the stack. The stack will now have two values on it, but the top of the stack points to the newest value pushed. Assuming the person who invoked the function was born in 2000, the stack will look like Figure 2-3.

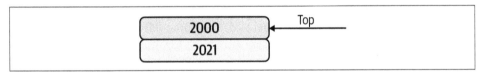

Figure 2-3. A stack with two values

The execution environment will press on as there is another instruction. This one is `i32.sub`. It represents the arithmetic subtraction of one i32 value from another. As it needs two values to make sense, it will consult the top two values on the stack by popping them off, resulting in an empty stack looking again like Figure 2-1. It then subtracts the second parameter from the first and pushes the result back to the top of the stack. The result is seen in Figure 2-4.

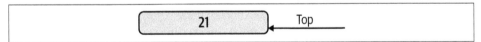

Figure 2-4. The result of the subtraction pushed back to the stack

At this point, there are no more instructions to execute and we are left with a single value at the top of the stack. In Example 2-2, we saw that our function defines an i32 return value. Whatever is at the top of the stack will be returned as the result of invoking the function.

This may seem like a lot of work to add two numbers, but consider that we have expressed a mathematical sequence of events in a platform-neutral way. When the code is ultimately converted to native instructions in a runtime host, the values will be loaded into CPU registers and an instruction will add them together using the mechanics of the CPU's instruction set. We do not have to worry about the details or idiosyncrasies of target platforms, but the conversion process will be fast and easy to conduct when it is time. Before that happens, however, we need to convert our text format to its binary representation.

Converting Wat to Wasm

Anyone who has been a programmer for more than a short time will notice all manner of potential problems with our implementation. We do not handle the case of someone inverting the parameters so that the function would return a negative number. In the interest of keeping the example simple, we are simply ignoring these realities. While this is not a super exciting function, we have investigated the mechanics of expressing some basic behavior via WebAssembly's native text format. The next step is to turn it into its binary executable form. You have several options for doing this, but we will focus on two approaches.

The first does not require you to install anything. In fact, you can go ahead and invoke your function to see it work! If you go to the online wat2wasm demo (*https:// oreil.ly/2Y1fp*), you will see a multipanel site. The upper left corner represents a *.wat* file. The upper right corner represents an annotated hex dump of the compiled *.wat* file. The lower left corner represents JavaScript code to invoke the behavior using the API we will introduce more fully later. The lower right corner represents the output from executing the code.

Copy and paste the code from Example 2-2 into the upper left panel labeled *WAT*. This will cause the text format to be converted into the binary format. Assuming you do not have any typos, you will also be able to download the binary format by pressing the Download button on that same panel. Do not worry about doing that yet.

Now, copy the code from Example 2-3 into the lower left panel. This will invoke the WebAssembly JavaScript API available in most modern browsers (and Node.js). We will discuss it more later, but for now we are retrieving the bytes of the binary module (available here via the `wasmModule` variable) and getting a reference to the `how_old` function so we can call it. As you can see, this function can be invoked like any other JavaScript function. The result of doing so will be printed out via `console.log()` to the lower right panel.

Example 2-3. Some JavaScript to invoke our function

```
const wasmInstance = new WebAssembly.Instance(wasmModule, {});
const { how_old } = wasmInstance.exports;
console.log(how_old(2021, 2000));
```

If everything goes well, you should see something like the screenshot in Figure 2-5. Try changing the dates for the current year and birth year parameters and make sure that your math is correct.

Figure 2-5. Converting a WebAssembly text file into a binary file and executing it

At this point, you can download the binary version of the file. By default it will be called *test.wasm*, but you can rename it to whatever you like. We will call it *hello.wasm*.

Another option you have to generate this binary form is to use the WebAssembly Binary Toolkit (WABT).[3] Consult the Appendix for instructions on installing WABT and other tools we will be using throughout the book.

Included with this installation is a command called wat2wasm. It does what the name says and converts the text file to the binary format:

```
brian@tweezer ~/g/w/s/ch02> wat2wasm hello.wat
brian@tweezer ~/g/w/s/ch02> ls -alF
total 24
drwxr-xr-x  5 brian  staff  160 Sep 13 12:54 ./
drwxr-xr-x  3 brian  staff   96 Sep 13 12:05 ../
-rw-r--r--  1 brian  staff   76 Sep 13 12:07 hello.c
-rw-r--r--  1 brian  staff   45 Sep 13 12:54 hello.wasm
-rw-r--r--  1 brian  staff  200 Sep 13 12:52 hello.wat
```

Look closely. Your eyes are not deceiving you. It does not do a whole lot, but the binary format is only 45 bytes long! I used to do a lot more Java programming and have had class names that were longer than that. We need a way of executing our function now that we are not in a browser. This is easy enough to do with the

---

3 Pronounced *wabbit* like that wascal, Bugs Bunny.

JavaScript API in Node.js, but we will use a different approach to show off a range of choices.

Running Wasm in a Repl

Another tool I show you how to install in the Appendix is wasm3 (*https://oreil.ly/5kAcT*), a WebAssembly interpreter written in C. It allows you to run Wasm modules and functions either on the command line or via an interactive mode conventionally called a "repl"[4] by the cool kids.

Once I execute the following command, I am given a wasm3 prompt. I pointed it to my Wasm file, so there is only one function I can call, but if there were other exported functions in the module, they would be available, too:

```
brian@tweezer ~/g/w/build> wasm3 --repl $HOME/hello.wasm
wasm3> how_old 2021 2000
Result: 21
wasm3> how_old 2021 1980
Result: 41
wasm3> $how_old 2021 2000
Error: function lookup failed ('$how_old')
wasm3> how_old 1980 2021
Result: 4294967255
wasm3>
```

Notice that I am only able to invoke the exported functions, not the inner functions. Also notice that we will fail poorly if we invert the order of parameters as anticipated. When you are building Wasm modules with higher-level languages, those will make it easier to do the right thing (although it is certainly possible to write this error-checking by hand in *.wat* files, life is too short for that kind of nonsense). To get out of the repl, you can simply type Ctrl-C or Ctrl-D.

Let's review what we just did, though. We expressed some arbitrary functionality via an instruction set that targets an abstract machine. We ran it in a browser. It should work with any of the major browsers on any of the major operating systems. Well, so should JavaScript. But we have also run it in a C executable running in an interactive mode on a macOS machine:

```
brian@tweezer ~/g/w/build> file wasm3
wasm3: Mach-O 64-bit executable x86_64
```

---

4 If you have never used an environment like this, you should check out this page on Wikipedia (*https://oreil.ly/IvMS1*).

Here it is running in the same application compiled as a Linux binary:

```
brian@bbfcfm:~/g/w/build> wasm3 --repl $HOME/hello.wasm
wasm3> how_old 2021 2000
Result: 21
wasm3> ^C
brian@bbfcfm:~/g/w/build> file wasm3

wasm3: ELF 64-bit LSB shared object, x86-64, version 1 (SYSV),
dynamically linked, interpreter /lib64/ld-linux-x86-64.so.2,
BuildID[sha1]=b5e98161d08d2d180d0725f973b338c2a340d015, for GNU/Linux
3.2.0, not stripped
```

There are actually several standalone WebAssembly environments written in Python, Rust, Scala, OCaml, Ruby, and more. Our function should be available and work in any of them.

Running Wasm in the Browser

For our next demonstration, I will show you how to invoke the behavior in a browser using the JavaScript API. We will not introduce the API just yet, but you will see a basic example. There are more sophisticated ways of compiling the modules and parameterizing them, but first we crawl, then we walk, then we run.

In Example 2-4, we see a reusable bit of code for instantiating a WebAssembly module instance. The JavaScript API for doing so is available in any environment supporting the WebAssembly MVP, but there are other environments that do not require JavaScript, such as the wasm3 runtime we just used. This code, however, will work in any WebAssembly-friendly browser[5] or Node.js. Notice the use of the Promise-based approach. If your JavaScript environment supports async/await, you could obviously use those too.

> The code in Example 2-4 is not the preferred way of instantiating WebAssembly modules if your browser supports the streaming compilation function. We will use it for the time being just so you can see the individual steps, but I will address the preferred approach later in the book.

Example 2-4. Instantiating a Wasm module in JavaScript

```
function fetchAndInstantiate(url, importObject) {
    return fetch(url).then(response =>
        response.arrayBuffer()
```

---

5 You can see which browser environments support WebAssembly (or other features) on "Can I use…" (*https://oreil.ly/y0JSO*).

```
    ).then(bytes =>
        WebAssembly.instantiate(bytes, importObject)
    ).then(results =>
        results.instance
    );
}
```

Once the function is available, it is easy enough to use from HTML. In Example 2-5, you can see how that process works.

Example 2-5. Instantiating a Wasm module from a web page

```
<!doctype html>
<html lang="en">
  <head>
    <meta charset="utf-8">
    <link rel="stylesheet" href="bootstrap.min.css">
    <title>Hello, World! (Sort of)</title>
    <script src="utils.js"></script>
  </head>
  <body>
    <div class="container">
      <h1>Hello, World! (Sort of)</h1>
      I think you are <span id="age"></span> years old.
    </div>

    <script>
      fetchAndInstantiate('hello.wasm').then(function(instance) {
          var ho = instance.exports.how_old(2021,2000);
          var ageEl = document.getElementById('age');
          ageEl.innerText=ho;
      });
    </script>
  </body>
</html>
```

In this example, we establish a <span> with an ID of age. It is currently empty. We are going to fill it with the result of invoking our WebAssembly function. There is nothing strange about the rest of our HTML file. We include our reusable instantiation code in the <head> element. Toward the bottom of this file we see an embedded <script> element, which calls the fetchAndInstantiate() function. It passes in a local reference to the *hello.wasm* file, so we will have to serve that up over HTTP as well.

The function returns a Promise. When that resolves, we receive a copy of the instantiated Wasm module instance and are able to invoke a method exposed through the module's exports section. Notice we are passing in regular JavaScript numeric literals, but these will be just fine to pass into the function. The number 21 is returned through the invocation process and then stored in the `innerText` of the empty `<span>` we noted earlier.

We need to serve the HTML, JavaScript, and Wasm module over HTTP to run in a browser. You can do that however you like, but with `python3` (or just `python` on non-Macs, probably) you can start up a server and specify which port to listen on:

```
brian@tweezer ~/g/w/s/ch02> python3 -m http.server 10003
Serving HTTP on :: port 10003 (http://[::]:10003/) ...
```

If you open up your browser and point it to *http://localhost:10003/index.html*, you should see something along the lines of Figure 2-6. Feel free to change the parameters in the embedded `<script>` element and verify that it continues to work.

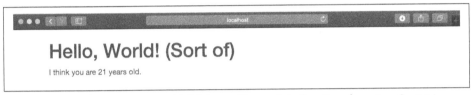

Figure 2-6. Invoking an exported WebAssembly module function from JavaScript in a web page

We obviously have a lot left to learn, but you have now seen the equivalent of a "Hello, World!" example and hopefully understand the basics of how WebAssembly can work.

## CHAPTER 3

WebAssembly Modules

A place for everything and everything in its place.
—Seventeenth-century proverb

An operating system runs a program usually contained in a compiled form.[1] Each operating system has its own format that defines where to start, what data is necessary, and what the instructions are for the different advertised bits of functionality. WebAssembly is no different. In this chapter, we are going to look at how the behavior is packaged up and how a host will know what to do with it.

It is possible that software engineers can spend their entire careers ignoring how programs are loaded and executed through this process. Their world starts and stops at `int main(int argc, char **argv)` or `static void main(String []args)` or even `if __name__ == "__main__":`. These are well-known entry points to programs in C, Java, and Python, thus this is where programmers assume responsibility for the control flow. Prior to programs being launched and after they exit, however, the operating system or programmatic runtime needs to set up and tear down the executable structure. The loader process needs to know where the instructions begin, how data elements are initialized, what other modules or libraries need to be loaded, and more.

These details are generally defined by the nature of the executable. On Linux, this is defined by the Executable and Linkable Format (ELF) (*https://oreil.ly/7cA9S*); on Windows, it's the Portable Executable (PE) format (*https://oreil.ly/jna93*); and on macOS, it is the Mach-O format (*https://oreil.ly/QQyC3*). These are obviously platform-specific formats for native executables. More portable systems like Java

---

1 I am ignoring scripting languages for the purpose of this discussion, but the engine that runs the scripts is still going to be some kind of compiled executable.

and .NET use an intermediate bytecode representation, but there is still a defined structure and they serve similar purposes.

One of the prime design considerations of the WebAssembly MVP was to define the module structure so that WebAssembly hosts know what to look for and validate, as well as where to begin when executing a unit of deployment.

In Chapter 2, you have already seen a more complicated module structure than we will start with in this chapter. We will introduce the sections incrementally and then show you some tools to explore the structure of a WebAssembly module both textually and visually. You have dealt briefly with the binary structure in the previous chapter. It is compact and fast for transferring and loading. You probably will not spend much time looking at the binary details on a regular basis as your focus will be on the software side of things. It is useful to be familiar with the module layout, however, so let's dig in.

Module Structure

The most basic WebAssembly module is an empty one. None of the sections are required, so it is possible to have a valid module such as you see in Example 3-1.

Example 3-1. An empty, but valid, WebAssembly module

```
(module)
```

Obviously it is not much to look at, but it is convertible to the binary form. You will note in the following output that it at least does not take up much room doing nothing:

```
brian@tweezer ~/g/w/s/ch03> wat2wasm empty.wat
brian@tweezer ~/g/w/s/ch03> ls -alF
total 16
drwxr-xr-x  4 brian  staff  128 Dec 21 14:45 ./
drwxr-xr-x  4 brian  staff  128 Dec 14 12:37 ../
-rw-r--r--  1 brian  staff    8 Dec 21 14:45 empty.wasm
-rw-r--r--  1 brian  staff    8 Dec 14 12:37 empty.wat
```

If you are visually oriented, you might enjoy using the WebAssembly Code Explorer that is available from the wasdk GitHub repo (*https://oreil.ly/kDOe7*). You can either use the explorer online (*https://oreil.ly/8Gial*) or download and run an HTTP server out of the cloned directory. In this case, I will use the distributed Python 3 web server as I did earlier:

```
brian@tweezer ~/g/wasmcodeexplorer> python3 -m http.server 10003
Serving HTTP on :: port 10003 (http://[::]:10003/) ...
```

Again, for an empty module, it will not look like much yet, but once we start adding some elements to it, this will be a useful summary. File formats are often identified by operating systems from the first few bytes of the file.[2] They are often called *magic numbers*. For WebAssembly, the bytes are \0asm encoded as 0x00 0x61 0x73 0x6D representing hex values for the characters *a*, *s*, and *m*. This is followed by the version number 1 (represented by the bytes 0x01 0x00 0x00 0x00).

In Figure 3-1, you can see these magic bytes as well as an indication that this is version 1 of the WebAssembly file format highlighted as a series of numbers on the left and the empty module structure on the right.

Figure 3-1. An empty module visualized in the WebAssembly Code Explorer

For command-line inspection of a module, you have several options, but the wasm-objdump executable from the Wabt toolkit is quite helpful. Please consult the Appendix for assistance in installing the various tools discussed in this book.

If you run the command without a switch, it will complain. As you will see momentarily, these make more of a difference when you have more details to explore:

```
brian@tweezer ~/g/w/s/ch03> wasm-objdump empty.wasm
At least one of the following switches must be given:
 -d/--disassemble
 -h/--headers
 -x/--details
 -s/--full-contents
```

For now, we will just verify that our module is useless but valid by using the details switch. This also indicates that we are dealing with version 1 of the format:

```
brian@tweezer ~/g/w/s/ch03> wasm-objdump -x empty.wasm

empty.wasm:     file format wasm 0x1

Section Details:
```

---

2 Many of the common formats (including WebAssembly) can be found in this list on Wikipedia (*https://oreil.ly/j5ekS*).

Exploring Module Sections

There is a circular dependency problem with respect to the concepts we are introducing. The module format must include support for all of the various elements that WebAssembly comprises, but we will not introduce some of those elements until later chapters. We will focus on the portions that we have seen primarily now, with a promise to revisit the other section elements soon.

The overall structure of the module is based upon a series of optional numbered sections that each address a particular feature of WebAssembly. In Table 3-1, we see a quick list of and description of these sections.

Table 3-1. WebAssembly module sections

Id	Name	Description
0	Custom	Debugging or metadata information for third-party uses
1	Type	Type definitions used in the modules
2	Import	Imported elements used by a module
3	Function	Type signatures associated with the functions in a module
4	Table	Tables that define indirect, immutable references used by a module
5	Memory	Linear memory structures used by a module
6	Global	Global variables
7	Export	Exported elements provided by a module
8	Start	An optional start function to initiate a module
9	Element	Elements defined by a module
10	Code	The body of the functions defined by a module
11	Data	The data elements defined by a module
12	Data Count	The number of data elements defined by the module

Here is our example from Chapter 2 again for reference.

Example 3-2. A simple WebAssembly text file

```
(module
    (func $how_old (param $year_now i32) (param $year_born i32) (result i32) ❶
        get_local $year_now
        get_local $year_born
        i32.sub)

    (export "how_old" (func $how_old)) ❷
)
```

❶ The internal function $how_old

---

❷ The exported function how_old

We converted it to its binary form with the wat2wasm tool. If we attempt to interrogate the structure generated by this conversion, we will see the following:

```
brian@tweezer ~/g/w/s/ch03> wasm-objdump -x hello.wasm

hello.wasm:     file format wasm 0x1

Section Details:

Type[1]:
 - type[0] (i32, i32) -> i32
Function[1]:
 - func[0] sig=0 <how_old>
Export[1]:
 - func[0] <how_old> -> "how_old"
Code[1]:
 - func[0] size=7 <how_old>
```

Notice there are quite a few more sections filled in compared to our empty module. To start with, we have a Type section that defines a single signature. It suggests a type that takes two i32s and returns an i32. That is an appropriate signature for our how_old method. The type is not given a name, but it can still be used to set expectations and validate them with respect to function configurations.

Next we have a Function section that links our type (type 0 from the Type section) to a named function. Because we export our function to make it available to our host environment or other modules, we see the inner function <how_old> is being exported via the name "how_old". Finally, we have a Code section that contains the actual instructions of our only function.

Figure 3-2 shows what our module looks like in the WebAssembly Code Explorer.[3]

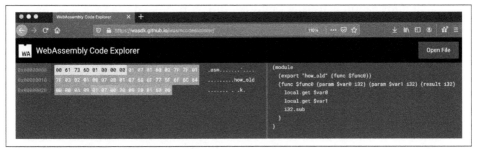

Figure 3-2. Our Hello, World! module visualized in the WebAssembly Code Explorer

---

3 The colors are not visible in the print version of this book, but you can follow along in WebAssembly.

The red colors indicate section boundaries, but you can also get more details by hovering over the various sections in the browser. The purple bytes of the Export section, for instance, should indicate the name of the exported function how_old if you place the mouse over one of them. You can see the actual instructions by hanging out over the green and blue bytes in the final Code section.

If you look closely at Example 3-2, you will notice that our variable names are not carried forth by default. The wasm-objdump also highlights this fact. In order to do so for debugging purposes, you will need to specify such during the wat2wasm command:

```
brian@tweezer ~/g/w/s/ch03> wat2wasm hello.wat -o hellodebug.wasm --debug-names
brian@tweezer ~/g/w/s/ch03> wasm-objdump -x hellodebug.wasm

hellodebug.wasm:        file format wasm 0x1

Section Details:

Type[1]:
 - type[0] (i32, i32) -> i32
Function[1]:
 - func[0] sig=0 <how_old>
Export[1]:
 - func[0] <how_old> -> "how_old"
Code[1]:
 - func[0] size=7 <how_old>
Custom:
 - name: "name"
 - func[0] <how_old>
 - func[0] local[0] <year_now>
 - func[0] local[1] <year_born>
```

Notice that wat2wasm uses the Custom section to preserve the function and local variable details. Other tools may use this section for their own purposes, but this is how debugging information is usually captured. In Figure 3-3, you can see that there are more bytes in the module because of this Custom section.

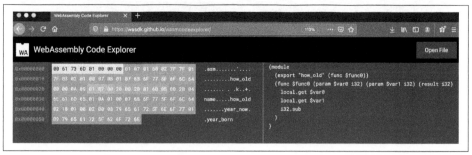

Figure 3-3. Our Hello, World! module with preserved debugging details visualized in the WebAssembly Code Explorer

Working with Modules

Once you understand the process of inspecting a WebAssembly module's static, binary structure, you will want to move on to working with it in a more dynamic way. We have seen the basics of instantiating a module via the JavaScript API in examples such as Example 2-4, but there are other things we can do as well.

Our code in Example 3-2 generates an Export section, but as we saw in Table 3-1, there is also a potential Import section for receiving elements from the hosting environment. This can eventually include Memory and Table instances, as we will see in subsequent chapters, but for now we can import a function to our module, allowing us to communicate with a console window from WebAssembly more directly. Please keep in mind we are still sorting through low-level details, and your day-to-day experiences with these technologies will likely be at a higher level.

Take a look at Example 3-3. This is a new version of our example so far that exports a second function. More importantly, it also imports a function.

Example 3-3. A WebAssembly module that imports a function

```
(module
    (func $log (import "imports" "log_func") (param i32)) ❶

    (func $how_old (param $year_now i32) (param $year_born i32) (result i32) ❷
        get_local $year_now
        get_local $year_born
        i32.sub)

    (func $log_how_old (param $year_now i32) (param $year_born i32) ❸
        get_local $year_now
        get_local $year_born
        call $how_old
        call $log
    )

    (export "how_old" (func $how_old)) ❹
    (export "log_how_old" (func $log_how_old)) ❺
)
```

❶ Importing a function from the host that expects a single i32 parameter

❷ Our same $how_old function as before

❸ A new function that takes two parameters and then calls our imported function

❹ Exporting our old how_old function as before

❺ Exporting our new `log_how_old` function

As you can see, we have a new function we can call in our module, but we cannot call it just yet. Our previous function is still available and has not changed. Our new function calls the old function to do the math but then expects there to be a function called `log_func` available for it to invoke the result with. To clarify some of the differences, let's generate the *.wasm* output and then dump the module structure:

```
brian@tweezer ~/g/w/s/ch03> wat2wasm hellolog.wat
brian@tweezer ~/g/w/s/ch03> wasm-objdump -x hellolog.wasm

hellolog.wasm:   file format wasm 0x1

Section Details:

Type[3]:
 - type[0] (i32) -> nil
 - type[1] (i32, i32) -> i32
 - type[2] (i32, i32) -> nil
Import[1]:
 - func[0] sig=0 <imports.log_func> <- imports.log_func
Function[2]:
 - func[1] sig=1 <how_old>
 - func[2] sig=2 <log_how_old>
Export[2]:
 - func[1] <how_old> -> "how_old"
 - func[2] <log_how_old> -> "log_how_old"
Code[2]:
 - func[1] size=7 <how_old>
 - func[2] size=10 <log_how_old>
```

For the first time, we have an entry for an Import section. It is defined to have a type we have not seen yet. If you look in the Type section, you will see we have three types specified now: one that takes an i32 but does not return anything, our existing type of two i32 parameters and an i32 return value, and another new one that takes two i32s and does not return anything.

The first of these types is defined in our import. We are expecting the host environment to give us a function we can invoke that will take an i32. The purpose of this function is to print out the argument somehow, not to return anything, so it does not need a return type. We are expecting to find this function from the importObject we have previously ignored on the JavaScript side. The second type is the same as before. The third one takes the parameters to call our $how_old function but will then log the results, so it also does not need a return value. The Import and Function sections show you the linkage between the functions and the signatures.

To provide elements via the importObject, we will need some HTML code like that shown in Example 3-4.

Example 3-4. An HTML file to instantiate our module with a method to call through the `importObject`

```
<!doctype html>

<html>
  <head>
    <meta charset="utf-8">
    <title>WASM Import test</title>
    <script src="utils.js"></script>
  </head>
  <body>
    <script>
      var importObject = {
        imports: {
          log_func: function(arg) {
            console.log("You are this old: " + arg + " years.");
          }
        }
      };

      fetchAndInstantiate('hellolog.wasm', importObject).then(
        function(instance) {
          console.log(instance.exports.log_how_old(2021, 2000));
        }
      );
    </script>
  </body>
</html>
```

Compare the `import` statement in Example 3-3 to this object structure. Notice the presence of an `imports` namespace with a function called `log_func`. That is the structure our `import` statement specifies.

The `$log_how_old` function pushes its two parameters to the top of the stack and then invokes our previous function with the `call $show_old` instruction. Keep in mind that function subtracts one parameter from the other and then returns the result on the top of the stack. At this point, we do not have to repush that value to the stack; we can simply invoke our imported function that we named `$log`. The result of the previous function will be the parameter for this new invocation. Take a moment to make sure you understand the relationship between parameters, return values, and functions.

If you copy the *utils.js* file from the previous chapter (which provides our `fetchAnd Instantiate()` function[4]) and then serve this all up over HTTP as we have done

---

4 Keep in mind we are still using the method to instantiate modules that is not recommended. One thing at a time!

previously, you can load the new HTML file in your browser. You will not see any-thing initially because our log_func simply dumps its argument to console.log(). If you view the console in your browser's developer tools, however, you should see something like Figure 3-4.

Figure 3-4. The results of calling our new function with an imported JavaScript function

If you change the importObject to look like Example 3-5 and then reload the HTML file in your browser, you will no longer see a message on the console; you should see an alert pop up with the message instead. Obviously there has been no change to our WebAssembly code—we simply passed a different function in from the JavaScript side of things and therefore see a different result. We will see much more complicated interactions as we delve deeper into this topic, but hopefully you are starting to see how WebAssembly and JavaScript code can interact via the Import and Export sections.

Example 3-5. The same WebAssembly module can be instantiated with a different method to call

```
var importObject = {
  imports: {
    log_func: function(arg) {
      alert("You are this old: " + arg + " years.");
    }
  }
};
```

Instantiating modules and invoking their functions are going to be your primary interaction with them via the JavaScript API, but there is additional behavior available to you. If you wanted to know what methods a module imports or exports, you can use the JavaScript API to interrogate a loaded module. Rather than invoking the fetchAndInstantiate() method from *utils.js*, if you change the HTML to have the code shown in Example 3-6, you will see the results in Figure 3-5.

Example 3-6. We can do more with the JavaScript API, including streaming compilation

```
WebAssembly.compileStreaming(fetch('hellolog.wasm'))
  .then(function(mod) {
    var imports = WebAssembly.Module.imports(mod);
    console.log(imports[0]);
    var exports = WebAssembly.Module.exports(mod);
    console.log(exports);
  }
);
```

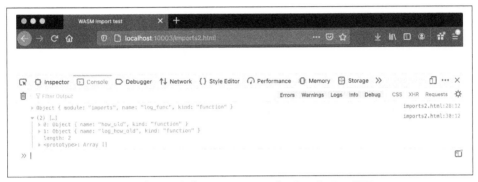

Figure 3-5. Interrogating the module structure via the JavaScript API

Once we learn a few more concepts and start to get into a higher-level language for expressing our behavior, the full power of WebAssembly will start to be evident.[5]

So far, we have been using a block of code in a file called *utils.js* that looked like what you see in Example 3-7. For simple modules, this is fine, but as your modules get larger, there are some built-in latencies that can be eliminated. Performance is not just about runtime performance; it is also about load-time performance.

Example 3-7. The simple way we have been instatiating modules

```
function fetchAndInstantiate(url, importObject) {
  return fetch(url).then(response =>
    response.arrayBuffer()
  ).then(bytes =>
    WebAssembly.instantiate(bytes, importObject)
  ).then(results =>
    results.instance
  );
}
```

5 Until then, if you want to explore further, the API is documented on GitHub (*https://oreil.ly/lNTvC*).

The issue here is that even though we are using Promises to avoid blocking the main thread, we are reading the module into an `ArrayBuffer` first and then instantiating it. We are in essence waiting until all of the network transfer is done before compiling the module. One of the first post-MVP capabilities added was the ability to support compilation while the bytes were still being pulled across the network. The module format structure lends itself to this optimization, so it is a shame not to use it.

While there is no "right way" to instantiate your modules (e.g., you may wish to instantiate multiple instances of modules in some scenarios), the majority of the time, the code in Example 3-8 is a slightly more efficient way to do so.

Example 3-8. The recommended way to instantiate modules most of the time

```
(async () => {
  const fetchPromise = fetch(url);
  const { instance } = await WebAssembly.instantiateStreaming(fetchPromise);
  // Use the module
  const result = instance.exports.method(param1, param2);
  console.log(result);
})();
```

Notice that we are not creating the `ArrayBuffer`; we are passing the `Promise` from the `fetch()` method into the `instantiateStreaming()` method on the `WebAssembly` object. This allows the baseline compiler to start to compile functions as they are appearing across the network. In most cases, the code compilation will happen faster than the network transfer, so that by the time you finish downloading the code, it should be validated and ready to use. When JavaScript finishes downloading, that is usually when the validation process begins, so we see an improvement in startup time.

There is not a formalized method for caching WebAssembly modules yet, but this too will become an unobtrusive way of improving startup time. Cache controls and other web artifact handling will avoid the need to redownload modules more often than necessary (e.g., if they have been updated).

Future ES6 Module Integration

While it is obviously useful to be able to work through the JavaScript API as we have seen, doing so is low-level and repetitive, which is why we put it in a reusable utility script file. In the future, we expect it will be even easier to use WebAssembly modules from HTML, because they will be available as ES6 modules.

This is a bit tricky because of the need for top-level asynchronous handling and how graphs of modules are loaded in three phases for construction, instantiation, and evaluation. There are slight differences between the binary WebAssembly and

JavaScript-based module validation processes, when compilation happens, and how module environment records are traversed and linked.

There is a proposal to add support to the platform to smooth over these differences. At the time of writing, this is in stage 2 of the proposal process.[6] Lin Clark has a nice walkthrough of the complexity on YouTube (*https://oreil.ly/Q9Qw0*).

The goal is to introduce a declarative form that would look something like what you see in Example 3-9.

Example 3-9. Proposed declarative form for loading WebAssembly Modules

```
import {something} from "./myModule.wasm";

something();
```

Not only will this have the benefit of simplifying the instantiation of WebAssembly modules, it will also facilitate their participation in graphs of JavaScript module dependencies. Developers will have an easier time intermixing behavior expressed in multiple languages as complete solutions if there are not distinctions to how they are managed as dependencies.

The proposal has a clean design and good support, but it involves a careful choreography across the HTML spec, the ES6 module spec, implementations, JavaScript bundlers, and the larger Node.js community. I suspect that it will not be much longer before we see some forward motion on this proposal.

Now that we have looked at the structural elements of a WebAssembly binary, you should feel comfortable inspecting your own and third-party modules either manually or programmatically. The next step is to look at the more dynamic elements of WebAssembly modules. We will start by focusing on `Memory` instances as the means of emulating the power of contiguous blocks of memory in a more conventional programming runtime.

---

6 If you are interested in the low-level proposal details, you can find them on GitHub (*https://oreil.ly/tS7qu*).

## CHAPTER 4

WebAssembly Memory

Perhaps one day this too will be pleasant to remember.
—Virgil

If WebAssembly is going to behave like a regular runtime environment, it needs a way to allocate and free memory for its data-handling activities. In this chapter, we will introduce you to how it emulates this behavior for efficiency but without the risk of typical memory manipulation problems seen with languages like C and C++ (even if that is what we are running). As we are potentially downloading arbitrary code over the internet, this is an important safety consideration.

The entire concept of computation usually involves some form of data processing. Whether we are spell-checking a document, manipulating an image, doing machine learning, sequencing proteins, playing video games, watching movies, or simply crunching numbers in a spreadsheet, we are generally interacting with arbitrary blocks of data. One of the most crucial performance considerations in these systems is how to get the data where it needs to be in order to interrogate or transform it somehow.

Central Processing Units (CPUs) work the fastest when data is available in a register or an on-chip cache.[1] Obviously these are very small containers, so large data sets are never going to be loaded onto the CPU in their entirety. We have to spend some effort moving data into and out of memory. The cost of waiting for the data to be loaded to one of these locations is an eternity in CPU clock time. This is one of the reasons they have gotten so complex. Modern chips have all manner of multipipeline, predictive branching, and instruction rewriting available to keep the chip busy while we are

---

[1] A register is an on-chip memory location that usually feeds an instruction what it needs to execute.

reading from a network into main memory, from there into multilevel caches, and finally to where it needs to be used.

Traditional programs have usually had stack memory to manage short-term variables of small or fixed sizes. They use heap-based memory for longer-term, arbitrarily sized blocks of data. These are generally just different areas of the memory allocated to a program that are treated differently. Stack memory gets overwritten frequently by the ebb and flow of functions being called during execution. Heap memory is used and cleaned up when it is no longer needed. If a program runs out of memory, it can ask for more, but it must be reasonably judicious about how it uses it.[2] These days virtual paging systems and cheaper memory make it entirely likely that a typical computer might have tens of gigabytes of memory. Being able to quickly and efficiently access individual bytes of potentially large data sets is a major key to decent software run-time performance.

WebAssembly programs need a way to simulate these blocks of memory without actually giving unfettered access to the privacy of our computer's memory. Fortunately, there is a good story to tell here that balances convenience, speed, and safety. It starts with making it possible for JavaScript to access individual bytes in memory, but will expand beyond JavaScript to be a generic way of sharing memory between host environments and WebAssembly modules.

TypedArrays

JavaScript has traditionally not been able to provide convenient access to individual bytes in memory. This is why time-sensitive, low-level functionality is often provided by the browser or some kind of plug-in. Even Node.js applications often have to implement some functionality in a language that handles memory manipulation better than JavaScript can. This complicates the situation, as JavaScript is an interpreted language and you would need an efficient mechanism for switching control flow back and forth between interpreted, portable code, and fast compiled code. This also makes deployments trickier because one part of the application is inherently portable and one needs native library support on different operating systems.

There is usually a trade-off in software development: languages are either fast or they are safe. When you need raw speed, you might choose C or C++ as they provide very few runtime checks in the use and manipulation of data in memory. Consequently, they are very fast. When you want safety, you might pick a language with runtime boundary checks on array references. The downside of the speed trade-off is that things are either slow or the burden of memory management falls to the

---

2 My first computer, an Atari 800, started off with only 16 kilobytes of memory. It was a big to-do the day my dad came home with a 32-kilobyte expansion card!

programmer. Unfortunately, it is extremely easy to mess up by forgetting to allocate space, reusing freed memory, or failing to deallocate the space when you are done. This is one of the reasons applications written in these fast languages are often buggy, crash easily, and serve as the source for many security vulnerabilities.[3]

Garbage-collected languages such as Java and JavaScript free developers from many of the burdens of managing memory, but often incur a performance burden at runtime as a trade-off. A piece of the runtime must constantly look for unused memory and release it. The performance overhead makes many such applications unpredictable and therefore unsuitable for embedded applications, financial systems, or other time-sensitive use cases.

Allocating memory is not a huge issue as long as what is created is a suitable size for what you want to put in it. The tricky part is knowing when to clean up. Obviously, freeing memory before a program is done with it is bad, but failing to do so when it is no longer needed is inefficient and you might run out of memory. Languages such as Rust strike a nice balance of convenience and safety. The compiler forces you to communicate your intentions more clearly, but when you do, it can be more effective in cleaning up after you.

How this is all managed at runtime is often one of the defining characteristics of a language and its runtime. As such, not every language requires the same level of support. This is one of the reasons WebAssembly's designers did not overspecify features such as garbage collection in the MVP.

JavaScript is a flexible and dynamic language, but it has not historically made it easy or efficient to deal with individual bytes of large data sets. This complicates the use of low-level libraries, as the data has to be copied into and out of JavaScript-native formats, which is inefficient. The `Array` class stores JavaScript objects, which means it has to be prepared to deal with arbitrary types. Many of Python's flexible containers are also similarly flexible and bloated.[4] Fast traversal and manipulation of memory through pointers is a product of the uniformity of the data types in contiguous blocks. Bytes are the minimum addressable unit, particularly when dealing with images, videos, and sound files.

Numerical data requires more effort. A 16-bit integer takes up two bytes. A 32-bit integer, four. Location 0 in a byte array might represent the first such number in an array of data, but the second one will start at location 4.

JavaScript added TypedArray interfaces to address these issues, initially in the context of improving WebGL performance. These are portions of memory available through

---

3 Ryan Levick highlights this point in his discussion of Microsoft's interest in Rust (*https://oreil.ly/uGU6m*).

4 The NumPy library helps solve this by reimplementing homogenous storage in C arrays and having compiled forms of the mathematical functions to run on those structures.

ArrayBuffer instances that can be treated as homogenous blocks of particular data types. The memory available is constrained to the ArrayBuffer instance, but it can be stored internally in a format that is convenient to pass to native libraries.

In Example 4-1, we see the basic functionality of creating a typed array of 32-bit unsigned integers.

Example 4-1. Ten 32-bit integers created in a Uint32Array

```
var u32arr = new Uint32Array(10);
u32arr[0] = 257;
console.log(u32arr);
console.log("u32arr length: " + u32arr.length);
```

The output of the invocation should look like this:

```
Uint32Array(10) [ 257, 0, 0, 0, 0, 0, 0, 0, 0, 0 ]
u32arr length: 10
```

As you can see, this works as you would expect an array of integers to. Keep in mind that these are 4-byte integers (thus the 32 in the type name). In Example 4-2, we retrieve the underlying ArrayBuffer from the Uint32Array and print it out. This shows us that its length is 40. Next we wrap the buffer with a Uint8Array representing an array of unsigned bytes and print out its contents and length.

Example 4-2. Accessing the 32-bit integers as a buffer of 8-bit bytes

```
var u32buf = u32arr.buffer;
var u8arr = new Uint8Array(u32buf);
console.log(u8arr);
console.log("u8arr length: " + u8arr.length);
```

The code produces the following output:

```
ArrayBuffer { byteLength: 40 }
Uint8Array(40) [ 1, 1, 0, 0, 0, 0, 0, 0, 0, 0, … ]
u8arr length: 40
```

The ArrayBuffer represents the raw underlying bytes. The TypedArray is an interpreted view of those bytes based upon the specified type size. So when we initialized the Uint32Array with a length of 10, that meant ten 32-bit integers, which requires 40 bytes to represent. The detached buffer is set to be this big so it can hold all 10 integers. The Uint8Array treats each byte as an individual element due to its size definition.

If you check out Figure 4-1, you will hopefully see what is going on. The first element (position 0) of the Uint32Array is simply the value 257. This is an interpreted view of the underlying bytes in the ArrayBuffer. The Uint8Array directly reflects the underlying bytes of the buffer. The bit patterns at the bottom of the diagram reflect the bits per byte for the first two bytes.

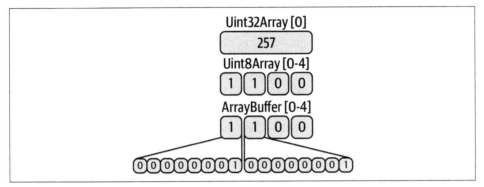

Figure 4-1. Representing the value 257

It may surprise you that there are 1s in the first two bytes. This is due to a confusing notion called *endianess* that shows up when we store numbers in memory.[5] In this case, a *little endian* system stores the least significant bytes first (the 1s). A *big endian* system would store the 0s first. In the grand scheme of things, it does not matter how they are stored, but different systems and protocols will pick one or the other. You just need to keep track of which format you are seeing.

As indicated earlier, TypedArray classes were introduced initially for WebGL, but since then, they have been adopted by other APIs including Canvas2D, XMLHttpRequest2, File, Binary WebSockets, and more. Notice these are all lower-level, performance-oriented I/O and visualization APIs that have to interface with native libraries. The underlying memory representation can be passed between these layers efficiently. It is for these reasons that they are useful for WebAssembly Memory instances as well.

WebAssembly Memory Instances

A WebAssembly Memory is an underlying ArrayBuffer (or SharedArrayBuffer, as we will see later) associated with a module. The MVP limits a module to having a single instance at the moment, but this is likely to change before long. A module may create its own Memory instance, or it may be given one from its host environment. These instances can be imported or exported just like we have done with functions so far. There is also an associated Memory section in the module structure that we skipped over in Chapter 3 because we had not covered the concept yet. We will fix that omission now.

---

5 This is a reference to *Gulliver's Travels* by Jonathan Swift (*https://oreil.ly/guM78*).

In Example 4-3, we have a Wat file that defines a Memory instance and exports it as the name "memory". This represents a contiguous block of memory constrained to a particular ArrayBuffer instance. It is the beginning of our ability to emulate C/C++-like homogenous arrays of bytes in memory. Each instance is made up of one or more 64-kilobyte blocks of memory pages. In the example, we initialize it to a single page but allow it to grow up to 10 pages for a total of 640 kilobytes, which ought to be enough for anyone.[6] You will see how to increase the available memory momentarily. For now, we are just going to write the bytes 1, 1, 0, and 0 to the beginning of the buffer. The i32.const instruction loads a constant value onto the stack. We want to write to the beginning of our buffer, so we use the value 0x0. The data instruction is a convenience for initializing portions of our Memory instance.

Example 4-3. Creating and exporting a Memory instance in a WebAssembly module

```
(module
  (memory (export "memory") 1 10)
  (data (i32.const 0x0) "\01\01\00\00")
)
```

If we compile this file to its binary representation with wat2wasm and then invoke wasm-objdump, we see some new details we have not yet encountered:

```
brian@tweezer ~/g/w/s/ch04> wasm-objdump -x memory.wasm

memory.wasm:    file format wasm 0x1

Section Details:

Memory[1]:
 - memory[0] pages: initial=1 max=10
Export[1]:
 - memory[0] -> "memory"
Data[1]:
 - segment[0] memory=0 size=4 - init i32=0
  - 0000000: 0101 0000
```

There is a configured Memory instance in the Memory section reflecting our initial size of one page and maximum size of 10 pages. We see that it is exported as "memory" in the Export section. We also see the fact that the Data section has initialized our memory instance with the four bytes we wrote into it.

Now we can use our exported memory by importing it into some JavaScript in the browser. For this example, we are going to load the module and fetch the Memory

---

6 Nice try, but no, Bill Gates never said it!

instance. We then display the buffer size in bytes, the number of pages, and what is currently in the memory buffer.

The basic structure of our HTML file is shown in Example 4-4. We have a series of <span> elements that will be populated with the details via a function called show Details(), which will take a reference to our memory instance.

Example 4-4. Display Memory details in the browser

```
<!doctype html>
<html lang="en">
  <head>
    <meta charset="utf-8">
    <link rel="stylesheet" href="bootstrap.min.css">
    <title>Memory</title>
    <script src="utils.js"></script>
  </head>
  <body>
    <div class="container">
      <h1>Memory</h1>
      <div>Your memory instance is <span id="mem"></span> bytes.</div>
      <div>It has this many pages: <span id="pages"></span>.</div>
      <div>Uint32Buffer[0] = <span id="firstint"></span>.</div>
      <div>Uint8Buffer[0-4] = <span id="firstbytes"></span>.</div>
    </div>

    <button id="expand">Expand</button>

    <script>
        <!-- Shown below -->
    </script>
  </body>
</html>
```

In Example 4-5, we see the JavaScript for our <script> element. First look at the fetchAndInstantiate() call. It behaves in the same way we have seen before in terms of loading the module. Here we get a reference to the Memory instance through the exports section. We attach an onClick() function for our button that we will address momentarily.

Example 4-5. The JavaScript code for our example

```
function showDetails(mem) {
  var buf = mem.buffer;
  var memEl = document.getElementById('mem');
  var pagesEl = document.getElementById('pages');
  var firstIntEl = document.getElementById('firstint');
  var firstBytesEl = document.getElementById('firstbytes');
```

```
      memEl.innerText=buf.byteLength;
      pagesEl.innerText=buf.byteLength / 65536;

      var i32 = new Uint32Array(buf);
      var u8 = new Uint8Array(buf);

      firstIntEl.innerText=i32[0];
      firstBytesEl.innerText= "[" + u8[0] + "," + u8[1] + "," +
                                    u8[2] + "," + u8[3] + "]";
    };

    fetchAndInstantiate('memory.wasm').then(function(instance) {
      var mem = instance.exports.memory;

      var button = document.getElementById("expand");
      button.onclick = function() {
        try {
          mem.grow(1);
          showDetails(mem);
        } catch(re) {
          alert("You cannot grow the Memory any more!");
        };
      };
      showDetails(mem);
    });
```

Finally, we call the `showDetails()` function and pass in our `mem` variable. This function will retrieve the underlying `ArrayBuffer` and references to our various `<span>`
elements to display the details. The buffer's length is stored in the `innerText` field of
our first `<span>`. The number of pages is this length divided by 64 KB to indicate the
number of pages. We then wrap the `ArrayBuffer` with a `Uint32Array`, which allows
us to fetch our memory values as 4-byte integers. The first element of this is shown in
the next `<span>`. We also wrap our `ArrayBuffer` in `Uint8Array` and show the first
four bytes. After our discussion earlier, the details shown in Figure 4-2 should not
surprise you.

Figure 4-2. Showing the details of our `Memory`

The onClick() function calls a method on the Memory instance to grow the allocated size by one page of memory. This causes the original ArrayBuffer to become detached from the instance, and the existing data is copied over. If we are successful, we reinvoke the showDetails() function and extract the new ArrayBuffer. If the button is pressed once, you should see that the instance now represents two pages of memory representing 128 KB of memory. The data at the beginning should not have changed.

If you press the button too many times, the number of allocated pages will exceed the maximum specified amount of 10 pages. At this point, it is no longer possible to expand the memory and a RangeError will be thrown. Our example will pop up an alert window when this happens.

Using the WebAssembly Memory API

The grow() method we used in the previous example is part of the WebAssembly JavaScript API that the MVP expects all host environments to provide. We can expand our use of this API and go in the other direction. that is, we can create a Memory instance in JavaScript and then make it available to a module. Keep in mind the current limit of one instance per module.

In subsequent chapters, we will see more elaborate uses of memory, but we will want to use a higher-level language than Wat to do anything serious. For now, we will keep our example on the simpler side but still try to expand beyond what we have seen.

We will start with the HTML so you can see the whole workflow, and then we will dive into the details of the new module. In Example 4-6, you can see that we are using a similar HTML structure to what we have used so far. There is a <div> element with the ID of container into which we will place a series of Fibonacci numbers (*https://oreil.ly/Aie3f*). If you are not familiar with these numbers, they are very important in a lot of natural systems, and you are encouraged to investigate them on your own. The first two numbers are defined to be 0 and 1. The subsequent numbers are set to the sum of the previous two. So the third number will be 1 (0 + 1). The fourth number will be "2" (1 + 1). The fifth number will be 3 (2 + 1), etc.

Example 4-6. Creating a Memory in JavaScript and importing it to the module

```
<!doctype html>
<html lang="en">
  <head>
    <meta charset="utf-8">
    <link rel="stylesheet" href="bootstrap.min.css">
    <title>Fibonacci</title>
    <script src="utils.js"></script>
  </head>
```

```
<body>
  <div id="container"></div>

  <script>
    var memory = new WebAssembly.Memory({initial:10, maximum:100});

    var importObject = {
      js: { mem: memory }
    };

    fetchAndInstantiate('memory2.wasm', importObject).then(function(instance) {
        var fibNum = 20;
        instance.exports.fibonacci(fibNum);
        var i32 = new Uint32Array(memory.buffer);

        var container = document.getElementById('container');

        for(var i = 0; i < fibNum; i++) {
            container.innerText += `Fib[${i}]: ${i32[i]}\n`;
        }
    });

  </script>
  </body>
</html>
```

The actual calculation is written in Wat and shown in Example 4-7, but before we get there, we see the creation of the Memory instance on the first line of the <script> element. We are using the JavaScript API, but the intent is the same as our use of the (memory) element in Example 4-3. We create an initial size of one page of memory and a maximum size of 10 pages. In this case, we will never need more than the one page, but you now see how to do it. The Memory instance is made available to the module via the importObject. As you will see momentarily, the function in the Wasm module will take a parameter indicating how many Fibonacci numbers to write into the Memory buffer. In this example, we will pass in a parameter of 20.

Once our module is instantiated, we call its exported fibonacci() function. We have access to the memory variable from above, so we can retrieve the underlying Array Buffer directly after the function invocation completes. Because Fibonacci numbers are integers, we wrap the buffer in a Uint32Array instance so we can iterate over the individual elements. As we retrieve the numbers, we do not have to worry about the fact that they are 4-byte integers. Upon reading each value, we extend the innerText of our container element with a string version of the number.

The calculation shown in Example 4-7 is going to be significantly more complicated than any Wat we have seen so far, but by approaching it in pieces you should be able to figure it out.

Example 4-7. Fibonacci calculations expressed in Wat

```
(module
  (memory (import "js" "mem") 1) ❶
  (func (export "fibonacci") (param $n i32) ❷
    (local $index i32) ❸
    (local $ptr i32) ❹

    (i32.store (i32.const 0) (i32.const 0)) ❺
    (i32.store (i32.const 4) (i32.const 1))

    (set_local $index (i32.const 2)) ❻
    (set_local $ptr (i32.const 8))

    (block $break ❼
      (loop $top ❽
        (br_if $break (i32.eq (get_local $n) (get_local $index))) ❾
        (i32.store ❿
          (get_local $ptr)
          (i32.add
            (i32.load (i32.sub (get_local $ptr) (i32.const 4)))
      (i32.load (i32.sub (get_local $ptr) (i32.const 8)))
          )
        )
        (set_local $ptr (i32.add (get_local $ptr) (i32.const 4))) ⓫
        (set_local $index (i32.add (get_local $index) (i32.const 1)))
        (br $top) ⓬
      )
    )
  )
)
```

❶ The Memory is imported from the host environment.

❷ The fibonacci function is defined and exported.

❸ $index is our number counter.

❹ $ptr is our current position in the Memory instance.

❺ The i32.store function writes a value to the specified location in the buffer.

❻ The $index variable is advanced to 2 and the $ptr is set to 8.

❼ We define a named block to return to in our loops.

❽ We define a named loop in our block.

❾ We break out of our loop when the $index variable equals the $n parameter.

⑩ We write the sum of the previous two elements to current location of `$ptr`.

⑪ We advance the `$ptr` variable by 4 and the `$index` variable by 1.

⑫ We break to the top of our loop.

Hopefully the numeric notes attached to Example 4-7 make sense, but given its complexity, it warrants a quick discussion. This is a stack-based virtual machine, so all of the instructions involve manipulating the top of the stack. In the first callout, we import the memory defined in the JavaScript. It represents the default allocation of one page, which should be enough for now. While this is a correct implementation, it is not an overly safe implementation. Bad inputs could mess up the flow, but we will be more concerned with that after we introduce higher-level language support where it is easier to handle those details.

The exported function is defined to take a parameter `$n` representing the number of Fibonacci numbers to calculate.[7] We use two local variables defined at the third and fourth callouts. The first represents which number we are working on and defaults to 0. The second will act as a pointer in memory. It will serve as the index into the `Memory` buffer. Remember, `i32` data values represent 4 bytes, so every advance of `$index` will involve advancing `$ptr` by 4. We do not have the benefit of `TypedArrays` on this side of the interaction, so we have to handle these details ourselves. Again, higher-level languages will shield us from many of these details.

By definition, the first two Fibonacci numbers are 0 and 1, so we write those into the buffer. `i32.store` writes an integer value to a location. It expects to find those values on the top of the stack, so the next two parts of the statement invoke the `i32.const` instruction, which pushes the specified values to the top of the stack. First, an offset of 0 indicates we want to write to the beginning of the buffer. The second one pushes the number 0 to the stack to indicate the value we want to write in position 0. The next line repeats the process for the next Fibonacci number. The `i32` from the previous line takes up 4 bytes, so we write value 1 to position 4.

The next step is to iterate over the remaining numbers, which are each defined as the sum of the previous two. This is why we need to start the process with the two we just wrote. We advance our `$index` variable to 2, so we will need $n - 2$ iterations of the loop. We have written two `i32` integers, so we advance our `$ptr` to 8.

Wat references several WebAssembly instructions that you will be introduced to over the course of the book. Here you can see some of the looping constructs. We define a

---

7 As a thought exercise, what could `$n` potentially be set to before our `i32` data type would overflow? How could you address that?

block at the seventh callout and give it a label of $break. The next step introduces a loop with an entry point called $top. The first instruction in the loop checks to see if $n and $index are equal, indicating we have handled all of our numbers. If so, it will break out of the loop. If not, it proceeds.

The i32.store instruction at the 10th callout writes to the $ptr location. The values of variables are pushed to the top of the stack with get_local. The value to write there is the addition of the values of the previous two numbers. i32.add expects to find its two addends at the top of the stack as well. So we load the integer location that is four less than $ptr. This represent $n – 1. We then load the integer stored at the location of $ptr minus 8, which represents $n – 2. i32.add pops these addends off the top of the stack and writes their sum back to the top. The stack now contains this value at the top and the location of the current $ptr value, which is what the i32.store is expecting.

The next step advances $ptr by four since we have now written another Fibonacci number to the buffer. We advance $n by one and then break to the top of the loop and repeat the process. Once we have written $n numbers to the buffer, the function returns. It does not need to return anything since the host environment has access to the Memory buffer and can read the results out directly with TypedArrays, as we saw earlier.

The result of loading our HTML into the browser and displaying the first 20 Fibonacci numbers is shown in Figure 4-3.

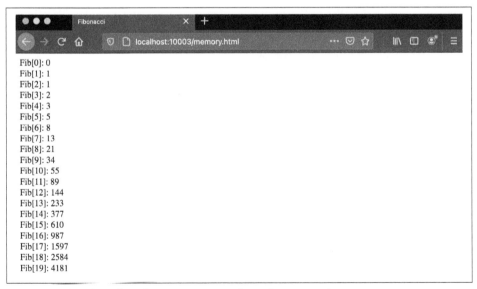

Figure 4-3. Reading the Fibonacci sequence from the Memory instance

This level of detail would be annoying to deal with regularly, but fortunately you will not have to. It is important to understand how things work at this level, though, and how we can emulate contiguous blocks of linear memory for efficient processing.

Strings at Last!

One final discussion before we move on is about how we can finally add strings to our repertoire! There are many more tools coming in later chapters of the book to make things even easier, but we can take advantage of some conveniences in Wat to write strings into Memory buffer and read them out on the JavaScript side.

In Example 4-8, you can see a very simple module that exports a one-page Memory instance. It then uses a data instruction to write a sequence of bytes into a location in the module's memory. It starts at location 0 and writes the bytes in the subsequent string. It is a convenience to not have to convert the multibyte strings into their component bytes, although you certainly can if you like. This string has a Japanese sentence and then its translation in English.[8]

Example 4-8. A simple use of strings in Wat

```
(module
 (memory (export "memory") 1)
 (data (i32.const 0x0) "私は横浜に住んでいました。I used to live in Yokohama.")
)
```

Once we compile the Wat to Wasm, we see that we have a new populated section in our module. You can see this with the wasm-objdump command:

```
brian@tweezer ~/g/w/s/ch04> wasm-objdump -x strings.wasm

strings.wasm:    file format wasm 0x1

Section Details:

Memory[1]:
 - memory[0] pages: initial=1
Export[1]:
 - memory[0] -> "memory"
Data[1]:
 - segment[0] memory=0 size=66 - init i32=0
  - 0000000: e7a7 81e3 81af e6a8 aae6 b59c e381 abe4  ................
  - 0000010: bd8f e382 93e3 81a7 e381 84e3 81be e381  ................
  - 0000020: 97e3 819f e380 8249 2075 7365 6420 746f  .......I used to
```

---

8 It's true!

```
   - 0000030: 206c 6976 6520 696e 2059 6f6b 6f68 616d   live in Yokoham
   - 0000040: 612e
```

The `Memory`, `Export`, and `Data` sections are filled in with the details of our strings written to memory. The instance is initialized this way so when a host environment reads from the buffer, the strings will already be there.

In Example 4-9, you see that we have one `<span>` for our Japanese sentence and one for our English sentence. To extract the individual bytes, we can wrap a `Uint8Array` around the `Memory` instance buffer that we have imported from the module. Notice that we only wrap the first 39 bytes. These bytes are decoded to a UTF-8 string via a `TextDecoder` instance, and then we set the `innerText` of the `<span>` designated for the Japanese sentence. We then wrap a separate `Uint8Array` around the portion of the buffer starting at position 39 and including the subsequent 26 bytes.

Example 4-9. Reading strings from an imported `Memory` instance

```
<!doctype html>
<html lang="en">
  <head>
    <meta charset="utf-8">
    <link rel="stylesheet" href="bootstrap.min.css">
    <title>Reading Strings From Memory</title>
    <script src="utils.js"></script>
  </head>
  <body>
    <div>
      <div>Japanese: <span id="japanese"></span></div>
      <div>English: <span id="english"></span></div>
    </div>
    <script>
      fetchAndInstantiate('strings.wasm').then(function(instance) {
          var mem = instance.exports.memory;

          var bytes = new Uint8Array(mem.buffer, 0, 39);
          var string = new TextDecoder('utf8').decode(bytes);
          var japanese = document.getElementById('japanese');
          japanese.innerText = string;

          bytes = new Uint8Array(mem.buffer, 39, 26);
          string = new TextDecoder('utf8').decode(bytes);
          var english = document.getElementById('english');
          english.innerText = string;
      });

    </script>
  </body>
</html>
```

In Figure 4-4, we see the successful results of reading the bytes out of the buffer and rendering them as UTF-8 strings.

Figure 4-4. Reading strings from the Memory instance

As cool as these results are, how did we know how many bytes to wrap and in which location to look for the strings? A little detective work can help. A capital letter "I" is represented as 49 in hexadecimal. The output from wasm-objdump gives us the offset in the Data segment for each byte. We see the value 49 for the first time on the row that begins with 0000020:. The 49 represents the seventh byte over, so the second sentence begins at position 27, which is 2 × 16 + 7 in decimal, so, 39. The Japanese string represents the bytes between 0 and 39. The English string begins at position 39.

But, wait a minute! It turns out we miscounted on the English sentence and we were off by one. This seems like a troublesome and error-prone amount of effort to get strings out of a WebAssembly module. Even doing things the hard way at this low level can be handled better. We will write out the locations of the strings first so we do not have to figure it out on our own.

Look at Example 4-10 to see how we can be more sophisticated. We have two data segments now. The first writes the starting position and length of the first string followed by the same information for the second one. Because we are using the same buffer for the indices and the strings, we have to be careful about locations.

As our strings are not very long, we can use single bytes as offsets and lengths. This is probably not a good strategy in general, but it will show off some additional flexibility. So, we write out the value 4 and the value 27. This represents an offset of 4 bytes and a length of 39. The offset is 4 because we have these four numbers (as single bytes) at the beginning of the buffer and will need to skip over them to get to the strings. As you now know, 27 is hexadecimal for 39, the length of the Japanese string. The English sentence will begin at index 4 + 39 = 43, which is 2b in hexadecimal (2 × 16 + 11) and is 27 bytes long, which is 1b in hexadecimal (1 × 16 + 11).

The second data segment starts at position 0x4 because we need to skip over those offsets and lengths.

Example 4-10. A more sophisticated use of strings in Wat

```
(module
 (memory (export "memory") 1)
 (data (i32.const 0x0) "\04\27\2b\1b")
 (data (i32.const 0x4) "私は横浜に住んでいました。I used to live in Yokohama.")
)
```

In Example 4-11, we see the other side of reading the strings out. It is certainly more complicated now, but it is also less manual as the module tells us exactly where to look. Another option when using `TypedArrays` is a `DataView`, which allows you to pull arbitrary data types out of the `Memory` buffer. They do not need to be homogenous like the normal `TypedArrays` (e.g., `Uint32Array`).

Example 4-11. Reading our indexed strings from the `Memory` buffer

```
<!doctype html>
<html lang="en">
  <head>
    <meta charset="utf-8">
    <link rel="stylesheet" href="bootstrap.min.css">
    <title>Reading Strings From Memory</title>
    <script src="utils.js"></script>
  </head>
  <body>
    <div>
      <div>Japanese: <span id="japanese"></span></div>
      <div>English: <span id="english"></span></div>
    </div>
    <script>
      fetchAndInstantiate('strings2.wasm').then(function(instance) {
          var mem = instance.exports.memory;

          var dv = new DataView(mem.buffer);
          var start = dv.getUint8(0);
          var end = dv.getUint8(1);

          var bytes = new Uint8Array(mem.buffer, start, end);
          var string = new TextDecoder('utf8').decode(bytes);
          var japanese = document.getElementById('japanese');
          japanese.innerText = string;

          start = dv.getUint8(2);
          end = dv.getUint8(3);

          bytes = new Uint8Array(mem.buffer, start, end);
          string = new TextDecoder('utf8').decode(bytes);
          var english = document.getElementById('english');
          english.innerText = string;
      });
```

```
    </script>
  </body>
</html>
```

We therefore wrap the exported `Memory` buffer with a `DataView` instance and read in the first two bytes by calling the `getUint8()` function once at location 0 and once at location 1. These represent the location and offset in the buffer for the Japanese string. Other than no longer using hardcoded numbers, the rest of our previous code is the same. Next we read out the two bytes at location 2 and 3, representing the location and length of the English sentence. This too is converted to a UTF-8 string and updated correctly this time, as seen in Figure 4-5.

Figure 4-5. Reading indices and strings from the Memory *instance*

As a homework assignment, try creating an even more flexible approach that tells you how many strings there are to read and what their locations and lengths are. The JavaScript to read it in can be made into a loop, and the whole process should be more flexible.

There is more to know about `Memory` instances as you shall see later, but for now, we have covered enough of the basics of WebAssembly that trying to do anything more sophisticated by hand in Wat will be too painful. Thus, it is time to use a higher-level language like C!

## CHAPTER 5

Using C/C++ and WebAssembly

The C programming language—a language which combines the flexibility of assembly language with the power of assembly language.
   —Anonymous

This begins a bit of a turning point in our discussion. Up until now, we have been focusing exclusively on WebAssembly and its immediate group of related tools and technologies. As we have seen, this is a useful way to explore what the platform offers, but it is an inefficient way to think about developing new software. Higher-level programming languages have long elevated our profession beyond the initial details of working with low-level instruction sets. It is simply easier and more efficient to express logic in syntactically clean and semantically rich languages.

To really appreciate what WebAssembly is providing, we need to consider one of the many source languages that compile down to it. The point is that not every problem is suitably expressed in JavaScript, so having the option to use another language for its performance, clarity of expression, or to simply reuse existing code is appealing.

The C language is one of the most important and widely used programming languages in the world.[1] I started playing around with it in high school on my Atari ST computer. I had read about it in *Computer Language* magazine and a friend gave me a copy of the seminal, eponymously named book *The C Programming Language* (*https://oreil.ly/XS4IG*) by Brian Kernighan and the late, great Dennis Ritchie.[2]

---

1 C's history (*https://oreil.ly/f22Gu*) is an integral part of our industry and the development of modern operating systems.

2 One of the most popular programming books ever.

There is an immense amount of software available in C, and much of it can simply be recompiled to WebAssembly. We will discuss porting existing libraries in Chapter 6, but for now we will learn a little C and how we can use it to improve some of the efforts we have tried so far.

Using C Functions

A C function is like a JavaScript function in many ways. It has its own lexical structure and it is not attached to a larger unit like a class or a struct. It may or may not take parameters. It can only return a single value and does not support exceptions, however, so error handling is often a little more primitive than in C++, Java, or JavaScript.

In Example 5-1, there is a C implementation of our age-calculating function from Chapter 2. Notice how much simpler it is to follow what is going on. This example even has some basic error handling to deal with the case of bad parameters where the birth year is bigger than the current year. Barring the appearance of a time-traveling visitor from the future, that should not happen and we should handle it. Higher-level languages are just easier for humans to use to express the logic of our business requirements.

Example 5-1. A simple C program

```c
#include <stdio.h>

int howOld(int currentYear, int yearBorn) {

  int retValue = -1;

  if(yearBorn <= currentYear) {
    retValue = currentYear - yearBorn;
  }

  return retValue;
}

int main() {
  int age = howOld(2021, 2000);

  if(age >= 0) {
    printf("You are %d!\n", age);
  } else {
    printf("You haven't been born yet.");
  }
}
```

Unfortunately, computers do not understand these higher-level languages, so we need to convert them to a binary machine representation for execution. If you have only ever done JavaScript programming, this process may be slightly foreign. As an interpreted language, you write JavaScript and simply run it. As with everything, there are trade-offs. What is convenient for developers is often significantly slower at runtime, and C and C++ have long held the mantle on performance.[3]

Given C's maturity and importance to our industry, there are many excellent commercial and open source compilers. These include the GNU/Linux C Compiler (GCC) and LLVM's Clang compiler. We are going to focus on the latter for reasons that will be clear shortly. You will want to install LLVM as described in the Appendix to run the following. Even on macOS, which uses Clang by default, not all of the commands will work out of the box without LLVM's WebAssembly support installed.

In its simplest form, we can convert our C program to an executable as follows:

```
brian@tweezer ~/g/w/s/ch05> clang howold.c
brian@tweezer ~/g/w/s/ch05> ls -laF
total 112
drwxr-xr-x  4 brian  staff    128 Feb 14 14:35 ./
drwxr-xr-x  6 brian  staff    192 Feb 14 14:32 ../
-rwxr-xr-x  1 brian  staff  49456 Feb 14 14:35 a.out*
-rw-r--r--  1 brian  staff    343 Feb 14 14:36 howold.c
```

For historical reasons, the executable generated is called a.out. You will see how to change that later. For now, we can execute the program:

```
brian@tweezer ~/g/w/s/ch05> ./a.out
You are 21!
```

This works because the executable generated has been turned into a suitable format that macOS knows how to run. It is a Mach-O executable that targets the Intel x86 instruction set on a 64-bit platform:

```
brian@tweezer ~/g/w/s/ch05> file a.out
a.out: Mach-O 64-bit executable x86_64
```

This program will not run on a Windows or Linux machine. Without their new emulation layer, it will not even run on Apple's new ARM-based machines. This is because a CPU has an instruction set that involves loading values into registers, invoking functionality on the CPU, and storing results in memory. Rerunning clang to produce assembly language output instead of a binary executable shows you what this looks like for this architecture:

```
brian@tweezer ~/g/w/s/ch05> clang -S howold.c
```

This produces the file shown in Example 5-2.

---

3 And the lion's share of security issues!

Example 5-2. Assembly language generated for our simple application

```
        .section        __TEXT,__text,regular,pure_instructions
        .build_version macos, 11, 0      sdk_version 11, 1
        .globl  _howOld                  ## -- Begin function howOld
        .p2align        4, 0x90
_howOld:                                 ## @howOld
        .cfi_startproc
## %bb.0:
        pushq   %rbp
        .cfi_def_cfa_offset 16
        .cfi_offset %rbp, -16
        movq    %rsp, %rbp
        .cfi_def_cfa_register %rbp
        movl    %edi, -4(%rbp)
        movl    %esi, -8(%rbp)
        movl    $-1, -12(%rbp)
        movl    -4(%rbp), %eax
        cmpl    -8(%rbp), %eax
        jg      LBB0_2
## %bb.1:
        movl    -8(%rbp), %eax
        subl    -4(%rbp), %eax
        movl    %eax, -12(%rbp)
LBB0_2:
        movl    -12(%rbp), %eax
        popq    %rbp
        retq
        .cfi_endproc
                                         ## -- End function
        .globl  _main                    ## -- Begin function main
        .p2align        4, 0x90
_main:                                   ## @main
        .cfi_startproc
## %bb.0:
        pushq   %rbp
        .cfi_def_cfa_offset 16
        .cfi_offset %rbp, -16
        movq    %rsp, %rbp
        .cfi_def_cfa_register %rbp
        subq    $16, %rsp
        movl    $0, -4(%rbp)
        movl    $2000, %edi              ## imm = 0x7D0
        movl    $2021, %esi              ## imm = 0x7E5
        callq   _howOld
        movl    %eax, -8(%rbp)
        cmpl    $0, -8(%rbp)
        jl      LBB1_2
## %bb.1:
        movl    -8(%rbp), %esi
        leaq    L_.str(%rip), %rdi
        movb    $0, %al
```

```
        callq   _printf
        jmp     LBB1_3
LBB1_2:
        leaq    L_.str.1(%rip), %rdi
        movb    $0, %al
        callq   _printf
LBB1_3:
        movl    -4(%rbp), %eax
        addq    $16, %rsp
        popq    %rbp
        retq
        .cfi_endproc
                                        ## -- End function
        .section        __TEXT,__cstring,cstring_literals
L_.str:                                 ## @.str
        .asciz  "You are %d\n!"

L_.str.1:                               ## @.str.1
        .asciz  "You haven't been born yet."

.subsections_via_symbols
```

As you can see, it is much more verbose than our C program. High-level constructs like function calls, loops, and conditional checks require many lower-level instructions to express. We will need an actual Intel x86 chip to run on, or at least an emulated one. At some level, however, this is conceptually similar to the Wat files we have seen in previous chapters.

The main reason we are discussing Clang as our example C compiler is because it has a modern, pluggable architecture based on the LLVM project.[4] This is incredibly important in the modern world of increasing numbers of competing instruction sets (e.g., x86, ARM, RISC-V), new programming languages (e.g., Rust, Julia, Swift), and an overall desire to reuse common optimizations regardless of source language.

In Figure 5-1, you can see this as a three-part process. Source code is parsed by a frontend processing step. This is going to be language-specific. The output of this step is an intermediate representation (IR), an instruction set of a hypothetical but not real machine. It captures the expressed logic in a format that can be manipulated by the optimization layer. This process involves applying one or more transformations that should have the effect of making the code faster or more efficient based purely on the expressed logic. Loops may be unrolled,[5] unused code may be eliminated, expressions involving constants may be evaluated by the compiler so they do not need to be evaluated at runtime, and more. The final step emits a native set of

---

4 LLVM (*https://llvm.org*) used to stand for Low-Level Virtual Machine, but these days it just means LLVM.

5 Loop unrolling (*https://oreil.ly/9d6qn*) is a common optimization in many programming languages.

instructions targeting a specific runtime. For our purposes, that was obviously the Mach-O x86 64-bit architecture.

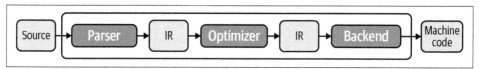

Figure 5-1. The LLVM pluggable compiler architecture

Any one of these layers may be swapped out for something else. As I mentioned, languages such as Rust, Julia, and Swift use the LLVM infrastructure. This keeps language authors from having to start from scratch every time. They need to write new frontend parsers, but can leverage much of the existing optimization and backend work. Compiler researchers can develop new optimizations and test them in isolation before making them available for use on the IR of arbitrary input languages. For our purposes, the backend is the most important swappable layer. On Linux or Windows, native versions of the same first two layers could be used, but there would also be a machine-specific backend.

You can usually generate a different backend than the native runtime of your computer through a process known as cross-compiling. This is useful for targeting embedded systems that may not have a developer toolchain installed. It is also useful in continuous integration and delivery systems so you can target multiple platforms from the same build environment. Otherwise, you might need a separate build environment for every target platform.

The Emscripten toolchain was developed for asm.js work and was based upon LLVM and Clang so it only had to emit the optimizable subset of JavaScript to allow C programs to run in the browser. When the WebAssembly instruction set and platform were ultimately defined, in essence, they merely had to add a WebAssembly backend to emit that instead. We will introduce this toolchain in the next chapter, but hopefully you are getting the picture of how higher-level languages can be compiled to a common form that can then be further transformed into an efficient native representation.

Our LLVM installation should natively support WebAssembly as a backend. To double-check, try the following:

```
brian@tweezer ~/g/w/s/ch05> llc --version
LLVM (http://llvm.org/):
  LLVM version 11.0.1
  Optimized build.
  Default target: x86_64-apple-darwin20.2.0
  Host CPU: skylake

  Registered Targets:
    aarch64    - AArch64 (little endian)
```

```
aarch64_32 - AArch64 (little endian ILP32)
aarch64_be - AArch64 (big endian)
arm        - ARM
arm64      - ARM64 (little endian)
arm64_32   - ARM64 (little endian ILP32)
nvptx      - NVIDIA PTX 32-bit
nvptx64    - NVIDIA PTX 64-bit
ppc32      - PowerPC 32
ppc64      - PowerPC 64
ppc64le    - PowerPC 64 LE
r600       - AMD GPUs HD2XXX-HD6XXX
riscv32    - 32-bit RISC-V
riscv64    - 64-bit RISC-V
wasm32     - WebAssembly 32-bit
wasm64     - WebAssembly 64-bit
x86        - 32-bit X86: Pentium-Pro and above
x86-64     - 64-bit X86: EM64T and AMD64
xcore      - XCore
```

I have edited the supported target list for length (it is much longer!), but still wanted to show that most of the major platforms are supported. To simplify our immediate usage, I am going to replace the standalone main() functionality in the program with just the age calculation function, as shown in Example 5-3.

Example 5-3. Just the howOld function

```
int howOld(int currentYear, int yearBorn) {

  int retValue = -1;

  if(yearBorn <= currentYear) {
    retValue = currentYear - yearBorn;
  }

  return retValue;
}
```

To compile this to WebAssembly, we can use the following:

```
brian@tweezer ~/g/w/s/ch05> clang --target=wasm32 -nostdlib -Wl,--no-entry ↵
-Wl,--export-all howold2.c -o howold.wasm
```

The --target=wasm32 directive targets the 32-bit WebAssembly platform. The -nostdlib tells it not to link against a standard library because we are not initially planning on running the function in a location where it will be directly available (i.e., a browser). The --not-entry and --export-all directives tell the linker not to expect a main() function and to keep all of the functions for export purposes. Without the latter hint, the optimization processes might eliminate unused functions as technically nothing is calling them. The -o howold.wasm names the output file.

What we are left with is a working Wasm module that we know how to explore and use from earlier chapters. There is quite a lot of new noise in the file, but the basics remain the same. We have our types, functions, and memory, as well as a variety of memory management details that we will ignore for now:

```
brian@tweezer ~/g/w/s/ch05> wasm-objdump -x howold.wasm

howold.wasm:    file format wasm 0x1

Section Details:

Type[2]:
 - type[0] () -> nil
 - type[1] (i32, i32) -> i32
Function[2]:
 - func[0] sig=0 <__wasm_call_ctors>
 - func[1] sig=1 <howOld>
Table[1]:
 - table[0] type=funcref initial=1 max=1
Memory[1]:
 - memory[0] pages: initial=2
Global[7]:
 - global[0] i32 mutable=1 - init i32=66560
 - global[1] i32 mutable=0 <__dso_handle> - init i32=1024
 - global[2] i32 mutable=0 <__data_end> - init i32=1024
 - global[3] i32 mutable=0 <__global_base> - init i32=1024
 - global[4] i32 mutable=0 <__heap_base> - init i32=66560
 - global[5] i32 mutable=0 <__memory_base> - init i32=0
 - global[6] i32 mutable=0 <__table_base> - init i32=1
Export[9]:
 - memory[0] -> "memory"
 - func[0] <__wasm_call_ctors> -> "__wasm_call_ctors"
 - func[1] <howOld> -> "howOld"
 - global[1] -> "__dso_handle"
 - global[2] -> "__data_end"
 - global[3] -> "__global_base"
 - global[4] -> "__heap_base"
 - global[5] -> "__memory_base"
 - global[6] -> "__table_base"
Code[2]:
 - func[0] size=2 <__wasm_call_ctors>
 - func[1] size=134 <howOld>
Custom:
 - name: "name"
 - func[0] <__wasm_call_ctors>
 - func[1] <howOld>
Custom:
 - name: "producers"
```

In Example 5-4, we use our new module to calculate an age based on an HTML input range setting. This is obviously not a function we would have to write in C, but we are keeping it simple momentarily. We have a range <input> element whose maximum value is set to the current year once the WebAssembly module is loaded. We arbitrarily set the minimum value to 100 years in the past. We have a function called update Labels to set the values on our elements when the value changes and another to recalculate someone's age when the slider value changes. The listener function calls into our module with the currentYear and the current value of the slider to calculate the difference.

Example 5-4. Using the howOld function in HTML

```
<!doctype html>
<html lang="en">
  <head>
    <meta charset="utf-8">
    <link rel="stylesheet" href="bootstrap.min.css">
    <title>How Old Are You?</title>
    <script src="utils.js"></script>
  </head>
  <body>
    <div id="container" class="container" style="width:  80%">
      <h1>How Old Are You?</h1>
      <label for="year" id="yearborn" class="form-label">Year Born</label>
      <input type="range" class="form-range" id="year" name="year" value="0"/>
      <div class="form-label">You are: <span id="age"/></div>
    </div>

    <script>
      var d = new Date();
      var currentYear = d.getFullYear();
      var slider = document.getElementById("year");
      var yearBorn = document.getElementById("yearborn");
      var ageSpan = document.getElementById("age");

      fetchAndInstantiate('howold.wasm').then(function(instance) {
          slider.setAttribute("min", currentYear - 100);
          slider.setAttribute("max", currentYear);

          var updateLabels = function(val, age) {
              yearBorn.innerText =  "Year Born: " + val;
              ageSpan.innerText = age;
          };

          var listener = function() {
              var age = instance.exports.howOld(currentYear, slider.value);
              updateLabels(slider.value, age);
          };
```

```
            slider.onchange = listener;
            slider.oninput = listener;
            slider.value = "1972";

            updateLabels(1972, 49);
        });
    </script>
  </body>
</html>
```

The rendered HTML should look something like Figure 5-2.

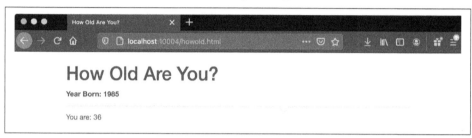

Figure 5-2. Our HTML application for calculating someone's age

Things Get Complicated

Now that you have seen the basics of using C with WebAssembly, the reality is that we have not used much of the language. I have shown you a simple example that passes a couple of numbers to a function that only returns a single number. That is not substantially different from what we have done so far.

More sophisticated C programs will have difficulty mapping quite so simply to the amount of the platform you have been exposed to. There is the issue we have raised already with respect to our "Hello, World!" program: there is no `printf()` function available to the program in the browser. There is also the issue of how C programs are structured and how memory is allocated and cleaned up. The process of linking the various compiled software files together is also fundamentally different in this world we are exploring.

The good news is that most of these issues can be handled by tools and the runtime platform. The bad news is that the details get rather complicated quickly. If you have never done any C programming before, there will be many new ideas. This book cannot teach you everything, but I will try to highlight specific interactions between this language and WebAssembly.[6]

---

6 There is a useful online C tutorial (*https://learn-c.org*) if you don't mind some annoying ads. Otherwise, Steve Oualline's *Practical C Programming* (O'Reilly) or *The C Programming Language* are good introductions.

Imagine a simple function that takes no parameters and returns the sum of an array. Example 5-5 has just such an example. Bear with me, I am keeping it arbitrarily simple for the moment. In this code we have no parameters and the compiler can tell how big the array needs to be because we initialize it with the first 10 digits.

Example 5-5. A simple C function

```
int addArray() {
  int retValue = 0;
  int array[] = {0, 1, 2, 3, 4, 5, 6, 7, 8, 9};

  for(int i = 0; i < 10; i++) {
    retValue += array[i];
  }

  return retValue;
}
```

If we try to compile this program, we will probably run into a warning because Clang is expecting there to be a main() program. Remember, this is how the operating system knows where to begin, as we discussed in Chapter 3. Because it cannot find a method with this name, it cannot link everything up into a standalone runtime:

```
brian@tweezer ~/g/w/s/ch05> clang simple.c -o simple.o
Undefined symbols for architecture x86_64:
  "_main", referenced from:
      implicit entry/start for main executable
ld: symbol(s) not found for architecture x86_64
clang-11: error: linker command failed with exit code 1 (use -v to see invocation)
```

No problem. This is an easy fix. We can simply tell Clang to compile the code but not link it with the -c option:

```
brian@tweezer ~/g/w/s/ch05> clang -c simple.c -o simple.o
brian@tweezer ~/g/w/s/ch05> ls -laF simple.*
-rw-r--r--  1 brian  staff   170 Feb 19 15:27 simple.c
-rw-r--r--  1 brian  staff  1060 Feb 19 15:43 simple.o
```

This has generated an object file that has the function definition in it. The nm command shows us what is in the compiled file:[7]

```
brian@tweezer ~/g/w/s/ch05> nm -a simple.o
                 U ___stack_chk_fail
                 U ___stack_chk_guard
0000000000000000 T _addArray
                 U _memcpy
00000000000000a0 s l___const.addArray.array
```

---

7 nm is a common tool in the world of C to print out the contents of binary files such as this.

This might be confusing at first, but the idea should be clear enough with some explanation. Our function, addArray(), is defined as a text segment symbol in the object file. The three items with a U symbol type indicate that they are undefined. These particular symbols refer to some buffer overflow protection methods linked in automatically for safety reasons and a function to copy memory from one location to another. The definitions of these functions will be required to make the code executable, but this is what the linking stage and reusable libraries like *libc* provide.

What we end up with is an incomplete executable, but a properly formed binary representation of our function. If we provide a main() method and link the executable, we can demonstrate how it works. In Example 5-6, our function is called by our driver program.

Example 5-6. A main() method to invoke our function

```c
#include <stdio.h>

extern int addArray();

int main() {
  int sum = addArray();

  printf("The array sum is: %d\n", sum);
}
```

Notice we have to tell the compiler about the definition of our addArray() function because it is not defined in this file. The extern keyword provides a promise that there will be something with this name that takes no arguments and returns an integer available. As such, it is OK to assign the result of this function to an integer variable called sum. This is then passed into the printf() function where it is formatted as a human-friendly output message indicating the accumulated sum.

To build the executable, we compile the *simplemain.c* and *simple.c* files and store the result in an executable called *simplemain*. Because we did not include the -c option, it does engage the linker. This no longer complains because we did provide a definition for the main() method:

```
brian@tweezer ~/g/w/s/ch05> clang simplemain.c simple.c -o simplemain
brian@tweezer ~/g/w/s/ch05> ls -laF simplemain
-rwxr-xr-x  1 brian  staff  49640 Feb 19 16:01 simplemain*
brian@tweezer ~/g/w/s/ch05> ./simplemain
The array sum is: 45
```

If we use the nm program on the final executable, you will notice that we have provided everything we need to this time. The undefined symbols will be expected to be provided by a dynamic library when the program runs. They are excluded from the binary to keep the size down:

```
brian@tweezer ~/g/w/s/ch05> nm -a simplemain
                 U ___stack_chk_fail
                 U ___stack_chk_guard
0000000100008018 d __dyld_private
0000000100000000 T __mh_execute_header
0000000100003ea0 T _addArray
0000000100003e70 T _main
                 U _memcpy
                 U _printf
                 U dyld_stub_binder
```

Now that we have a working program, let us return to our function shown in Example 5-5. This works because we used a literal syntax to initialize the array. We did not specify how big the array needed to be because the compiler could figure it out. In memory it has allocated enough space to hold that many integers. This allocation is done on the stack so when we return from the function, there is no additional cleanup necessary. We end up with a sufficiently large location in memory to store our numbers to sum up, as shown in Figure 5-3.

Figure 5-3. A C array is just a named portion of memory storing our data

What happens if we tell the compiler how big it needs to be but then give it more numbers than that? In Example 5-7, we tell the compiler we are only expecting 5 integers in the array but then give it 10. This is known as a *blivet* in some circles.[8] With the following discussion I am hoping to show you how a compiler can help you come to a more correct solution as you make edits to your code by providing feedback on your mistakes. This happens well before we try to run the code, which is usually where we find problems in interpreted languages.

Example 5-7. A broken version of our function

```
int addArray() {
  int retValue = 0;
  int array[5] = {0, 1, 2, 3, 4, 5, 6, 7, 8, 9};

  for(int i = 0; i < 10; i++) {
    retValue += array[i];
  }

  return retValue;
}
```

---

8 Sometimes referred to as "ten pounds of manure in a five-pound bag." It will not fit!

Fortunately, this is also something easy for a compiler to detect. It will point out that we are being silly and give us a warning:

```
brian@tweezer ~/g/w/s/ch05> clang -c simple.c -o simple.o
   int array[5] = {0, 1, 2, 3, 4, 5, 6, 7, 8, 9};
                               ^

1 warning generated.
```

What happens if we want to return an array from our function? In Example 5-8, we attempt this but quickly see that it will not work.

Example 5-8. An unsuccessful attempt to return an array from a function

```
int[] generateArray() {
  int array[] = {0, 1, 2, 3, 4, 5, 6, 7, 8, 9};
  return array;
}
```

Even though what we are doing seems reasonable, the compiler again informs us that we are not doing it right:

```
brian@tweezer ~/g/w/s/ch05> clang -c simple2.c -o simple2.o
simple2.c:1:22: error: brackets are not allowed here; to declare an array, place
the brackets after the identifier
int[] generateArray() {
   ~~                 ^
                     []
simple2.c:1:20: error: function cannot return array type 'int []'
int[] generateArray() {
                   ^
simple2.c:3:10: warning: incompatible pointer to integer conversion returning
'int [10]' from a function with result type 'int' [-Wint-conversion]
   return array;
          ^~~~~
simple2.c:3:10: warning: address of stack memory associated with local variable
'array' returned [-Wreturn-stack-address]
   return array;
          ^~~~~
2 warnings and 2 errors generated.
```

Array names are special variables in C. They are placeholders for the address of a contiguous block in memory that stores these values. We can introduce a pointer to an integer and assign it to the location of the beginning of the array. In order to access the value at that location, we must use the dereference operator, *.

In Example 5-9, you can see us define a pointer to an integer and assign the array address to it. When we print out a, we use a special formatting structure of %p to indicate this is a memory reference.

Example 5-9. Using a pointer to an array

```c
#include <stdio.h>

void generateArray() {
  int array[] = {0, 1, 2, 3, 4, 5, 6, 7, 8, 9};
  int * a = array;
  printf("a is %p\n", a);
  printf("The first value is: %d\n", *(a));
  printf("The second value is: %d\n", *(a + 1));
  printf("The third value is: %d\n", *(a + 2));
}

int main() {
  generateArray();
}
```

The first value in the array is located at the beginning of the array, so we can access it with *a. The second integer is one memory address over, so we add one to the base of the array before dereferencing it. The third value is two over.

Compiling our program and running it shows us the output we expect. Your value for a as an address is unlikely to be the same, but it should look similar:

```
brian@tweezer ~/g/w/s/ch05> clang simple3.c -o simple3
brian@tweezer ~/g/w/s/ch05> ./simple3
a is 0x7ffeef3a9720
The first value is: 0
The second value is: 1
The third value is: 2
```

The reason the compiler yelled at us with the code in Example 5-8 is because you cannot return an array like we tried. Instead, you have to return a pointer. We try once again in Example 5-10 to return our array.

Example 5-10. Another unsuccessful attempt to return an array from a function

```c
#include <stdio.h>

int * generateArray() {
  int array[] = {0, 1, 2, 3, 4, 5, 6, 7, 8, 9};
  return array;
}

int main() {
  int * a = generateArray();
  printf("a is %p\n", a);
  printf("The first value is: %d\n", *a);
  printf("The second value is: %d\n", *(a + 1));
  printf("The third value is: %d\n", *(a + 2));
}
```

And once again, we fail:

```
brian@tweezer ~/g/w/s/ch05> clang simple4.c -o simple4
simple4.c:5:10: warning: address of stack memory associated with local variable
'array' returned [-Wreturn-stack-address]
  return array;
         ^~~~~
1 warning generated.
```

This time the compiler is telling us that we are returning a reference to memory on the stack. If you remember what I said previously about what happens when we return from the function, our pointer is pointing to memory that is going to be thrown away before we even get a chance to use it.

This is why we need the ability to allocate memory on the heap. It will be valid until we tell the C runtime that we do not need it anymore. The easiest way to allocate memory on the heap is to use the `malloc()` function.

We finally have a working code sample in Example 5-11. The `malloc()` function is provided by the standard library, so we include another header with its definition. We need to tell this function how much memory to allocate, so we use some multiple of the size of an integer. The good news is that we can also create arbitrarily large arrays now. You can see here we double the size to 20 and then iterate over the numbers between 0 and 19 to fill our array. Finally, we return the result and capture it as an `int *` in the `main()` method. This behaves just like our `int *` in Example 5-9, even though we are pointing to the heap now instead of the stack.

Example 5-11. A successful (but still flawed) attempt to return an array from a function

```
#include <stdio.h>
#include <stdlib.h>

int * generateArray() {
  int * array = (int *) malloc(sizeof(int) * 20);
  for(int i = 0; i < 20; i++) {
    array[i] = i;
  }

  return array;
}

int main() {
  int * a = generateArray();
  printf("a is %p\n", a);
  printf("The first value is: %d\n", *a);
  printf("The second value is: %d\n", *(a + 1));
  printf("The third value is: %d\n", *(a + 2));
}
```

Compiling and running our new program finally gives us some joy:

```
brian@tweezer ~/g/w/s/ch05> clang simple5.c -o simple5
brian@tweezer ~/g/w/s/ch05> ./simple5
a is 0x7fae22c059e0
The first value is: 0
The second value is: 1
The third value is: 2
```

Before you get too comfortable, however, there remains a flaw in our program. Because we print out the results and quit, it is not a huge issue, but it is the kind of issue that drives C programmers (and their users) bonkers. We forgot to free up the memory we allocated! If this were a server or a long-running program and we called our function many times, we might eventually run out of memory.

To solve the problem, we just need to call the free() function to tell the runtime we are done with that memory. Once we do, we cannot touch it again. This highlights some of the many issues you need to consider when writing programs in C:

- Do not use memory before you have allocated it.
- Do not create blivets with the memory you have allocated. Make sure they are big enough.
- Do not forget to free your memory once you are done with it.
- Do not use your memory after you have freed it.

Forgetting any one of these rules is likely to cause your program to crash or run out of memory. If this seems like a big hassle, you will appreciate languages such as Java, Python, and JavaScript, which alleviate some of these issues for you. The downside is that there is usually a performance trade-off, which is why Rust is so compelling. It gives you the speed of a language like C without the danger of a language like C. We will introduce Rust in Chapter 10.

Until then, we need to figure out what all of this means for WebAssembly.

C/C++ and WebAssembly

For this next section, I am going to be using a more complex infrastructure based upon a sample project provided by Petter Strandmark (*https://oreil.ly/ejhrx*) for using Clang and WebAssembly together. In the next chapter, we will introduce the Emscripten toolchain to make it easier to port existing code to WebAssembly. Eventually, we will introduce the WebAssembly System Interface (WASI) to handle these details, but until then we need the infrastructure to help us overcome the obstacles we have seen so far.

There are several pieces to this infrastructure, but it is largely self-contained and I think ultimately pretty clear. For reasons that are not worth going into at the moment, we are going to use the C++ version of the Clang compiler. We do not have time to teach you C++ in this chapter as well, so I am not going to focus on too many specifics. There are cases where we need to make the C++ code behave like C, however, so just stick with me on this one.

We will start with some C/C++ code. The two languages are quite closely related, but C++ provides object-oriented programming features that make it a little easier to model a domain using natural concepts (e.g., orders, accounts, users, etc.). We are not going to focus on any of these distinctions, however, which is why I keep referring to the languages together. In Example 5-12, you can see some of the functionality we are going to use. To keep things manageable, I won't show you everything at this point.

Example 5-12. Some C/C++ functions for us to call

```
#include "nanolibc/libc.h"
#include "nanolibc/libc_extra.h"

#define WASM_EXPORT __attribute__((visibility("default"))) extern "C"

WASM_EXPORT int* get_memory_for_int_array(int size) {
  return new int[size];
}

WASM_EXPORT void free_memory_for_int_array(int* arr) {
  delete[] arr;
}

WASM_EXPORT void mergeSort(char *p, int length) {
  int c, d, swap;

  for(c = 0; c < length - 1; c++ ) {
    for( d = 0; d < length - c - 1; d++) {
      if(p[d] > p[d+1]) {
        swap = p[d];
        p[d] = p[d+1];
        p[d+1] = swap;
      }
    }
  }
}

WASM_EXPORT void reverse(unsigned char* p, int len) {
  for( int i = 0; i < len / 2; i++ ) {
    unsigned char temp = p[i];
    p[i] = p[len - i - 1];
    p[len - i - 1] = temp;
```

```
    }
}
```

The first thing that will jump out at you is the `#include` statements. This code uses a very small implementation of the *libc* library, which provides us with working versions of `malloc()`, `free()`, and even `printf()` (but hold that thought for a moment). Header files in C/C++ allow us to advertise the signatures of functions so the compiler knows what to expect.

As you see in Example 5-13, we have a collection of functions available for us to link against. To make sure they are visible as C functions, we use the `extern "C"` keyword to keep the C++ compiler from mangling their names.[9]

Example 5-13. The header file for a small implementation of libc

```
#ifndef _NANOLIB_C_H
#define _NANOLIB_C_H
#include <stdarg.h>
#include <stddef.h>

extern "C" {
  void* memcpy(void* dest, const void* src, size_t count);
  void* memset (void * dest, int value, size_t count);

  int puts ( const char * str );
  int printf(const char* format, ...);
  int sprintf(char* buffer, const char* format, ...);
  int snprintf(char* buffer, size_t count, const char* format, ...);
  int vsnprintf(char* buffer, size_t count, const char* format, va_list va);

  void* malloc(size_t amount);
  void* realloc(void *ptr, size_t size);
  void* calloc(size_t num, size_t size);
  void free(void* mem);
}

#endif
```

Looking back at Example 5-12, we have a method called `get_memory` `_for_int_array()` that takes a `size` parameter to tell us how much memory to allocate. If you look closely at the implementation, it is using C++'s new operator. For our purposes, just assume that means the same things as a `malloc()` call. The `free_mem` `ory_for_int_array()` function serves a similar role to a `free()` call by using the `delete` operator.

---

9 It is outside of the scope of this book to cover these details, but you can find more online (*https://oreil.ly/ FBc4R*) if you are interested.

There is a #define macro that gives these functions external visibility, which will make sure they are available to our JavaScript code that is going to invoke them.

We next have a function providing an implementation of a merge sort and another that reverses an array of numbers.[10]

The build systems for C/C++ applications and libraries are not as modern and friendly as, say, Rust's cargo command, but they are solid and flexible. We are going to use a simple *Makefile*-based approach. This is another detail we do not have time to cover in depth, but basically we define a set of rules to build the target. When source code changes, it causes the dependencies to be reevaluated and builds anything that needs to be built. The contents of this file are available through the book's Git repo (*https://github.com/bsletten/wasm_tdg*) if you want to see how it works.

To build our code, we will use the make command and it will let us know how it goes:

```
brian@tweezer ~/g/w/s/c/helloworld> make
... Lots of noise goes by...
brian@tweezer ~/g/w/s/c/helloworld> ls -laF *.wasm
-rwxr-xr-x  1 brian  staff  5309 Feb 19 20:03 library.wasm*
```

I will leave it to you to explore the contents of the module in detail, but I want to highlight a few quick points for part of it. Notice our module exports its own memory. You can change this behavior to import a Memory instance from the JavaScript side of things, but we are not going to do that for now.

All you need to focus on for the moment is that our C/C++ code has a tiny implementation of *libc* that will allocate and free memory from an exported Memory instance, which, after Chapter 4, should start to get your gears turning:

```
brian@tweezer ~/g/w/s/c/helloworld> wasm-objdump -x library.wasm
...
Export[11]:
 - memory[0] -> "memory"
 - func[1] <get_memory_for_int_array> -> "get_memory_for_int_array"
 - func[14] <_Znam> -> "_Znam"
 - func[3] <free_memory_for_int_array> -> "free_memory_for_int_array"
 - func[16] <_ZdaPv> -> "_ZdaPv"
 - func[5] <debug_dump_memory> -> "debug_dump_memory"
 - func[7] <mergeSort> -> "mergeSort"
 - func[8] <reverse> -> "reverse"
 - func[9] <helloWorld> -> "helloWorld"
 - func[11] <_Znwm> -> "_Znwm"
 - func[15] <_ZdlPv> -> "_ZdlPv"
...
```

---

10 Merge sort (*https://oreil.ly/cInzP*) is a utility-sorting algorithm with O(n log n) complexity. It is easy to implement, which is why I chose it.

Next we will need some HTML code to invoke our C/C++ behavior. Much of the structure is similar to what we have seen previously, but I will highlight the parts you need to understand in Example 5-14.

Example 5-14. The relevant portions of our HTML file

```
<script>
let wasm;

...

WebAssembly.instantiateStreaming(fetch('library.wasm'), importObject).then(
  function(obj) { ❶
    wasm = obj; ❷

    const ptr = wasm.instance.exports.get_memory_for_int_array(10); ❸
    const memory = new Uint8Array(wasm.instance.exports.memory.buffer); ❹
    const nums = memory.subarray(ptr); ❺

    for(var i = 0; i < 10; i++) {
      nums[i] = i;
    }

    console.log(nums);

    wasm.instance.exports.reverse(ptr, 10); ❻

    console.log(nums);

    var arr = [0, 1, 2, 3, 4, 5, 6, 7, 8, 9, 10]; ❼

    shuffleArray(arr);

    for(var i = 0; i < 10; i++) {
      nums[i] = arr[i];
    }

    console.log(nums);

    wasm.instance.exports.mergeSort(ptr, 10); ❽

    console.log(nums);

    wasm.instance.exports.free_memory_for_int_array(ptr); ❾

    ...
}

</script>
```

❶ The module is created in the JavaScript host the same way as usual.

❷ We want access to the module instance elsewhere once it is available.

❸ Enough space is initialized in the module for 10 integers. We capture the "pointer" that is returned.

❹ The underlying buffer is wrapped with a Uint8Array.

❺ A sub-Uint8Array is created that covers the portion referenced by the previously returned "pointer."

❻ The reverse() method from the module is invoked.

❼ We rely upon JavaScript functionality to shuffle some data.

❽ The mergeSort() method is invoked with a reference to the "pointer."

❾ The memory is freed on the module side.

We start off by serving up the HTML and WebAssembly module over HTTP as we have done previously. The module is loaded and instantiated using the same utility library as before, even though it was generated via a completely different process. Once the module instance is available, we assign the variable to another variable defined outside of the lexical scope of this block so we can use it elsewhere.

Because the C/C++ side of our code does not realize what is going on, we have to allocate enough memory from its perspective to store some data from the JavaScript side. Previously we just wrote data directly into the exported Memory instances. Because we are going to be emulating pointers, we have to create something on that side that will look appropriate. We invoke the get_memory_for_int_array() function and ask it to allocate room for 10 integers. The function returns a pointer on the C/C++ side. From this side it is more rightly considered a "pointer." It is not directly a reference to a location in the heap as you saw earlier. Instead, it is an index into the underlying buffer that the small *libc* implementation allocated the data into. We will use this reference as an offset into the memory when we pass it back to the other side.

We surround the underlying ArrayBuffer with a Uint8Array wrapper so we can write 8-bit integers easily from this side. If you revisit the code in Example 5-12, you might notice that our sorting and reversing functions accept char *. C can be pretty flexible by doing automatic type coercions between ints, chars, addresses, booleans, and more. It is extremely flexible and often very buggy. These chars cannot be bigger than 8 bits, so they have a max size of 255. We wrap the buffer with a Uint8Array for the convenience of not having to worry about that.

After this, a subarray of type `Uint8Array` is generated for the portion beginning at our "pointer." This allows us to ignore everything that might have been allocated before our array, and we can start writing into it conveniently using JavaScript numbers. The results of this are dumped to the console to show you what is going on.

The next step is to invoke the `reverse()` function. This implementation is written with the perception that it is just swapping values in memory and, remarkably, it does not have to change. We do not need a return value from this function because the array was reversed in place. This is one of the reasons C can be so fast. It avoids creating a lot of unnecessary memory and has very low overhead to retrieve values and iterate through memory locations. On the JavaScript side, our "pointer" will still point to the beginning of the newly reversed array, which is dumped to the console for clarity.

In order to show off the sorting functionality, we need some shuffled data. It certainly would have been possible to write code like that in C, but we need to rely on a random number generator for the shuffling algorithm. That would have complicated things for us dependency-wise, so we just rely on JavaScript's support for random number generation. You are likely to rely on behavior from the browser sometimes and rely on code expressed in a WebAssembly module at other times.

A newly created array is filled, shuffled, and dumped to the console. We write the shuffled values back into our C/C++ array at the location indicated by our "pointer" and then invoke the `mergeSort()` functionality. This too is written assuming it has access to a location in memory so it efficiently reorders the data to be sorted.

When we return to JavaScript, we dump the results to the console and then free up the memory we allocated as we are no longer using it.

In Figure 5-4, you see the remarkable results of our most complicated example so far. We are getting the benefits of reusing code that performs at near native speed in the browser. For small data sets, the overhead is probably still not worth it, but it is easy to make the case in other situations that it is.

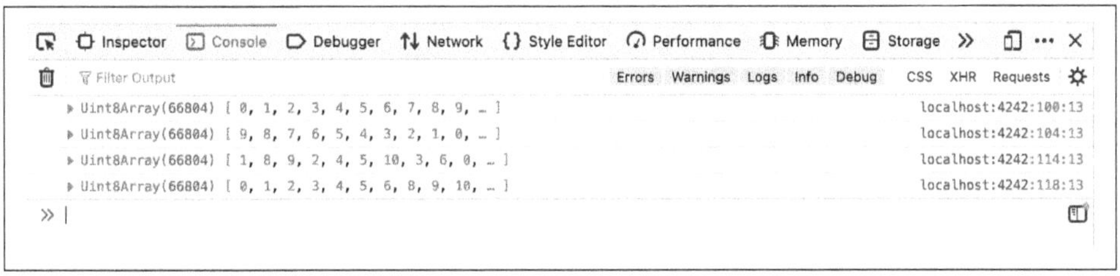

Figure 5-4. The results of intermixing our JavaScript and C/C++ via WebAssembly

Finally, "Hello, World!" in WebAssembly

This has been a bit of a beast of an effort, but I hope the reality of what is possible is starting to become clear. We still have a lot more to show you, but it is high time I honored my promise to give you a "Hello, World!" example. To keep it simple, I am not going to have a typical `main()` program. Instead, I will expose the behavior as another function in our *library.cpp* file. Example 5-15 shows you how simple this is.

Example 5-15. "Hello, World!" as a function in our C/C++ code

```
WASM_EXPORT void helloWorld() {
  printf("Hello, World!\n");
}
```

If I add a call to this new function after the other code in the HTML, you can see the results in Figure 5-5.

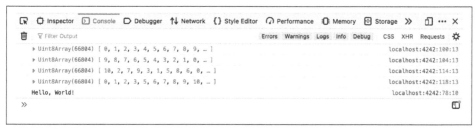

Figure 5-5. The previously promised "Hello, World!" results in all of their glory

How the heck did this work!?! And if it was so easy, why did we have to wait until the end of Chapter 5 to see it?

Let me show you some more details from the HTML in Example 5-16. There is a new function call, `get_memory()`, that simply returns a `Uint8Array` instance. There are `decoder` and `encoder` variables available for converting to and from UTF-8 representations of strings.[11] There is a function called `charPtrToString()` that will convert a "character pointer" (i.e., C string) into a UTF-8 string for JavaScript to use.

Farther down we have a function called `printString()` that will be invoked with a JavaScript string to be dumped to the console. Our `importObject` is configured to have a method in it called `print_string`, which will convert a "character pointer" to a string before invoking the method to dump it to the console. The `importObject`, you will recall, allows us to share functionality and data with our module instance.

---

11 Petter's example at the previously listed GitHub repo does more with strings moving back and forth from JavaScript and C.

Example 5-16. Behind-the-scenes machinery to make "Hello, World!" work

```
<script>
function get_memory() {
  return new Uint8Array(wasm.instance.exports.memory.buffer);
}

const decoder = new TextDecoder("utf-8");
const encoder = new TextEncoder("utf-8");

function charPtrToString(str) {
  const memory = get_memory();
  let length=0;
  for (; memory[str + length] !== 0 ;++length) {}
  return decoder.decode(memory.subarray(str, str + length));
}

let printString = function(str) {
  console.log(str);
};

const importObject = {
  env: {
    print_string: function(str) {
      printString(charPtrToString(str));
    }
  }
};
...
</script>
```

This covers the JavaScript side. On the C/C++ side, we see in Example 5-17 that the nanolibc/libc_extra.h header defines a function called print_string() that takes a char *.

Example 5-17. Exposing JavaScript functions as C functions

```
#ifndef _NANOLIB_C_EXTRA_H
#define _NANOLIB_C_EXTRA_H

extern "C" {
  // Will be provided by Javascript.
  void print_string(const char* str);
}

#endif
```

There is a file that defines our printf() instance in the *nanolibc* directory. The details there are complicated, so I do not want to go into them, but I will point out that it calls puts() to put a char * to the output console. Normally this is a low-level service provided by the operating system, but based on what you have seen so far, our Java-Script handlers will route it to its console once we hook the final piece up in Example 5-18.

Example 5-18. Exposing JavaScript functions as C functions

```
int puts ( const char * str ) {
  print_string(str); ❶
  return 0;
}
```

❶ puts() calls the JavaScript function with a char *.

At long last, we see how this works. Our function calls printf(), which calls puts(), which is defined to call the provided function. I am not going to describe how that gets hooked in right now, but I hope the result is still satisfying. There is more to know about using C/C++ with WebAssembly, but that is the subject of the forthcoming chapters. Until then, you have just crossed an important chasm for understanding how WebAssembly works behind the scenes. Next, we will learn how to port existing software to run in the browser.

## CHAPTER 6

Applied WebAssembly: Legacy Code in the Browser

No matter where you go, there you are.
—Buckaroo Banzai

It is time we look more closely at the process of invoking C/C++ code in the browser. Most code in these languages was never intended to run in the browser in a downloaded form. But as the leader of the Hong Kong Cavaliers tells us in the quotation at the beginning of this chapter, occasionally you will find yourself somewhere unexpected and new, but it is still just you there.[1]

We are interested in invoking C/C++ code in the browser for a variety of reasons. Replacing JavaScript is not one of them. At least not for most people. Instead, we have an enormous base of legacy code out there written in languages such as C and C++. A lot of it is very useful and it would be great to have access to it within our web applications. Some of it may be tying organizations to legacy systems. Being able to distribute this code via the browser would be a big step forward!

Additionally, there are simply some problems that are not well suited to be written in JavaScript. Having the option of writing that portion of your application in another language without requiring a separate runtime is very compelling. And, as our final use case demonstrates, there is real value in having trusted code from trusted sources providing provenance for sensitive and tricky software such as encryption algorithms. Being able to simply recompile existing code from people you know who know what they are doing is a useful capability to have as well.

---

1 *The Adventures of Buckaroo Banzai Across the 8th Dimension* (*https://oreil.ly/leejd*) is one of the best cult sci-fi movies ever.

In the previous chapter, we showed that it is possible to use a regular WebAssembly-enabled C compiler like clang and some header and library dependency management to achieve basic integration. Having to provide our own versions of the standard library and manually linking C code to provided JavaScript is going to get old really quickly, however.

Fortunately, the Emscripten project (*https://emscripten.org*) has laid the foundation for making this an easier process than it might otherwise be. This is not surprising because its main developers, Alon Zakai and Luke Wagner, have been behind much of the work, starting with asm.js, extending into the WebAssembly MVP, and to the specification advancements that continue to this day. The Emscripten[2] toolchain has been there for much of the journey.

The project is based upon the LLVM platform. In earlier chapters, I indicated that it initially had a custom backend that emitted the optimizable subset of JavaScript for asm.js. Once the WebAssembly platform was defined, a new backend was able to emit Wasm binaries.

Unfortunately, that is only part of the solution. There also needs to be support for getting data into and out of memory, linking modules, wrapping existing libraries, and more. A C program that provides a user interface or listens for network requests often spins in a fairly tight loop responding to input activity. Given that a browser is a single-threaded environment by default, there would be an operational mismatch with that kind of main loop. The Emscripten toolchain has been modified to solve many types of issues that might arise in trying to port native C/C++ to run in our web environment. As with most topics, this book cannot be a comprehensive introduction to everything this project does, but I will try to get you started quickly.

Proper "Hello, World!"

So, first a confession: we could have had a working, unmodified "Hello, World!" example in the browser way back in Chapter 2. For the final time, we will show you the code in Example 6-1.

Example 6-1. The typical "Hello, World!" program as expressed in C

```
#include <stdio.h>

int main() {
  printf("Hello, World!\n");
  return 0;
}
```

---

2 The name is a linguistic mashup of JavaScript and the word "embiggen," made popular by *The Simpsons*.

Using the Emscripten C compiler (installation instructions can be found in Appendix), we simply need to tell it to compile the C code and generate some JavaScript scaffolding. After that, it runs in Node.js unmodified:

```
brian@tweezer ~/g/w/s/ch06> emcc hello.c -o hello.js
brian@tweezer ~/g/w/s/ch06> ls -laF
total 520
drwxr-xr-x  7 brian  staff     224 Mar  1 14:45 ./
drwxr-xr-x  7 brian  staff     224 Mar  1 13:02 ../
-rw-r--r--  1 brian  staff  121457 Mar  1 13:05 bootstrap.min.css
-rw-r--r--  1 brian  staff      76 Mar  1 13:02 hello.c
-rw-r--r--  1 brian  staff     388 Mar  1 13:07 hello.html
-rw-r--r--  1 brian  staff  121686 Mar  1 14:45 hello.js
-rwxr-xr-x  1 brian  staff   11711 Mar  1 14:45 hello.wasm*
brian@tweezer ~/g/w/s/ch06> node hello.js
Hello, World!
```

The HTML file in Example 6-2 was not generated by this process and is suspiciously different than what we have seen before. There is a single `<script>` element that loads our generated JavaScript. We are not using the *utils.js* file we have used so far. Instead, we have a much longer JavaScript file produced by the previous command. Look at that file listing! It is over 120 kilobytes! It is over 2,000 lines of code. If you take a look at it, you might find yourself getting lost pretty quickly. This is why I did not want to start there in earlier chapters.

Example 6-2. A substantially different HTML file than we have seen

```
<!doctype html>
<html lang="en">
  <head>
    <meta charset="utf-8">
    <link rel="stylesheet" href="bootstrap.min.css">
    <title>Hello, World!</title>
  </head>
  <body>
    <div class="container">
      <h1>Hello, World!</h1>
    </div>
    <script src="hello.js"></script>
  </body>
</html>
```

And yet, if we serve up this directory via HTTP, open a browser, and open the Java-Script console, you will see something very similar to Figure 6-1.

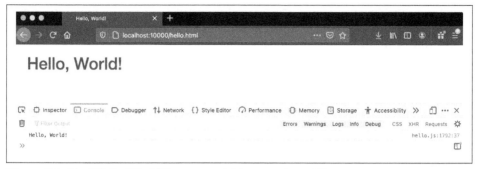

Figure 6-1. The "Hello, World!" you were told was not possible

If you use the `wasm-objdump` command on the file *hello.wasm*, you will notice that there is an exported `main()` function. The generated code has quickly outgrown our ability to show entire files, so I will highlight just the `Export` section:

```
...
Export[13]:
 - memory[0] -> "memory"
 - func[3] <__wasm_call_ctors> -> "__wasm_call_ctors"
 - func[5] <main> -> "main"
 - func[6] <__errno_location> -> "__errno_location"
 - func[50] <fflush> -> "fflush"
 - func[47] <stackSave> -> "stackSave"
 - func[48] <stackRestore> -> "stackRestore"
 - func[49] <stackAlloc> -> "stackAlloc"
 - func[44] <emscripten_stack_init> -> "emscripten_stack_init"
 - func[45] <emscripten_stack_get_free> -> "emscripten_stack_get_free"
 - func[46] <emscripten_stack_get_end> -> "emscripten_stack_get_end"
 - table[0] -> "__indirect_function_table"
 - func[53] <dynCall_jiji> -> "dynCall_jiji"
...
```

You see that there is quite a bit of generated scaffolding to make this all work. The details are fairly complicated, but if you wanted to trace your way through it, I would recommend generating the corresponding Wat file with `wasm2wat`. From there, trace through the `main()` function (numbered 5 in the previous code sample). You will see something like Example 6-3.

Example 6-3. The main method in Wat

```
...
  (func (;5;) (type 5) (param i32 i32) (result i32)
    (local i32)
    call 4
    local.set 2
    local.get 2
```

```
      return)
...
```

Eventually, you will find your way back to the generated JavaScript file. In there is a function called `fd_write`, as shown in Example 6-4. This is added to a namespace called `wasi_snapshot_preview1`. As the name suggests, this is a bit of a preview we will cover in later discussions, but the main point is that the Emscripten toolchain is generating code to solve some of the low-level hassles we have seen in the previous chapters. We will discover similar tooling with the Rust ecosystem in Chapter 10.

Example 6-4. Part of the printf solution

```
...
  function _fd_write(fd, iov, iovcnt, pnum) {
    // hack to support printf in SYSCALLS_REQUIRE_FILESYSTEM=0
    var num = 0;
    for (var i = 0; i < iovcnt; i++) {
      var ptr = HEAP32[(((iov)+(i*8))>>2)];
      var len = HEAP32[(((iov)+(i*8 + 4))>>2)];
      for (var j = 0; j < len; j++) {
        SYSCALLS.printChar(fd, HEAPU8[ptr+j]);
      }
      num += len;
    }
    HEAP32[((pnum)>>2)] = num
    return 0;
  }
...
```

It is certainly not necessary to get down in the weeds to see exactly how all of this works. It's important for you to understand that we are not actually calling `printf()` in a typical standard library sense, but that this function has been rewritten to call the generated code. In the browser, it will route the characters to the JavaScript console associated with developer tools. In a Node.js environment, it will get routed to the underlying system console. What is important at this stage is the fact that our legacy application did not have to change to run in this new environment, but we are also not encumbered with the terrifying prospect of running native C and C++ directly. We are striking a crucial balance of portability, safety, and performance, which is what WebAssembly is all about.

The generated code has a `Module` object in the JavaScript, which defines the runtime environment our WebAssembly code will occupy. There are comments at the top of the JavaScript file that describe this object and its role as an interface between the two worlds. To keep things manageable, however, we are going to focus on a much smaller portion of this.

One of the options available to us is the use of compiler directives to turn on or sur-press certain generated behavior. For example, we might not want our C program to run immediately when the JavaScript code is loaded. If you try compiling without the INVOKE_RUN=0 directive, you will see the typical greeting as you did in the previous example. In the following snippet, notice nothing is printed out to the command line when the code is loaded in Node.js:

```
brian@tweezer ~/g/w/s/ch06> emcc hello.c -o hello.js -s INVOKE_RUN=0
brian@tweezer ~/g/w/s/ch06> node hello.js
brian@tweezer ~/g/w/s/ch06>
```

Obviously, if you suppress the automatic execution, you will want to be able to indicate when the application should be executable. This can be accomplished with another directive:

```
brian@tweezer ~/g/w/s/ch06> emcc hello.c -o hello.js ↵
    -s INVOKE_RUN=0 -s EXTRA_EXPORTED_RUNTIME_METHODS="['callMain']"
```

In Example 6-5, you can see us invoking the main() function in response to a button click.

Example 6-5. A delayed main() method invocation

```
<!doctype html>
<html lang="en">
  <head>
    <meta charset="utf-8">
    <link rel="stylesheet" href="bootstrap.min.css">
    <title>Hello, World!</title>
  </head>
  <body>
    <div class="container">
      <h1>Hello, World!</h1>
      <button id="press">Press Me</button>
    </div>
    <script src="hello.js"></script>
    <script>
        var button = document.getElementById("press");
        button.onclick = function() {
            try {
                Module.callMain();
            } catch(re) {
            };
        };
    </script>
  </body>
</html>
```

In Figure 6-2, the friendly message is seen printing to the console when the button is pressed. Firefox is not displaying each identical message, but it shows that I have pressed the button seven times off to the right. Your browser may show one printed message per invocation.

Figure 6-2. The "Hello, World!" triggered by pressing the button

Porting Third-Party Code

We are now going to dive into bringing some existing code into the browser. This code was never intended to run on the web and does things you would normally not expect to work in a browser, such as writing to the filesystem. Do not fret, we are not going to break the browser security model, but you will see how this C++ code can run basically unmodified.

Emscripten has a tremendous number of options for porting third-party code to WebAssembly. There are effectively drop-in replacements for cc, make, and configure, which often makes the porting process trivial. In reality, you will likely have to work your way through the issues you encounter, but you are probably going to be surprised at how easy the process is. The project's website (*https://oreil.ly/BlnlK*) has great documentation to assist you with it. My favorite introduction to the topic, however, has been Robert Aboukhalil's fantastic Level Up With WebAssembly material (*https://levelupwasm.com*). He walks you through the process of porting several different open source projects to WebAssembly to run them in the browser. This includes games like *Tetris*, *Pong*, and *Pac-Man*. Rather than attempt to re-create what he has already done masterfully, I am going to focus on a relatively simple and clean project.

I spent some time looking for good candidate code. I wanted something meaty but not overwhelming. Eventually I found Arash Partow's collection of elegant, clean, suitably licensed, and useful C++ code at his website (*https://www.partow.net*). If you go there, you will find quite a lot of interesting material. I was originally going to use the computational geometry library but decided that the Bitmap library was better suited to a book like this.

To start off, fetch the code from Partow's site (*https://oreil.ly/KR2oX*). Once you download the ZIP file and uncompress it, you will see three files. A *Makefile* is an old-school Unix build file that has directions to assemble the software in question. We will explore that process momentarily. The *bitmap_image.hpp* file is the main library, and *bitmap_test.cpp* is a comprehensive collection of tests that generate a bunch of interesting Windows Bitmap images. This code does not require any platform-specific libraries:

```
brian@tweezer ~/g/w/s/c/bitmap> ls -alF
total 536
drwxr-xr-x@  5 brian  staff     160 Dec 31  1999 ./
drwxr-xr-x  11 brian  staff     352 Mar  6 13:56 ../
-rw-r--r--@  1 brian  staff     770 Dec 31  1999 Makefile
-rw-r--r--@  1 brian  staff  247721 Dec 31  1999 bitmap_image.hpp
-rw-r--r--@  1 brian  staff   20479 Dec 31  1999 bitmap_test.cpp
```

I have removed some of the comments and license details from Example 6-6 for space. What remains is the structure of the rules for building the test app, *bitmap_test*. A *Makefile* works by establishing a target followed by the dependencies and rules to build the target. As a convention, there is often an `all` rule that specifies the target file name mentioned earlier. It is dependent upon the *.cpp* and *.hpp* files. If either of those are modified, our executable needs to be rebuilt. To do that, the `make` tool will execute the file in the `COMPILER` variable with the options in the `OPTIONS` variable. As a C/C++ program, it will also need to be linked against the libraries specified in the `LINKER_OPT` variable. In this case, we want to link against the standard C++ library and a basic collection of mathematical functions. This is about as independent as you get library-wise. The `clean` target just removes the derived results.

 Makefiles are often sensitive to spaces versus tabs. Make sure to use tabs to start indented rule lines. The code in the repository for the book does this, but if you are modifying it in any way, you will want to make sure to use tabs.

Example 6-6. Makefile for our test program

```
COMPILER     = -c++
OPTIONS      = -ansi -pedantic-errors -Wall -Wall -Werror -Wextra -o
LINKER_OPT   = -L/usr/lib -lstdc++ -lm

all: bitmap_test

bitmap_test: bitmap_test.cpp bitmap_image.hpp
        $(COMPILER) $(OPTIONS) bitmap_test bitmap_test.cpp $(LINKER_OPT)
```

```
clean:
        rm -f core *.o *.bak *stackdump *~
```

As long as you have a functioning C++ environment installed, you should be able to build the test program:

```
brian@tweezer ~/g/w/s/c/bitmap> make
c++ -ansi -pedantic-errors -Wall -Wall -Werror -Wextra -o bitmap_test ↵
    bitmap_test.cpp -L/usr/lib -lstdc++ -lm
brian@tweezer ~/g/w/s/c/bitmap> ls -alF
total 944
drwxr-xr-x@  6 brian  staff     192 Mar  6 14:35 ./
drwxr-xr-x  11 brian  staff     352 Mar  6 13:56 ../
-rw-r--r--@  1 brian  staff     770 Dec 31  1999 Makefile
-rw-r--r--@  1 brian  staff  247721 Dec 31  1999 bitmap_image.hpp
-rwxr-xr-x   1 brian  staff  205032 Mar  6 14:35 bitmap_test*
-rw-r--r--@  1 brian  staff   20479 Dec 31  1999 bitmap_test.cpp
```

Now this test program requires an example *image.bmp* file in the current directory. I just found one online and dropped it in place with that name. After running the command, you will end up with a ton of generated images, as shown in Figure 6-3.

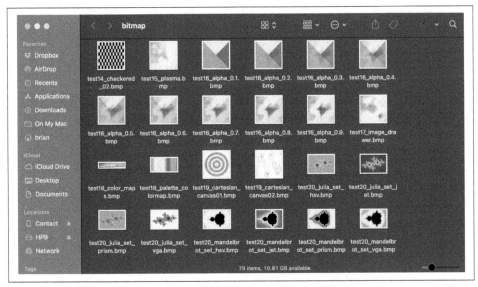

Figure 6-3. The images generated by the bitmap_test executable

OK, so it works. It is clean code. I am not going to teach you C++ or walk you through the code, but I will show you some working examples that you can try without entirely understanding what is going on.

First things first. We need to modify the Makefile to use the Emscripten compiler, rather than whatever you used to build the test program. This is as simple as updating the COMPILER variable as shown in Example 6-7.

Example 6-7. Updating the Makefile for our test program to build with Emscripten

```
...
COMPILER     = -em++
...
```

The clean step of the Makefile does not remove the executable. So, manually delete *bitmap_test* (or better yet, modify the Makefile!) and rerun make now. You should see something like the following:

```
brian@tweezer ~/g/w/s/c/bitmap> make
em++ -ansi -pedantic-errors -Wall -Wall -Werror -Wextra -o bitmap_test ↵
    bitmap_test.cpp -L/usr/lib -lstdc++ -lm
brian@tweezer ~/g/w/s/c/bitmap> ls -alF
total 1848
drwxr-xr-x@  8 brian  staff     256 Mar  6 15:21 ./
drwxr-xr-x  12 brian  staff     384 Mar  6 14:47 ../
-rw-r--r--@  1 brian  staff     771 Mar  6 15:20 Makefile
-rw-r--r--@  1 brian  staff  247721 Dec 31  1999 bitmap_image.hpp
-rw-r--r--   1 brian  staff  248314 Mar  6 15:21 bitmap_test
-rw-r--r--@  1 brian  staff   20479 Dec 31  1999 bitmap_test.cpp
-rwxr-xr-x   1 brian  staff  296743 Mar  6 15:21 bitmap_test.wasm*
-rw-r--r--@  1 brian  staff  120054 Mar  6 14:39 image.bmp
```

Uhm. That was easy. Sadly, we are not quite done yet. While that did compile, it is not going to work for a variety of reasons. The first of which is that the library expects to be able to write to the filesystem. It should come as no surprise that this is not possible. However, there is a really cool filesystem abstraction that writes to local storage available to us by adding a compiler directive. Now, just like taking care of printf() calls, the Emscripten toolchain will simulate a filesystem. You can unlock this support by adding the directive -s FORCE_FILESYSTEM=1 to your Makefile. I will show you the final form below.

The second problem is that the Memory instance that will be generated by default will not be allowed to grow. If we expect this library to generate some rather large images in memory, it will need to be able to ask for enough memory. So, we can use another directive to allow for this. This is something I showed you how to do manually in Chapter 4. It is the kind of detail that Emscripten can take care of for us. In order to have more control over the process, we will tell Emscripten not to automatically execute the program and to also export the main() method so we can call it when we want. Because we are not generating a standalone binary, we also want to tell the Emscripten compiler to generate a JavaScript file called *bitmap_test.js*. The command for the bitmap_test rule should now look like Example 6-8.

In the following code, I indicate line continuation with the carriage return character (↵) so the command fits on the page. Do not type those in, just keep the line going in your file.

Example 6-8. Modified Makefile with all of our Emscripten options

```
bitmap_test: bitmap_test.cpp bitmap_image.hpp
        $(COMPILER) $(OPTIONS) bitmap_test.js bitmap_test.cpp $(LINKER_OPT) ↵
            -s FORCE_FILESYSTEM=1 ↵
            -s ALLOW_MEMORY_GROWTH=1 ↵
            -s INVOKE_RUN=0 ↵
            -s EXTRA_EXPORTED_RUNTIME_METHODS="['callMain']"
```

That solves the specific problems that would prevent the example from working. However, there is one remaining issue. This test runs 20 relatively time-consuming tests. As JavaScript is a single-threaded environment, while the WebAssembly module is doing its thing, the browser is likely to start freaking out about things taking too long.

We will address this eventually, but for the time being, I am just going to remove calls to the rest of the tests and only call my favorite, `test20()`.

The `main()` method now looks like Example 6-9.

Example 6-9. Main method to call one test

```
int main()
{
    test20();
    return 0;
}
```

If you rerun the `make` command, you should see the generated Wasm and JavaScript files. I am going to generate some basic HTML scaffolding for us to use. In Example 6-10, you can see I have a button and a `<canvas>` element that we will use to render the bitmap. For now, save this file to the same directory as your Wasm and JavaScript files and serve it up over HTTP as we have done throughout the book.

Example 6-10. HTML scaffolding for our Bitmap generator

```
<!doctype html>
<html lang="en">
  <head>
    <meta charset="utf-8">
    <title>C++-rendered Image in the Browser</title>
  </head>
```

```
<body>
  <div class="container">
    <h1>C++-rendered Image in the Browser</h1>
  </div>
  <button id="load">Load</button>
  <canvas id="output"></canvas>
  <script src="bitmap_test.js"></script>
  <script>
    var button = document.getElementById("load");
    button.onclick = function() {
      Module.callMain();
      console.log("Done rendering.");
    };
  </script>
</body>
</html>
```

Once you load the HTML into your browser, open up the developer console and press the button. This will generate a variety of files and write them out to "disk." It will take a little while and I fully expect your browser will complain about this. Just tell it to wait as many times as it asks. Once it is done, you should see the message printed to the console. At this point, in the console, you can do something that might surprise you, as shown in Figure 6-4.

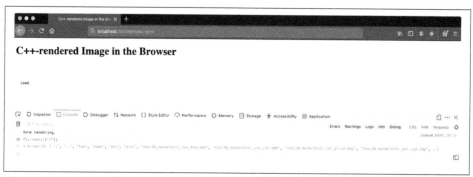

Figure 6-4. Writing files to the "filesystem" in the browser

Our third-party code used the Standard C++ library to write to the "filesystem." Emscripten provided an abstraction layer over local storage in the browser to make this possible. From C++, we could easily read it back in. From JavaScript, it is not much harder, as shown in Example 6-11.

Example 6-11. JavaScript to read "files" in from "disk" with the filesystem abstraction

```
>> var image = FS.readFile("./test20_julia_set_vga.bmp");
<- undefined
>> image
<- Uint8Array(2880054) [ 66, 77, 54, 242, 43, 0, 0, 0, 0, 0, ... ]
```

We just got a `Uint8Array` back from calling the `FS.readFile()` function. This is going to make it easy to deal with the bytes from the file. There is only one problem. Browsers do not support displaying Windows Bitmap files!

Fortunately, this is a documented format and someone has done us a solid and provided the code to do so. We could have relied on some existing C or C++ code, but just to show you some options, we will use the JavaScript code provided (*https:// oreil.ly/HQwQL*).

Fortunately, after Chapter 4 you are equipped to understand most of what is shown in Example 6-12. We pass the underlying `ArrayBuffer` returned from the `FS.read File()` function to a method called `getMBP()`. This creates a `DataView` around the buffer and pulls out the various image details before shoving them into a more convenient JavaScript representation.

Once the Bitmap file is read in, we convert the JavaScript structure to an `ImageData` instance via the `convertToImageData()` function from the same website. After that we set the `<canvas>` size to match its height and width and use its `putImageData()` method to render the pixels.

Example 6-12. JavaScript to read our Bitmap file back in and render it in the `<canvas>` element

```
<script>
  // Code taken from https://tinyurl.com/bitmap-in-javascript
  // Written by Ian Elliott
  function getBMP(buffer) {
    var datav = new DataView(buffer);
    var bitmap = {};
    bitmap.fileheader = {};
    bitmap.fileheader.bfType = datav.getUint16(0, true);
    bitmap.fileheader.bfSize = datav.getUint32(2, true);
    bitmap.fileheader.bfReserved1 = datav.getUint16(6, true);
    bitmap.fileheader.bfReserved2 = datav.getUint16(8, true);
    bitmap.fileheader.bfOffBits = datav.getUint32(10, true);
    bitmap.infoheader = {};
    bitmap.infoheader.biSize = datav.getUint32(14, true);
    bitmap.infoheader.biWidth = datav.getUint32(18, true);
    bitmap.infoheader.biHeight = datav.getUint32(22, true);

    bitmap.infoheader.biPlanes = datav.getUint16(26, true);
    bitmap.infoheader.biBitCount = datav.getUint16(28, true);
    bitmap.infoheader.biCompression = datav.getUint32(30, true);
    bitmap.infoheader.biSizeImage = datav.getUint32(34, true);
    bitmap.infoheader.biXPelsPerMeter = datav.getUint32(38, true);
    bitmap.infoheader.biYPelsPerMeter = datav.getUint32(42, true);
    bitmap.infoheader.biClrUsed = datav.getUint32(46, true);
    bitmap.infoheader.biClrImportant = datav.getUint32(50, true);
    var start = bitmap.fileheader.bfOffBits;
```

```
        bitmap.stride = Math.floor((bitmap.infoheader.biBitCount
            *bitmap.infoheader.biWidth + 31) / 32) * 4;
        bitmap.pixels = new Uint8Array(buffer, start);
        return bitmap;
      }

      // Code taken from https://tinyurl.com/bitmap-in-javascript
      // Written by Ian Elliott
      function convertToImageData(bitmap) {
        var canvas = document.createElement("canvas");
        var ctx = canvas.getContext("2d");
        var width = bitmap.infoheader.biWidth;
        var height = bitmap.infoheader.biHeight;
        var imageData = ctx.createImageData(width, height);

        var data = imageData.data;
        var bmpdata = bitmap.pixels;
        var stride = bitmap.stride;

        for (var y = 0; y < height; ++y) {
          for (var x = 0; x < width; ++x) {
            var index1 = (x+width*(height-y))*4;
            var index2 = x * 3 + stride * y;
            data[index1] = bmpdata[index2 + 2];
            data[index1 + 1] = bmpdata[index2 + 1];
            data[index1 + 2] = bmpdata[index2];
            data[index1 + 3] = 255;
          }
        }
        return imageData;
      }

      var button = document.getElementById("load");
      button.onclick = function() {
        Module.callMain();
        var canvas = document.getElementById("output");
        var context = canvas.getContext('2d');

        var image = FS.readFile("./test20_julia_set_vga.bmp");
        var bmp = getBMP(image.buffer);
        var imageData = convertToImageData(bmp);

        canvas.width = bmp.infoheader.biWidth;
        canvas.height = bmp.infoheader.biHeight;

        context.putImageData(imageData, 0, 0);

        console.log(image);
      };
    </script>
  </body>
</html>
```

The result of calling our C++ application and rendering the results in a canvas after reading it back in via JavaScript can be seen in Figure 6-5.

Figure 6-5. The result of rendering our Bitmap file in the canvas

I hope you are at least a little impressed. It is pretty cool how little we had to do to run this C++ code in the browser! There are still some issues with respect to performance and threading, but you have come a long way from adding two numbers together.

One thing we could do is add a command-line parameter to the execution to select which of the tests to run. For the time being, we are not going to worry about the tests that read in the sample image.[3]

To accept parameters on the command line, we need to modify the `main()` method to what you see in Example 6-13.

Example 6-13. Modified main() method to accept parameters for test selection

```
int main(int argc, char **argv)
{
  int which = 20;

  if(argc > 1) {
```

---

3 It is your homework assignment to make that work.

```
      std::string::size_type sz;
      which = std::stoi(argv[1], &sz);
    }

    switch(which) {
    case 0:
    case 1:
    case 2:
    case 3:
    case 4:
    case 5:
    case 6:
    case 7:
    case 8:
    case 10:
    case 11:
    case 12:
    case 13:
    case 16:
      printf("%s requires reading in a file which we don't support yet.\n", argv[1]);
      break;
    case 9:
      test09();
      break;
    case 14:
      test14();
      break;
    case 15:
      test15();
      break;
    case 17:
      test17();
      break;
    case 18:
      test18();
      break;
    case 19:
      test19();
      break;
    case 20:
      test20();
      break;
    default:
      printf("Sorry, %s is an unknown test number.\n", argv[1]);
    }

    return 0;
}
```

The first thing you will notice is that the signature of main() has been modified to accept an integer representing the number of command-line parameters and effectively an array of strings. Keep in mind that in C/C++ this is implemented as a pointer to a bunch of pointers, which is why there are two asterisks. We can index them as you would an array.

By default, the first argument will be the name of the executable. As we start counting at 0, the first passed-in argument will be at position 1. We set a default test number to 20, as I have indicated that this is my favorite of the tests. However, if you pass in a string representing a number, it will be converted into an integer. Once we have determined whether we will use the default value or not, we switch on this value. As mentioned, we skip over the tests that require the input image. There are still several others you can run.

 If you are going to go back and forth between native code and WebAssembly, you will probably want to maintain two different Makefiles at this point. When you are more comfortable, you can create flexible Makefiles that support both targets. You can specify which file to use with the -f <file> parameters, as seen in the following example.

If you want, recompile the native executable and try out the new parameter handling:

```
brian@tweezer ~/g/w/s/c/bitmap> make -f Makefile.orig
c++ -ansi -pedantic-errors -Wall -Wall -Werror -Wextra -o bitmap_test ↵
   bitmap_test.cpp -L/usr/lib -lstdc++ -lm
brian@tweezer ~/g/w/s/c/bitmap> ./bitmap_test 1
1 requires reading in a file which we don't support yet.
brian@tweezer ~/g/w/s/c/bitmap> ./bitmap_test 9
brian@tweezer ~/g/w/s/c/bitmap> ls -laF
total 7608
drwxr-xr-x@ 14 brian   staff      448 Mar  7 22:55 ./
drwxr-xr-x  12 brian   staff      384 Mar  6 14:47 ../
-rw-r--r--@  1 brian   staff      893 Mar  7 17:42 Makefile
-rw-r--r--@  1 brian   staff      776 Mar  7 20:10 Makefile.orig
-rw-r--r--@  1 brian   staff   247721 Dec 31  1999 bitmap_image.hpp
-rwxr-xr-x   1 brian   staff   205264 Mar  7 22:55 bitmap_test*
-rw-r--r--@  1 brian   staff    20954 Mar  7 20:16 bitmap_test.cpp
-rw-r--r--   1 brian   staff   249546 Mar  7 20:16 bitmap_test.js
-rw-r--r--@  1 brian   staff   120054 Mar  6 14:39 image.bmp
-rw-r--r--   1 brian   staff     3127 Mar  7 17:26 index.html
-rw-r--r--   1 brian   staff  3000054 Mar  7 22:55 test09_color_map_image.bmp
```

As you can see, it works. After passing in a 9, you see the corresponding test image written out.

Now, let's invoke the program from JavaScript with parameters. We need to rebuild our Wasm module and JavaScript scaffolding:

```
brian@tweezer ~/g/w/s/c/bitmap> make
em++ -ansi -pedantic-errors -Wall -Wall -Werror -Wextra -o bitmap_test.js ↵
   bitmap_test.cpp -L/usr/lib -lstdc++ -lm -s FORCE_FILESYSTEM=1 ↵
```

```
            -s ALLOW_MEMORY_GROWTH=1 -s INVOKE_RUN=0 ↵
            -s EXTRA_EXPORTED_RUNTIME_METHODS="['callMain']"
brian@tweezer ~/g/w/s/c/bitmap> ls -alF
total 1840
drwxr-xr-x@ 13 brian  staff      416 Mar  7 23:00 ./
drwxr-xr-x  12 brian  staff      384 Mar  6 14:47 ../
-rw-r--r--@  1 brian  staff      893 Mar  7 17:42 Makefile
-rw-r--r--@  1 brian  staff      776 Mar  7 20:10 Makefile.orig
-rw-r--r--@  1 brian  staff   247721 Dec 31  1999 bitmap_image.hpp
-rw-r--r--@  1 brian  staff    20954 Mar  7 20:16 bitmap_test.cpp
-rw-r--r--   1 brian  staff   249546 Mar  7 23:00 bitmap_test.js
-rwxr-xr-x   1 brian  staff   257810 Mar  7 23:00 bitmap_test.wasm*
-rw-r--r--@  1 brian  staff   120054 Mar  6 14:39 image.bmp
-rw-r--r--   1 brian  staff     3127 Mar  7 17:26 index.html
```

The good news is that we do not have to do much to our JavaScript code! Because the signature has changed, we can now pass strings into our method to invoke the main() method. Rather than dumping out only moderately different JavaScript in HTML, in Figure 6-6 you can see the results of invoking the executable with parameters from the developer console.

Figure 6-6. Invoking our Bitmap generator with command-line parameters in the browser

In addition to selecting tests based upon command-line parameters, you might also want to run the tests just as functions. This requires a little more discussion, however.

We will start by adding a method to our test file called run_test() that will take a single argument. There is no need to repeat the actual code at this point, so we will just print out a string indicating which test was requested to run. You can see this function defined in Example 6-14.

Example 6-14. Exporting a function to call from JavaScript

```
void run_test(int i) {
  printf("Running test %d!\n", i);
}
```

By default, only the `main()` method is exported, as that is the only function we need to kick off our program. We need to add an `EXPORTED_FUNCTIONS` directive as shown next. The function names are defined with a leading underscore character. If you want `main()` to still be callable, you will need to include that as well, which we do not do in Example 6-15.

Example 6-15. Modified Makefile to export additional methods

```
bitmap_test: bitmap_test.cpp bitmap_image.hpp
        $(COMPILER) $(OPTIONS) bitmap_test.js bitmap_test.cpp $(LINKER_OPT) ↵
              -s FORCE_FILESYSTEM=1 ↵
              -s ALLOW_MEMORY_GROWTH=1 ↵
              -s INVOKE_RUN=0 ↵
              -s EXPORTED_FUNCTIONS="['_main', '_run_test']" ↵
              -s EXTRA_EXPORTED_RUNTIME_METHODS="['callMain']"
```

Unfortunately, that will not work because we are using C++. The generated function names are further mangled by the compiler for reasons that are not worth going into here.[4] To avoid this problem, we need to tell the compiler to suppress this behavior and use C linkage. To engage this behavior, we need to modify our function definition to look like Example 6-16.

Example 6-16. Exporting a function to call from JavaScript with C linkage

```
extern "C"
void run_test(int i) {
  printf("Running test %d!\n", i);
}
```

That should solve that problem, but I will make one more change to show you another option you have. There is a convenience method from the Emscripten toolchain called `cwrap` that will generate a JavaScript function for invoking a particular C function. We add that to the `EXTRA_EXPORTED_RUNTIME_METHODS` directive in Example 6-17.

---

[4] If you would like to know more about C++ name mangling, please check out this description on Wikipedia (*https://oreil.ly/FBc4R*).

Example 6-17. Updated Makefile to use `cwrap`

```
bitmap_test: bitmap_test.cpp bitmap_image.hpp
        $(COMPILER) $(OPTIONS) bitmap_test.js bitmap_test.cpp $(LINKER_OPT) ↵
                -s FORCE_FILESYSTEM=1 ↵
                -s ALLOW_MEMORY_GROWTH=1 ↵
                -s INVOKE_RUN=0 ↵
                -s EXPORTED_FUNCTIONS="['_main', '_run_test']" ↵
                -s EXTRA_EXPORTED_RUNTIME_METHODS="['callMain', 'cwrap']"
```

If you rebuild and reload your HTML, you will be able to invoke this function from the JavaScript developer console. See the results of doing so in Figure 6-7.

Figure 6-7. Invoking our functions from JavaScript directly and via `cwrap()`

Notice that the `cwrap()` invocation returns a proper JavaScript function that we can invoke as usual. You could move the `switch` statement to this method and have the same ability to invoke arbitrary tests.

For some additional practice, try adding a method that writes out a Bitmap file called *image.bmp*. Export this method from your C++ code and invoke it from the browser. This could then allow you to read the file back in for the tests that need it. You could modify the `switch` statement to allow those methods to be called.

Finally, imagine some other user interface elements allowing you to pick which test to run. Once run, imagine a list of files to display in a `<canvas>` element. You have almost all of the pieces you would need to do this, so give it a try!

libsodium

Before we wrap up this chapter, I want to draw your attention to a project called libsodium (*https://doc.libsodium.org*). We are not going to do anything directly with it, but it demonstrates additional motivation for mixing languages such as C and C++ with the browser via WebAssembly.

This is based upon another library called Networking and Cryptography library (NaCl).[5] It is a high-performance, modern encryption library written by people who know what they are doing. Many of the features of this NaCl are not necessarily available to JavaScript runtimes yet. New ciphersuites, including Authenticated Encryption with Additional Data (AEAD), might show up here long before they are ported to JavaScript or available to the browser through the operating system.[6] One compelling use case for WebAssembly is the ability to basically recompile such modern support and bring it to the browser immediately without having to wait for updates.

A second motivation is that the authors of the NaCl library know what they are doing. It is extremely easy to undermine the efficacy of an encryption library with a poor implementation. Even something as subtle as comparing whether two hash values are the same can leak details if not implemented correctly. Frustratingly, the correct implementation of this comparison will fly in the face of how developers would normally compare two hashes. My point is that there is a provenance to the NaCl codebase. If a JavaScript developer without the background to understand these details tries to implement the functionality, there is a good chance it might have these vulnerabilities. When you have a trusted codebase, being able to recompile it and use it directly is another reason to consider the topics of this chapter.

So, libsodium is basically a project designed to export the NaCl library via WebAssembly into JavaScript environments without a need to rewrite or compromise on performance. It is designed to be maintained as a WebAssembly project. I think once people get a better idea of what it means to use WebAssembly in this way, we will start to see more projects that can be used as native libraries or WebAssembly modules depending upon your configuration needs. That will be a great opportunity for code reuse. We will see another example of this approach in Chapter 10.

Until then, there is still more to learn about WebAssembly.

---

5 Please note this has nothing to do with the Native Client (NaCl) we mentioned in Chapter 1. You can find more details about this one online (*http://nacl.cr.yp.to*).

6 A ciphersuite is a collection of cryptographic primitives providing a set of capabilities to an encryption engine.

## CHAPTER 7

WebAssembly Tables

The dinner table is the center for the teaching and practicing not just of table manners but of conversation, consideration, tolerance, family feeling, and just about all the other accomplishments of polite society except the minuet.
  —Judith Martin

The dinner table is a great metaphor for the sharing of ideas and stories. It is always more fun to join others than to eat by yourself. If you bring a bunch of people together from all walks of life, you can spur glorious, energetic conversation on a near infinite number of topics. Nobody has all of the stories. Some participants may share some aspects of the same stories. Others may have their own version. In order to function, however, there does have to be a certain amount of decorum, restraint, and willingness to accept what is given by the other participants. Dinner guests who misbehave, do not stop talking, or step on each other's lines are going to ruin it for everyone.

Tables are another feature of WebAssembly that allow it to be a modern software system with functional dependencies that will be satisfied by additional modules. They provide the equivalent capability of a dynamic shared library compared to a statically linked library. The idea is that not every module needs to provide everything it requires to do its work. That would be horribly inefficient. Instead, it is written against the promise of some other module satisfying the need at runtime. That is called dynamic linking in the C and C++ world. Obviously, my dinner table metaphor is simply a play on the word *table*, but just like there needs to be some coordination around sharing ideas over a meal, we need this for sharing behavior between libraries. Let's explore that idea more closely and then see how WebAssembly supports it.

Static Versus Dynamic Linking

Anyone who follows me on Twitter knows what an amazing cook my wife is. She comes from a great family of cooks and has had the opportunity to learn from a large number of generous mentors. People often see posts I make of the culinary art she produces and ask me for the recipe. This is not usually as easy as just sending a link, because she often combines ideas from multiple sources and then puts her own spin on things.

In our house, she could rely on the cookbook library she has amassed. She could say, "Make this sauce from that book. Prepare the beef with the technique described in that other book. After it reaches the doneness you want, add these additional ingredients that I thought would make it better."

Within our house, she can make references to steps and ingredient lists from known sources and amend the process with her additional steps. But when she wants to give the recipe to someone else, she cannot rely on their having these books. In that case, she would have to copy the recipes from her sources into a new recipe document that was self-contained. At this point, all the steps and ingredients would be defined in one place and the recipe could be sent to someone else.

That is basically the difference between static and dynamic linking. A typical program needs to read and write the contents of files, open windows, collect input from the user, or send messages across the network. These are common enough tasks that they are usually available as functionality in libraries provided by the operating system. When you wish to use a function from one of them, you would tell the linker to allow for runtime linking. Otherwise, it would complain about missing symbol references.

At runtime, the operating system will search its configuration path that tells it where to find these shared libraries. Prior to initiating the program, it will map the functionality from the libraries into a memory location that can be dynamically linked to the rest of the code.

There are many reasons for this approach. The first is just efficiency. Let's say you have a function called a() that is referenced by a dozen or more other programs. With static linking, each executable has its own copy. Programs take up more disk space. Their memory footprints at runtime are also going to be larger. It is just not an efficient use of space.

If the dynamic library is loaded into a shared memory space, then presumably we only need one copy of one version of the file on disk. Depending on the complexity of your operating system, you might only need one copy in memory at a time too.

Dynamically linked libraries often have their own release cycles. If you were using a system library from one of your executable programs, you might update your operating system and get a new version of the library with a patch for a security issue. As long as the numbering mechanism works out and it is backward-compatible, presumably you could strengthen the security of your application by using the patched version without having to do anything else.

Look at Example 7-1. This is a function on its own without a `main()` function. It is intended to be used as a library. We could compile it into a static library, but for now we will just create the object code and link our `main()` program against it. Note that this function also relies on `printf()`, so it must import the *stdio.h* header.

Example 7-1. A library with a function to call

```
#include <stdio.h>

void sayHello(char *message) {
  printf("%s\n", message);
}
```

In Example 7-2, you will see the `main()` function that will first call `printf()` and then call our function, which also calls `printf()`.

Example 7-2. A sample main() method to call our library function

```
#include <stdio.h>

extern void sayHello(char *message);

int main() {
  printf("Hello, world.\n");
  sayHello("How are you?");
  return 0;
}
```

By default, if you compile these two files with `clang`, it will generate an output file. I left it to use the default name. When we run it, we see the behavior we expect. By default, the compiler will use dynamic linking for the system library for all of the reasons I already outlined:

```
brian@tweezer ~/g/w/s/ch07> clang main.c library.c
brian@tweezer ~/g/w/s/ch07> ls
a.out*     library.c  main.c
brian@tweezer ~/g/w/s/ch07> ./a.out
Hello, world.
How are you?
```

You can verify that we are using dynamic linking here with the `nm` command. First, we see that our binary file provides definitions for `main()` and `sayHello()`, but not `printf()`. That is the reused function from the standard library:

```
brian@tweezer ~/g/w/s/ch07> nm a.out
0000000100008008 d __dyld_private
0000000100000000 T __mh_execute_header
0000000100003f10 T _main
                 U _printf
0000000100003f50 T _sayHello
                 U dyld_stub_binder
```

On Linux, you can see that the same build steps yield a binary with additional functions mentioned. This is natural as it is a different operating system with a different runtime and a different binary format. The salient point is that our methods are provided in our binary, but printf() is not:

```
brian@bbfcfm:~/src/hello$ nm a.out
0000000000404030 B __bss_start
0000000000404030 b completed.8060
0000000000404020 D __data_start
0000000000404020 W data_start
0000000000401080 t deregister_tm_clones
0000000000401070 T _dl_relocate_static_pie
00000000004010f0 t __do_global_dtors_aux
0000000000403e08 d __do_global_dtors_aux_fini_array_entry
0000000000404028 D __dso_handle
0000000000403e10 d _DYNAMIC
0000000000404030 D _edata
0000000000404038 B _end
0000000000401218 T _fini
0000000000401120 t frame_dummy
0000000000403e00 d __frame_dummy_init_array_entry
000000000040216c r __FRAME_END__
0000000000404000 d _GLOBAL_OFFSET_TABLE_
                 w __gmon_start__
0000000000402024 r __GNU_EH_FRAME_HDR
0000000000401000 T _init
0000000000403e08 d __init_array_end
0000000000403e00 d __init_array_start
0000000000402000 R _IO_stdin_used
0000000000401210 T __libc_csu_fini
00000000004011a0 T __libc_csu_init
                 U __libc_start_main@@GLIBC_2.2.5
0000000000401130 T main
                 U printf@@GLIBC_2.2.5
00000000004010b0 t register_tm_clones
0000000000401170 T sayHello
0000000000401040 T _start
0000000000404030 D __TMC_END__
```

The otool command is another command that can be used on macOS to show you which dynamic libraries are required for the successful execution of your binary. The macOS version of the system library is shown:

```
brian@tweezer ~/g/w/s/ch07> otool -L a.out
a.out:
    /usr/lib/libSystem.B.dylib (compatibility vers 1.0.0, current vers 1292.60.1)
```

otool does not exist for Linux, but we can see similar results by using objdump. I have removed some of the output for space, but the relevant portion is shown in the following snippet. As you can see, we need *libc.so.6* to satisfy the needs of our binary. There will be similar tools on Windows to check your DLL dependencies:

```
brian@bbfcfm:~/src/hello$ objdump -x a.out

a.out:      file format elf64-x86-64
a.out
architecture: i386:x86-64, flags 0x00000112:
EXEC_P, HAS_SYMS, D_PAGED
start address 0x0000000000401040


...

Dynamic Section:
  NEEDED               libc.so.6
  INIT                 0x0000000000401000
  FINI                 0x0000000000401218
  INIT_ARRAY           0x0000000000403e00
  INIT_ARRAYSZ         0x0000000000000008
  FINI_ARRAY           0x0000000000403e08
  FINI_ARRAYSZ         0x0000000000000008
  HASH                 0x00000000004002e8
  GNU_HASH             0x0000000000400310
  STRTAB               0x0000000000400390
  SYMTAB               0x0000000000400330
  STRSZ                0x000000000000003f
  SYMENT               0x0000000000000018
  DEBUG                0x0000000000000000
  PLTGOT               0x0000000000404000
  PLTRELSZ             0x0000000000000018
  PLTREL               0x0000000000000007
  JMPREL               0x0000000000400428
  RELA                 0x00000000004003f8
  RELASZ               0x0000000000000030
  RELAENT              0x0000000000000018
  VERNEED              0x00000000004003d8
  VERNEEDNUM           0x0000000000000001
  VERSYM               0x00000000004003d0

Version References:
  required from libc.so.6:
    0x09691a75 0x00 02 GLIBC_2.2.5


...
```

WebAssembly is not the same thing as an operating system, obviously, but it benefits from a similar concept. Our choices are the same: put all function definitions into a single module so it stands on its own or invoke behavior from another module in order to meet our needs. Given that we are going to be downloading WebAssembly modules over the network frequently, having them be on the smaller side is desirable. This also affects disk storage, module validation, loading the instances in memory, etc. For that, we have `Table` instances.

Creating Tables in Modules

`Table` instances have some similar characteristics to the `Memory` instances we introduced in Chapter 4. There can currently only be one per module, but it can either be defined in the module or passed in through an imported object. The single-instance-per-module restriction is likely to be lifted in the future, but it is something we must abide by for the time being.

Part of the reason we have this structure in WebAssembly rather than just using `Memory` instances is because the latter can be manipulated by a module. If we are trying to have a proper dinner conversation, we do not want any individual participant rewriting the rules of polite company. The same is true in the land of shared modules. If we have loaded in and validated a module with exported functions through `Table` instances, we do not want another module to be able to mess it up for anyone else. Thus, all you can do is make indirect function calls to function references stored in the table. Currently, function references are the only thing that can be stored in `Table` instances, but that is also expected to change in the future.

Rather than overly complicate things at this point, I am going to go back to simple function definitions in Wat to demonstrate the way to create `Table` instances and export them.

In Example 7-3, I have created two functions. The `$add` function takes two parameters, adds them together, and returns the result. The `$sub` function takes two parameters, subtracts the second from the first, and then returns the result. So far, as they say, so what? This is just retrodden territory from earlier chapters. The difference here is what happens next.

Example 7-3. A module that exports its `Table` instance

```
(module
  (func $add (param $a i32) (param $b i32) (result i32)
      get_local $a
      get_local $b
      i32.add)

  (func $sub (param $a i32) (param $b i32) (result i32)
```

```
      get_local $a
      get_local $b
      i32.sub)

  (table (export "tbl") anyfunc (elem $add $sub))
)
```

We introduce a new Wat keyword, `table`. This defines a collection of function references. Notice the inline `export` command. We will allow our host environment to
invoke methods through the $add and $sub functions, but not via their names. The
host can only invoke the behavior through the `Table` instance. The `anyfunc` type is
currently the only allowed type for this structure, as we noted previously. Based on
the ordering in the `elem` reference, $add will be in the 0th position and $sub will be in
the 1th[1] position.

As you know by now, we can turn our Wat file into a Wasm module and check out its
contents as follows. Notice the `Table` section, the `Type` section, and the `Export`
section:

```
brian@tweezer ~/g/w/s/ch07> wat2wasm math.wat
brian@tweezer ~/g/w/s/ch07> wasm-objdump -x math.wasm

math.wasm:      file format wasm 0x1

Section Details:

Type[1]:
 - type[0] (i32, i32) -> i32
Function[2]:
 - func[0] sig=0
 - func[1] sig=0
Table[1]:
 - table[0] type=funcref initial=2 max=2
Export[1]:
 - table[0] -> "tbl"
Elem[1]:
 - segment[0] flags=0 table=0 count=2 - init i32=0
  - elem[0] = func[0]
  - elem[1] = func[1]
Code[2]:
 - func[0] size=7
 - func[1] size=7
```

---

1 I declared this to be a word on Twitter. It is therefore on the internet, so it must be real. I'm using it to disam-
  biguate the second position in a 0-based collection. If I said *first*, you might get confused. If I make up a word,
  maybe you won't.

The JavaScript in Example 7-4 instantiates our module like we did in the early chapters. From there it extracts the Table instance from the module's export section.

Example 7-4. Using an exported Table instance from JavaScript

```
<!doctype html>
<html>
  <head>
    <meta charset="utf-8">
    <title>WASM Table test</title>
    <script src="utils.js"></script>
  </head>
  <body>
    <script>
      fetchAndInstantiate('math.wasm').then(function(instance) {
        var tbl = instance.exports.tbl;
        console.log("3 + 1 = " + tbl.get(0)(3,1));
        console.log("3 - 1 = " + tbl.get(1)(3,1));
      });
    </script>
  </body>
</html>
```

After we fetch the reference, we can retrieve the function associated with the 0th position and invoke it. Keep in mind that what comes back from the get() invocation is a reference to a function. To invoke it, we submit the parameters in the second set of parentheses and then print out the result to the console. We then do so for the function in the 1th position as well.

Serve the HTML up over HTTP and open up the JavaScript console. When your browser executes the code, it should look something like Figure 7-1.

Figure 7-1. The output from invoking methods through Table instances

The Table instance is only defined to have two references. If you attempt to access a position beyond tbl.length, it will cause an exception.

Dynamic Linking in WebAssembly

Our final example is going to be a trivial example of using dynamic linking in WebAssembly. We are going to define two modules. One is going to contain our previously defined $add and $sub methods. The first module is shown in Example 7-5. The main difference to what we have seen before is that this module is importing a Table from the host. We place the arithmetic functions into this table with the elem instruction. The addition function is stored in position 0. The subtraction function is stored in position 1.

Example 7-5. A dynamically linked module

```
(module
  (import "js" "table" (table 2 anyfunc))

  (func $add (param $a i32) (param $b i32) (result i32)
      get_local $a
      get_local $b
      i32.add)

  (func $sub (param $a i32) (param $b i32) (result i32)
      get_local $a
      get_local $b
      i32.sub)

  (elem (i32.const 0) $add)
  (elem (i32.const 1) $sub)
)
```

Our second module is going to export two functions, myadd and mysub. It is advertising the ability to add and subtract two numbers to its clients. Internally, it is going to call the function references in an import Table instance, which we also import from the host JavaScript environment.

The implementations of our advertised functionality are shown in Example 7-6. Both functions invoke the call_indirect instruction. In earlier chapters, we saw the use of the call instruction to call a function defined in the current module. The call_indirect instruction invokes a function by identifying which element of the Table you would like to invoke.

Example 7-6. A module dependent upon the dynamically linked module

```
(module
  (import "js" "table" (table 2 anyfunc))

  (type $sig (func (param $a i32) (param $b i32) (result i32)))
```

```
(func (export "myadd") (param $a i32) (param $b i32) (result i32)
    (call_indirect (type $sig) (get_local $a) (get_local $b) (i32.const 0))
)

(func (export "mysub") (param $a i32) (param $b i32) (result i32)
    (call_indirect (type $sig) (get_local $a) (get_local $b) (i32.const 1))
)
)
```

One of the things that is going to jump out at you is the use of the `type` instruction. This is going to define the signature of a function to provide a modicum of type safety in WebAssembly. The idea is that an imported `Table` function should have the signature you are looking to invoke.

In this case, we define a function signature that takes two `i32s` and returns an `i32`. When we invoke the methods through the `Table`, we indicate that this is the type we are expecting. After the signature, we push the parameters to our function onto the stack before finally pushing the `Table` position number. For addition, that is the constant value of 0, representing the first position in the `Table`. For subtraction, it will be the second position.

We put it all together in Example 7-7. The first thing we do is create a shared `Table` instance. This will be passed in via the `importObject` to both modules. The difference is that the *math2.wat* module writes its functions, $add and $sub, into positions 0 and 1, respectively. The *mymath.wat* module invokes these positions indirectly when `myadd` and `mysub` are invoked from the host JavaScript environment. As part of the invocation, they will also pass the parameters they have been given to the dynamically linked functions.

Because we are dealing with two modules, our instantiation mechanism is slightly different. Rather than waiting on a single `Promise`, we invoke the `Promise.all()` method, which blocks until all of the subordinate `Promises` are met. In this case, it means that both modules are loaded and ready to go.

Example 7-7. Instantiating two modules with dynamic linking between them

```
<!doctype html>
<html>
  <head>
    <meta charset="utf-8">
    <title>WASM Dynamic Linking test</title>
    <script src="utils.js"></script>
  </head>
  <body>
    <script>
      var importObject = {
        js: {
```

```
        table: new WebAssembly.Table({ initial:2, element:"anyfunc" })
      }
    };

    Promise.all([
      fetchAndInstantiate('math2.wasm', importObject),
      fetchAndInstantiate('mymath.wasm', importObject)
    ]).then(function(instances) {
      console.log("4 + 3 = " + instances[1].exports.myadd(4,3));
      console.log("4 - 3 = " + instances[1].exports.mysub(4,3));
    });
  </script>
 </body>
</html>
```

Once the modules are both available, this code invokes the myadd and mysub methods with some parameters. Notice we are choosing the second module instance, representing our versions of the behavior. It is an array of the instances rather than a single one.

After they are served over HTTP, the results in the browser should look something like what you see in Figure 7-2. One module is calling behavior implemented in another module indirectly through the shared Table instance.

Figure 7-2. The output from invoking our dynamically linked functions

This ends our introduction to the main functional elements of WebAssembly as a platform. The remainder of the book will build upon these fundamentals and show you several examples of how WebAssembly is being used now and how it will be used in the future. This includes some of the more advanced features that we have yet to cover.

## CHAPTER 8

WebAssembly in the Server

I felt extremely uncomfortable as the focal point, in the spotlight. I really like the behind-the-scenes role, because all my freedom is there.
—Brian Eno

My career started in the user interface world. I first worked on an X/Motif application to control Network Matrix Switches.[1] From there, I went on to a Whole Earth visualization environment capable of displaying terabytes of terrain data and hyperspectral imagery. Not only was this fun from a 3D visualization perspective, but we were inspired by Doug Young at Silicon Graphics to build the entire application around the Command Pattern[2] a year before the "Gang of Four" *Design Patterns* book emerged.

Working on software that humans sat down and used was a fun and rewarding experience most of the time. You could genuinely make people's lives easier and less stressful by putting some thought into how they went about their work tasks. Despite these positives, it had its drawbacks as well. While everyone had opinions on user interface decisions, only some of them were informed opinions.

I imagine in some small way, this is what Brian Eno was referring to in the above quotation. He was notably one of the cofounders of Roxy Music, a darling of music nerds everywhere. But, despite his glam outfits and makeup, he did not really care to be in the spotlight and, after frequent clashes with Bryan Ferry, he went his own way, focusing more on composition and production than on being a typical rock star performer.

---

1 Motif (*https://oreil.ly/N8ZoI*) built on top of the Xt Intrinsics libraries and the X Window System.

2 The Command Pattern (*https://oreil.ly/AcQLh*) separates the triggering event for execution of code from the actual code allowing for, among other things, macro recording and playback.

My career shifted and I began to focus on design, architecture, backend services, and the like. I strayed away from the spotlight of user interfaces and enjoyed the relative freedom of backend server work. It was not as attention-getting as user-facing activities, but it also had the benefit of not being as attention-getting as user-facing activities.

For most of its existence, WebAssembly has been positioned as a client-side technology. It has been seen primarily as a way to extend and expand what is possible in the browser, a universal client no longer restricted to extension only via JavaScript. There is a much bigger role for WebAssembly than being simply a frontend darling. It is going to have an extremely important role as a technology outside of the browser as well. In fact, it has been positioned for that all along with Node.js supporting WebAssembly modules almost the entire time.

It may not be obvious why this makes as much sense on the server, where performance is so crucial and you generally have the freedom to pick your implementation technologies. At the confluence of hardware heterogeneity and evolution, developer productivity, business value, security, and the capacity for architecture to serve as a design choice to minimize infrastructure and network costs, however, lies a glowing opportunity that WebAssembly is rapidly expanding to fill. Over the remainder of the book we will fill in that story, but for now we will simply focus on the basics of running WebAssembly outside of the browser.

Native Extensions to Node.js

Node.js emerged as, among other things, a response to the fact that developers would use one language and set of frameworks on the client side in the browser, and another set on the server. Previous efforts to gain reusable code everywhere (via Java itself and the Google Web Toolkit [GWT]) had attempted to travel the other direction, from server to client. This was a movement in the other direction. Most of the excitement in the software development space was happening in the browser and in the explosion of techniques and frameworks from Ajax to jQuery to Angular and more. It was maddening to have to write code that ran in the browser and then rewrite it to run on the server in a different language.

Node.js quickly grew in popularity and became a darling of the software developers, who now had further reach and greater reusability. As a JavaScript-based environment, applications written to run on it were intrinsically portable as long as the environment was. At its core, Node.js was the highly performant V8 JavaScript engine from Google, libuv (the basis of its event loop and abstraction layer over lower-level functionality), and a set of APIs built on top of all of this. This was an inherently portable environment.

The problem remained that not everything is a good fit to be implemented in Java-Script even with the high-powered V8 engine at its core. Naturally, it allowed for an extension mechanism with native libraries implemented in C and C++. Given the complex relationship between JavaScript object life cycles and native code structures, this makes for much trickier software development. On top of that, you suddenly have a native library management problem. If you install a Node.js application with native library extensions, there needs to be a process to get them to compile on Linux, Windows, macOS, etc.

So many WebAssembly tutorials demonstrate adding two numbers together. Obviously, this would not be a good use case for employing a native library unless you were talking about machine learning–levels of math. In Chapter 9, we will discuss that scenario in more depth. For now, we will just highlight the relative complexity of integrating Node.js with native libraries even for this simple, poorly justified example.

The issue is largely the fact that C and C++ code has direct access to memory but JavaScript code does not. In the Node.js environment, the V8 engine manages memory for the JavaScript code that runs in it. This makes passing strings, structures, arguments, and other elements that take up space in memory trickier to send between the JavaScript and native portions of the engine. V8 was intended to isolate JavaScript from one page in the browser being able to interfere with memory allocated for other code on a different page. This isolation is maintained when it is embedded in the Node.js environment.

Server-side frameworks are often extensible, so we can add additional response behaviors, filters, authorization models, and data processing workflows. In the Java world, there are a series of ways server developers can deploy behavior. There are servlets, Spring beans, reactive systems, and more. The structure of these extensions is often defined by standards or well-established conventions.

In Node.js, there has historically been middleware like Express and then native add-ons written in C and C++. The majority of applications in this environment do not have native add-ons because the JavaScript engines have become quite performant and there is a seemingly limitless supply of open source libraries tackling various needs. For the case where JavaScript performance is not suitable, however, it is possible to create an extension and make it callable from the JavaScript side of things.

This is not a simple activity, unfortunately. First of all, many JavaScript developers are not accomplished C and C++ programmers. There are big differences between the languages and runtimes and passing memory back and forth from the unrestricted world of C and C++ to the isolated, garbage-collected JavaScript world requires significant hoop jumping. Even when the developers are effective in these lower-level languages, the adoption of native libraries complicates the build process. Suddenly, the program artifacts are no longer intrinsically portable and we need to keep track of Linux, macOS, and Windows versions of the native libraries.

Let's look at a simple example that we have seen multiple times so far in this book. The Node.js documentation on add-ons (*https://oreil.ly/Bhl6Y*) has a great example for us to make the comparison. First, be sure the node and node-gyp commands are installed as per the Appendix. Then take a look at Example 8-1, where you will see a single function to add two numbers together.

Example 8-1. A Node.js add-on from the Node website

```
// addon.cc
// Taken from https://nodejs.org/api/addons.html#addons_addon_examples

#include <node.h>

namespace demo {

using v8::Exception;
using v8::FunctionCallbackInfo;
using v8::Isolate;
using v8::Local;
using v8::Number;
using v8::Object;
using v8::String;
using v8::Value;

// This is the implementation of the "add" method
// Input arguments are passed using the
// const FunctionCallbackInfo<Value>& args struct
void Add(const FunctionCallbackInfo<Value>& args) {
  Isolate* isolate = args.GetIsolate();

  // Check the number of arguments passed.
  if (args.Length() < 2) {
    // Throw an Error that is passed back to JavaScript
    isolate->ThrowException(Exception::TypeError(
        String::NewFromUtf8(isolate,
                            "Wrong number of arguments").ToLocalChecked()));
    return;
  }

  // Check the argument types
  if (!args[0]->IsNumber() || !args[1]->IsNumber()) {
    isolate->ThrowException(Exception::TypeError(
        String::NewFromUtf8(isolate,
                            "Wrong arguments").ToLocalChecked()));
    return;
  }

  // Perform the operation
  double value =
      args[0].As<Number>()->Value() + args[1].As<Number>()->Value();
```

```
  Local<Number> num = Number::New(isolate, value);

  // Set the return value (using the passed in
  // FunctionCallbackInfo<Value>&)
  args.GetReturnValue().Set(num);
}

void Init(Local<Object> exports) {
  NODE_SET_METHOD(exports, "add", Add);
}

NODE_MODULE(NODE_GYP_MODULE_NAME, Init)

} // namespace demo
```

The method is called `Add()`, and it takes a `FunctionCallbackInfo<Value>&` reference. From this, we retrieve the `Isolate` instance, which is the handle we have to the memory subsystem that V8 is maintaining for this instance. If there are not two arguments or if they are not numeric types, we throw an exception. Otherwise, we retrieve the values as numbers and add them together before creating a new location to hold the value, then set it as the return type for the function. In addition to all of this, we need to register the module with Node.js via the `Init()` method.

The next step is to build the add-on. In Example 8-2, you can see the *binding.gyp* file, which instructs the `node-gyp` command in how to perform the build. This can be a much more detailed process, but our needs here are fairly simple.

Example 8-2. Build instructions for the add-on

```
{
  "targets": [
    {
      "target_name": "addon",
      "sources": [ "addon.cc" ]
    }
  ]
}
```

The build command is straightforward enough (I have hidden some of the details):

```
brian@tweezer ~/g/w/s/c/node-addon> node-gyp configure build
gyp info it worked if it ends with ok
gyp info using node-gyp@8.0.0
gyp info using node@15.4.0 | darwin | x64
gyp info find Python using Python version 3.8.3 found at "/usr/local/bin/python3"
gyp http GET https://nodejs.org/download/release/v15.4.0/node-v15.4.0-hdrs.tar.gz
gyp http 200 https://nodejs.org/download/release/v15.4.0/node-v15.4.0-hdrs.tar.gz
gyp http GET https://nodejs.org/download/release/v15.4.0/SHASUMS256.txt
gyp http 200 https://nodejs.org/download/release/v15.4.0/SHASUMS256.txt
...
```

```
gyp info spawn args [ 'BUILDTYPE=Release', '-C', 'build' ]
  CXX(target) Release/obj.target/addon/addon.o
  SOLINK_MODULE(target) Release/addon.node
```

At this point, the add-on has been built. We can test it with the code shown in Example 8-3.

Example 8-3. JavaScript code to test the native add-on

```
// test.js
const addon = require('./build/Release/addon');

console.log('This should be eight:', addon.add(3, 5));
```

On the surface, the use of the add-on feels quite similar to calling a WebAssembly module, but clearly the implementation is significantly more complicated than the C code we have invoked to add two numbers elsewhere. The real issue is that the complexity of native libraries is kind of a pain to manage. Now, with WebAssembly, there is no real need for this anymore, and you can understand why the Node.js community is excited about WebAssembly versions of libraries. They provide good performance gains but are completely portable and simplify their deployment model.

WebAssembly and Node.js

While most people think of WebAssembly as a client-side browser technology, Node.js has had support for invoking functions from WebAssembly modules almost as long as the browsers have. I am not going to create any actual "servers," as I think that may distract from the points I want to make, but you clearly could set up a REST API or something similar and still use the features I am mentioning.

Let's start with a simple example in Example 8-4.

Example 8-4. A simple program to add two numbers

```
#include <stdio.h>

int add(int x, int y) {
  return x + y;
}

int main() {
  printf("The sum of 2 and 3 is: %d\n", add(2,3));
  return 0;
}
```

With `clang`, this is trivially compiled and executed:

```
brian@tweezer ~/g/w/s/c/node> clang add.c
brian@tweezer ~/g/w/s/c/node> ./a.out
The sum of 2 and 3 is: 5
```

If we update the source code to include some Emscripten-related macros, we can easily run it in Node.js as we have seen previously. I also removed the `main()` method so our module will no longer expect an implementation of the `printf()` function, since we will be operating in the world of server-side JavaScript. The updated code is in Example 8-5.

Example 8-5. A simple program to add two numbers with Emscripten macros

```
#include <emscripten.h>  ❶

EMSCRIPTEN_KEEPALIVE int add(int x, int y) {  ❷
  return x + y;
}
```

❶ Include the Emscripten header for the macro definition.

❷ Tell the Emscripten compiler to keep the `add()` method around.

Now we can recompile with `emcc` and run it with Node.js:

```
brian@tweezer ~/g/w/s/c/node> emcc add.c
brian@tweezer ~/g/w/s/c/node> ls -alF
total 376
drwxr-xr-x   6 brian  staff     192 Apr 18 15:05 ./
drwxr-xr-x  10 brian  staff     320 Apr 18 13:08 ../
-rwxr-xr-x   1 brian  staff   49456 Apr 18 15:05 a.out*
-rw-r--r--   1 brian  staff  121686 Apr 18 15:05 a.out.js
-rwxr-xr-x   1 brian  staff   11805 Apr 18 15:05 a.out.wasm*
-rw-r--r--   1 brian  staff     141 Apr 18 15:05 add.c
brian@tweezer ~/g/w/s/c/node> node a.out.js
The sum of 2 and 3 is: 5
```

If you investigate the file *a.out.js*, you will see all of the setup the Emscripten toolchain has handled for us.

There is a proper JavaScript-based WebAssembly API available via the Node.js runtime such as we have seen in the browser. This allows you to load and instantiate modules and invoke behavior on them as you see fit. Behind the scenes, this is what the Emscripten toolchain is generating for us.

However, we are also interested in simplifying the loading and instantiation of WebAssembly modules in the server just as in the browser. Node.js provides experimental support for loading them as ES6 modules, too, as you can see in Example 8-6.

Example 8-6. Loading WebAssembly modules as ES6 modules

```
import * as Module from './a.out.wasm';

console.log('The sum of 6 and 2 is: ' + Module.add(6,2));
```

Depending on when you attempt to run the following, you may need the experimental feature flags, but notice how much easier it is to deal with than what we have seen before. The expression of the behavior is also dramatically simpler than what we saw in the previous discussion on native add-ons. You can see why this community is excited about continued WebAssembly support being added over time:

```
brian@tweezer ~/g/w/s/c/node> node --experimental-modules ↵
  --experimental-wasm-modules index.mjs
(node:74571) ExperimentalWarning: Importing Web Assembly modules is an
experimental feature. This feature could change at any time (Use `node
--trace-warnings ...` to show where the warning was created)
The sum of 6 and 2 is: 8
```

As a final example, I want to pull in a more sophisticated third-party library. For reasons that I will explain at the end of this chapter, finding a good example that did not open up too many cans of worms was tricky. There are things we have not introduced yet but are starting to lay the foundation for in this chapter.

Supply Chain Attacks

This brings us to another consideration. We are facing a very serious problem in the world of secure software systems called supply chain attacks. They are not a new problem, but they are getting worse and more frequent.

There is no single way to build a secure system, certainly not simply by turning on encryption or a similar security feature. Those may be necessary for a secure system, but are most definitely insufficient. Usually through the combination of defense-in-depth,[3] the principle of least privilege,[4] and a deliberate attempt to accept the responsibility for security organizationally, you can start to head in the right direction.

For us, the problem is that we are running potentially untrusted code from untrusted third parties with the privileges we normally give ourselves in production. Out of the box, Node provides no protection against this, and that is a serious problem that is opening up new attack vectors for phishing, data exfiltration, and other attacks.

---

3 A combination of overlapping security controls (*https://oreil.ly/ftxt0*) can help you protect against unexpected vulnerabilities.

4 Only assigning the minimum privileges necessary to users (*https://oreil.ly/D8bkY*) is part of how this technique helps.

Hayden Parker wrote about a supply chain attack in 2018 (*https://oreil.ly/1MFGd*). The basic idea is that an attacker will produce a moderately useful bit of open source functionality and let it start to get used. Developers often add dependencies without considering their source, or the transitive collection of sources for dependencies. Once the code gains sufficient use in the ecosystem, a minor update under carefully controlled circumstances starts to expose the attack in subtle and hard to anticipate ways. Basically, the code may start looking for cryptocurrency private keys or other useful and sensitive information.

One of the only real solutions to this problem involves an active and attentive software developer community that hand checks every update to every dependency (and its corresponding comprehensive list of transitive dependencies), which is pretty much guaranteed to never happen. The other solution is to run in a scenario where arbitrary code is not given the privilege to do whatever it likes. Node.js has traditionally allowed this model, which is one of the reasons its creator, Ryan Dahl, has moved on to create something new and more secure.

Enter Deno.

WebAssembly and Deno

Deno is basically a more secure runtime for JavaScript and Typescript than Node.js is likely to become.[5] Even though both were initially built by the same person, security was not as much of a consideration with Node.js and would therefore be difficult to tack on after the fact. Deno starts off with security as a default position. Code running in a Deno runtime cannot access the filesystem or open up network connection unless given permission to do so.

This is obviously not a new idea. Java has had a secure permission model at its core almost the entire time it has been a thing. The problem is that Java's permission model can be somewhat Byzantine and hard to get right. If anything is going to kill security, complexity is at the top of the list. As you will see below, Deno has a simpler way of handling this using a capability-based approach.[6]

Beyond security, Deno "runs TypeScript" natively, whereas it is usually transpiled into some flavor of JavaScript first. While Deno is compiling it behind the scenes and caching the compiled form, it feels more like native support. This improves things with respect to the quality of JavaScript development (which also has security implications) by allowing for improved type-checking. Problems that would normally arise

---

5 There is a lot to like about Deno (*https://deno.land*) beyond security.

6 Capability-based security systems (*https://oreil.ly/mLml3*) generally require actors to demonstrate that they have an unforgeable permission to conduct an operation.

at runtime can be detected at compile time because of the robust type systems available in TypeScript.

Let's start with our WebAssembly module from Example 8-5 that adds two numbers together. In Example 8-7, you can see our first attempt to use Deno's WebAssembly support. Super simple!

Example 8-7. Loading WebAssembly modules in Deno

```
const wasmCode = await Deno.readFile("./a.out.wasm");
const wasmModule = new WebAssembly.Module(wasmCode);
const wasmInstance = new WebAssembly.Instance(wasmModule);
const add = wasmInstance.exports.add as CallableFunction

console.log("2 + 3 =  " + add(2,3));
```

Unfortunately, our excitement is short-lived. At least the problem is clear. We are attempting to read from the filesystem, but we do not have permission to do so. We see Deno's security advantage immediately:

```
brian@tweezer ~/g/w/s/c/deno> deno run main.ts
error: Uncaught (in promise) PermissionDenied: Requires read access to
"./a.out.wasm", run again with the --allow-read flag

const wasmCode = await Deno.readFile("./a.out.wasm");
                     ^
    at unwrapOpResult (deno:core/core.js:100:13)
    at async open (deno:runtime/js/40_files.js:46:17)
    at async Object.readFile (deno:runtime/js/40_read_file.js:19:18)
    at async file:///Users/brian/git-personal/wasm_tdg/src/ch08/deno/main.ts:1:18
```

If we rerun with the following command, things are much more pleasant:

```
brian@tweezer ~/g/w/s/c/deno> deno run --allow-read main.ts
Check file:///Users/brian/git-personal/wasm_tdg/src/ch08/deno/main.ts
2 + 3 =  5
```

While I did not want to get super distracted with the details of running Node.js and Deno HTTP servers, I do admit that it is more than a bit pathetic that I have not run a server yet in a chapter about servers. So, here is a simple HTTP server. To get more sophisticated would require us to get into Deno middleware.

In Example 8-8, however, you see how Deno allows you to pull versioned modules over HTTP for use. In this case, we are pulling a basic HTTP server from the Deno standard library.

Example 8-8. Using WebAssembly in a Deno HTTP server

```
import { serve } from "https://deno.land/std@0.93.0/http/server.ts";

const wasmCode = await Deno.readFile("./a.out.wasm");
const wasmModule = new WebAssembly.Module(wasmCode);
const wasmInstance = new WebAssembly.Instance(wasmModule);
const add = wasmInstance.exports.add as CallableFunction

const server = serve({ hostname: "0.0.0.0", port: 9000 });
console.log(`HTTP webserver running.  Access it at:  http://localhost:9000/`);

for await (const request of server) {
  let bodyContent = "2 + 3 = " + add(2,3);
  request.respond({ status: 200, body: bodyContent });
}
```

Prepare yourself for quick disappointment! Just as we could not run TypeScript code that read from the filesystem without giving our application permission to do so, we cannot listen to network connections without permission to do so either!

```
brian@tweezer ~/g/w/s/c/deno> deno run --allow-read main-serve.ts
error: Uncaught (in promise) PermissionDenied: Requires net access to
"0.0.0.0:9000", run again with the --allow-net flag
  const listener = Deno.listen(addr);
                   ^
    at unwrapOpResult (deno:core/core.js:100:13)
    at Object.opSync (deno:core/core.js:114:12)
    at opListen (deno:runtime/js/30_net.js:18:17)
    at Object.listen (deno:runtime/js/30_net.js:184:17)
    at serve (https://deno.land/std@0.93.0/http/server.ts:303:25)
    at file:///Users/brian/git-personal/wasm_tdg/src/ch08/deno/main-serve.ts:8:16
```

Fortunately, we are told what to do and that it is an easy problem to fix:

```
brian@tweezer ~/g/w/s/c/deno> deno run --allow-read --allow-net main-serve.ts
HTTP webserver running.  Access it at:  http://localhost:9000/
```

Now a simple HTTP client can fetch our result:

```
brian@tweezer ~> http http://localhost:9000
HTTP/1.1 200 OK
content-length: 9

2 + 3 = 5
```

Next we will look at one final example of Deno and WebAssembly. I have been a bit cagey about showing certain types of functionality until we have a chance to discuss the WebAssembly System Interface (WASI) standard in Chapter 11. For the time being, I want to show a use of WebAssembly with Deno that is not going to require too many additional details.

Tilman Roeder[7] has created an in-memory SQLite WebAssembly module and wrapped it for use in JavaScript and TypeScript, which you can access on GitHub (*https://oreil.ly/FtA3r*). The details for how it works will have to wait, but using it is quite straightforward, as you see in Example 8-9.

Example 8-9. Using a WebAssembly SQLite wrapper in a Deno HTTP server

```
import { DB } from "https://deno.land/x/sqlite/mod.ts";
import { serve } from "https://deno.land/std@0.93.0/http/server.ts";

// Create the Database. This requires write access!

const db = new DB("pl.db");
db.query(
  "CREATE TABLE IF NOT EXISTS languages (id INTEGER PRIMARY KEY AUTOINCREMENT,
      name TEXT)",
);

const names = ["C", "C++", "Rust", "TypeScript"]

// Populate the database

for (const name of names) {
  db.query("INSERT INTO languages (name) VALUES (?)", [name]);
}

// Close out the connection

db.close();

const server = serve({ hostname: "0.0.0.0", port: 9000 });
console.log(`HTTP webserver running.  Access it at:  http://localhost:9000/`);

for await (const request of server) {
  // Re-open the Database

  const db = new DB("pl.db");
  let bodyContent = "Programming Languages that work with WebAssembly:\n\n";

  for(const [name] of db.query("SELECT name FROM languages")) {
    bodyContent += name + "\n";
  }

  bodyContent += "\n";
  request.respond({ status: 200, body: bodyContent });

  // Close the Database
```

---

7 @dyedgreen on Twitter and Github

```
  db.close();
}
```

We start by creating the database file. I hope your intuition kicked in that this is going to require another runtime permission, because it does as you see below. After that, we load some data into the database and close out the connection.

Once we start up the server, upon receiving a suitable HTTP request, we will open up the database again, run a query, generate a result, and then close the database. I am not suggesting that this is quality production code yet, but it is quite remarkable that this code runs securely in Deno and will do so across the various platforms that Deno supports. Even though we are dealing with a wrapped C library (i.e., SQLite3), WebAssembly makes the code portable while still being fairly performant. I hope the idea of extending server infrastructure with safe, fast, and portable WebAssembly code makes more sense.

The following command will start up the server with suitable permissions:

```
brian@tweezer ~/g/w/s/c/deno> deno run --allow-read --allow-write ↵
  --allow-net db-serve.ts
HTTP webserver running.  Access it at:  http://localhost:9000/
```

A request from an HTTP client produces what we would expect:

```
brian@tweezer ~> http http://localhost:9000
HTTP/1.1 200 OK
content-length: 74

Programming Languages that work with WebAssembly:

C
C++
Rust
TypeScript
```

A Look Forward

As big of a leap out of the browser as this chapter represented, this is just the beginning. While we gave up the security restrictions of running in that constrained environment (except for a similarly locked-down Deno instance), we also gave up the rich functionality of the browser. There is a tremendous amount of functionality available to the JavaScript environment in any modern browser platform. This includes JavaScript engines, hardware accelerated 2D/3D graphics and video playback, sound, font support, the ability to make network requests, and more. By default, neither Node.js nor Deno provides all of the functionality of the browser, although Deno is trying to support most of it. This makes it harder to write WebAssembly-based applications that will work inside and outside of the browser.

WebAssembly makes the code portable. We need another strategy for making applications portable by providing consistent service interfaces to functionality we would expect in a modern computing platform. This is why I have been a bit circumspect about the kinds of examples I can show you. A real solution to the problem will be introduced in Chapter 11. Until then, be patient, but we have a bunch more to discuss on our way.

## CHAPTER 9

Applied WebAssembly: TensorFlow.js

*Now, the world don't move
to the beat of just one drum,
What might be right for you,
May not be right for some.*
—Theme to *Diff'rent Strokes*

This is the first of our "Applied WebAssembly" chapters, where I highlight potential use cases for the technology. As you will see over the course of the book, there is no single use. Instead, the designers have crafted a platform with increasing reach into just about all aspects of the software development industry. So follow along. I will not be teaching new features per se. Instead, I hope to help shape your understanding of how our industry is changing rapidly and how WebAssembly will assist.

To begin, I want you to stop for a moment and think about programming languages and machine learning. What is the first programming language that comes to mind? There is probably a good chance your answer was not JavaScript. Why would it be? Machine learning is an incredibly performance-oriented activity with monumental computational workloads these days.

Languages such as Python are much more strongly associated with machine learning than JavaScript is. If we are being honest, that is a bit of a stretch too. Python is a horrible numerics language on its own. It strikes a nice balance, however, of readability, flexible programming style (functional, object-oriented, procedural), and wide-ranging coverage of algorithms, visualization, and data-wrangling features. If you can make it run faster, then it checks an awful lot of boxes. NumPy, native libraries, clustered cloud environments, and more can give it the computational horsepower to make the training process happen.

Most organizations do not run Python operationally, though, so chances are you will need to serialize the model into some other format so it can be loaded into a C/C++,

C#, Java, or JavaScript application. This is becoming easier because of open formats such as Open Neural Network Exchange (ONNX) (*https://onnx.ai*), but many frameworks such as TensorFlow naturally support this form of mixed use.

The first step is to train our models. The second step is inference. Until a few years ago, TensorFlow required you to train in Python, but you could save the model out to disk and load it into other environments. These days you have the choice of training in Python, JavaScript, or Swift with TensorFlow.

We are going to discuss TensorFlow.js, which is designed as a way of providing machine learning capabilities in and out of the browser in JavaScript environments. Using JavaScript for machine learning (particularly in the browser) makes more sense than you might think. In order to understand the relationship between machine learning and JavaScript and WebAssembly, however, we must first have a quick discussion about hardware and how it is changing our industry.

Hardware

The typical programmer thinks of their job as writing software that runs on computers containing a Central Processing Unit (CPU), main memory, a storage system, a display, and some input devices. While this still covers a significant amount of software development, we have a richer ecosystem of computational runtimes than most people realize. Computers, tablets, game consoles, networking equipment, smartphones, watches, embedded systems, Internet of Things (IoT) devices, and systems on chip (SOC) provide a menagerie of hardware systems that execute software.

Herb Sutter of C++ fame has written an excellent essay called "Welcome to the Jungle" (*https://oreil.ly/b93Cm*) that is worth your time.[1] In it, he highlights the impact of hardware developments on the software industry over the last several decades. For approximately 30 years, Moore's law translated higher density into faster chips.[2] If your software was slow, you simply waited 18 to 24 months and it would get faster.

Once we stopped being able to make faster, more complex chips, we used the extra density to make simpler chips. Multicore systems became the norm. Unlike the previous "free lunch" period, developers now had to write crazy concurrent code to benefit from the extra processing power, and not every problem fits this mold nicely. Also, this is tricky code and easy to get wrong. This has largely pushed us toward functional programming languages and immutable data structures.

---

1 In it, he cites another essay he wrote called "The Free Lunch is Over," also worth your time.

2 Moore's law (*https://oreil.ly/3GI3L*) is a famous observation about manufacturing trends in the density of silicon chips.

Other developments include the emergence of cloud computing to meet elastic demand, edge computing to distribute it geographically for low-latency customer experiences, and heterogenous computing environments. This includes graphics processing units (GPUs), field-programmable gate arrays (FPGAs), and application-specific integrated circuits (ASICs).

Tied up in all of this is the idea that it takes time and power to compute things. A big part of a successful IT strategy moving forward is going to be about minimizing time costs, power costs, and latency costs. This is going to influence where things run. It makes sense to push large amounts of data into the cloud for elastic, bursty training sessions. But if this results in large models, those are not as easily distributed to the desktop/mobile experience because of size. At the same time, we do not want internet sensors and car brakes making cloud calls at crucial times.

We are facing an absolute explosion of data, which is going to make all of this more crucial. In order to process data in reasonable amounts of time, we need access to hardware acceleration. This parallelizes the math so it is tractable. It is in this world that we finally can explore the concept of JavaScript-based machine learning in the browser.

Playground

TensorFlow Playground (*https://oreil.ly/gRvLh*) is an experimental environment for nonexperts to gain intuition about how neural networks work through direct manipulation.[3] The idea is that these models are increasingly driving systems with real-world consequences, but the background needed to understand them is beyond the typical nonacademic researcher. By working with visual representations, nontechnical users are able to gain a sense of cause and effect.

The problem is that the JavaScript environment is single-threaded and the numerics support is not great for the kind of math that training neural networks requires. The Playground environment allows you to change all hyperparameters of the training process via simple user interface actions. While it is easy and fun to experiment with changing these parameters, they can have significant impacts on the quality of the results. To see the effect quickly and in real time, the runtime needs to recalculate significant portions of the code; otherwise, the whole point of direct manipulation is lost. Fortunately, they were able to eke out enough performance to make it all work by relying on the presence of WebGL in the browser. We will discuss this idea more in a moment.

---

3 Direct manipulation (*https://oreil.ly/NQzq5*) is a style of user interface in which a user has controls that allow for safe, exploratory manipulation of an application and its data.

TensorFlow.js

Out of the success of Playground came an appreciation of what was necessary and possible to bring deep learning systems to the browser. It may strike you as a bit odd to want to run such computationally intensive systems on potentially lower-end devices such as phones or tablets. Even just running in the browser on a powerful desktop machine is a slightly odd concept. There are quite a few benefits to the idea, though.

Unsurprisingly, the experience of clicking on a link and downloading a deep learning–based application is a lot easier than having to install a potentially large number of required libraries. There is zero installation to load a web page. It is easier to share research and practical applications when it is this easy. This broadens the potential for interaction among deep learning researchers and makes it easier to target end users with applications that employ these capabilities.

Given the popularity of JavaScript, it is a bit of a steep request that web developers learn Python in order to do machine learning. There is an overwhelming amount of open source JavaScript code for building all manner of software systems. Being able to take advantage of it all would be a benefit to developers of machine learning systems in the other direction.

Our phones and tablets have quickly become something much more than mobile portable electronic devices. They have become diagnostic tools, part of our banking systems, methods of identification, and more. New software is being written to detect the onset of dementia or the presence of strokes by analyzing video from their cameras. Both for the quality of the user experience and for privacy law compliance with respect to the results of diagnostic outcomes, being able to push apps to the device will be much less encumbered by regulatory burdens than trying to take data off of the device.

Finally, many of the devices that these downloaded apps might run on have powerful and sophisticated GPUs available for use. Not only could it be possible to do deep learning systems in the browser, it might actually perform well.

So, why are we discussing all of this?

The design of the TensorFlow.js framework is elegant and results in clean APIs that work across a wide range of devices. Rather than limiting the implementation to what is available everywhere, the designers chose to create a pluggable backend to cover the widest number of systems.

The basic version of the backend is a CPU-based JavaScript implementation that will run anywhere. All of the code executes directly on the CPU without benefit of optimizing instruction sets such as the Advanced Vector Extensions (AVX).[4] It does not perform effectively anywhere, but it will run basically everywhere. Other options are better first choices, but this is a decent fallback position.

The next major backend is accelerated by WebGL. There is no direct support for accessing GPUs from JavaScript, but there is via WebGL, which is supported in nearly every browser. By pretending to do 3D graphics, the developers can execute calculations on the GPU and write the results into the textures. This produces a fast and convenient implementation that runs well on just about every major modern browser. It is similar to what was done with the TensorFlow Playground application mentioned earlier.

 This is not as strange a scenario as it sounds. Prior to the availability of GPU computation libraries such as CUDA, OpenCL, Metal, and Vulkan, researchers would do this with OpenGL to get access to comparatively cheap computation. These APIs that specifically allow the use of GPUs for arbitrary computation were part of what accelerated the machine learning and deep learning systems we enjoy these days.

Servers with deep learning needs can be implemented in Node.js, so the next backend is designed to run in a freer environment than the browser. Apps running in Node.js can read from and write to the filesystem, load and use native libraries, and communicate directly with the normal native TensorFlow libraries. These can take advantage of multicore systems, GPUs, or other hardware accelerating devices such as Google's Tensor Processing Units (TPUs).

You can see the basic structure of the API design in Figure 9-1.

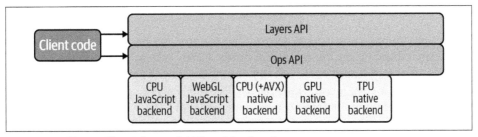

Figure 9-1. TensorFlow.js layered API and backends

There is quite a lot to unpack here. First of all, the lower-level operators are exposed via the Ops API shown above. Developers who need to get down into the details have

---

4 AVX/AVX2 (*https://oreil.ly/8eWWz*) are extensions to the Intel x86 instruction set architecture (ISA) that provide parallel optimizations of the kind of math we are using here.

the option of entering the API at that level. Above that, however, is a Keras-inspired Layers API that is designed with a pleasant developer experience in mind. This is a simple API for defining complex neural network architectures using a simplified stacked layer approach. It hides many of the details but still exposes powerful behavior through a relatively straightforward mechanism.

Regardless of which layer of the API the client code uses to enter TensorFlow.js, the applications written against those APIs will be portable across all of the environments covered by the backends. That includes in the browser, out of the browser, with hardware acceleration and without. This is a remarkable enough design achievement, but the code will also run exceptionally well in the different environments when it is able to take advantage of hardware acceleration. As we have seen, this can come in a variety of forms, but we are not writing against the least common denominator environment and the application code need not be encumbered by a bunch of features-testing code to see what the environment provides.

The results of a single inference using MobileNet averaged over one hundred runs are shown in Table 9-1.[5] This data is taken from the paper that introduced the world to TensorFlow.js, "TensorFlow.js: Machine Learning for the Web and Beyond" (*https://oreil.ly/Wn9AE*).[6]

Table 9-1. Summary of Tensorflow.js performance results

Backend	Time(ms)	Speedup
CPU JavaScript	3426	1x
WebGL (Intel Iris Pro)	49	71x
WebGL (GTX 1080)	5	685x
Node.js CPU w/ AVX2	87	39x
Node.js CUDA (GTX 1080)	3	1105x

The results are not surprising as a trend, but the specifics kind of are. It takes nearly 3.5 seconds running on the raw JavaScript backend with no hardware acceleration. Simply swap out the backend to one that is optimized by the presence of WebGL support and even a very modest integrated GPU yields a 71x speedup running in the browser. On a desktop machine with a more powerful GPU, we achieve nearly a 700x speedup. A server application running without benefit of a GPU but with the benefit of a CPU with optimized AVX instructions has a nearly 40x improvement. The same environment backed by a more powerful GPU produces a jaw-dropping 1,000x+

---

5 The MobileNet collection of models (*https://oreil.ly/BwNOJ*) is designed for efficient mobile and embedded vision applications.

6 The paper is a good read and worth your time.

speedup. Keep in mind that nothing has changed in the application, simply the environment it runs in.

This is my larger point. The move from the "free lunch" period to the multicore period forced a significant change in how developers had to program in order to take advantage of these extra resources. If we had to adjust for custom acceleration, the presence of multiple CPUs, cloud hosting environments, and running in the browser, our deep learning applications would be a rat's nest of unmaintainable code. Instead, what we see is a strategy for isolating the bits that change and taking advantage of the hardware options available to us. This leads us to the final backend we will consider.

WebAssembly Backend

Not too long after TensorFlow.js was released, the team released a new backend written in WebAssembly. It may surprise you that they felt the need to do so given the coverage we just discussed. However, by now I hope you realize that this probably did not mean starting from scratch. Clearly there was work to do, but a fair amount of the effort was handled by relying on existing code. In particular, the XNNPack library was extended to support WebAssembly builds.[7]

This extends our collection of backends to include the one shown in Figure 9-2.

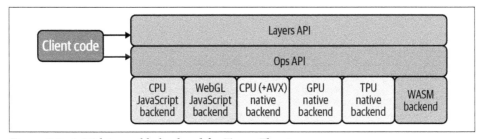

Figure 9-2. A WebAssembly backend for TensorFlow.js

This example highlights a prominent use case for WebAssembly. It is not about replacing JavaScript, at least not in all cases. It is about extending what is possible in the browser without having to wait for consensus from the browser vendor community. WebGPU[8] or something like it is coming through the standards process, but this can take years. An existing library written in C++ and designed to be optimized and portable across many platforms is able to bring a good portion of that power to browsers now without waiting.

---

7 XNNPack is available on GitHub (*https://oreil.ly/xK1nM*), although it is not intended to be used directly by deep learning researchers.

8 This emerging standard (*https://oreil.ly/Q57ko*) will directly expose GPU support to browsers in a cross-platform manner.

The WebAssembly backend broadens the computational runtime to include older devices without powerful GPUs. The code can be optimized to still run well across a wide range of platforms. Additionally, the WebAssembly designers are in the process of adopting two advanced features that we will discuss in later chapters, which are the use of Single Instruction Multiple Data (SIMD) parallelization and the use of multiple threads.[9]

In Figure 9-3, we have a similar use of MobileNet as before. Clearly, the WebAssembly backend on its own does not perform as well as the WebGL-backed one. You are encouraged to use the Wasm backend instead of the plain JavaScript one as it will perform much better everywhere. Depending on the model size, the Wasm backend makes more sense than the WebGL one because of some fixed costs with respect to WebGL execution. Note the dramatic improvement in performance for the platforms that support them when threading and SIMD parallelization are added to the Wasm mix.

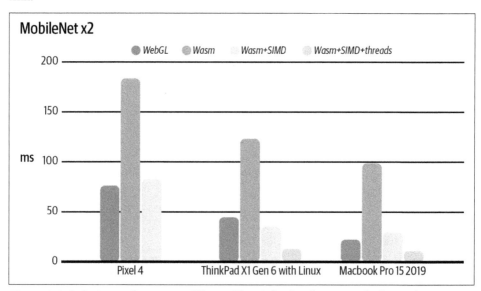

Figure 9-3. Relative performance of TensorFlow.js backends across platforms (source: https://oreil.ly/0Nq29)

In Figure 9-4, we see the results for a different model with a smaller number of parameters. In this scenario, the Wasm backend makes more sense. Notice the comparable performance on the Pixel 4 and the dramatically better performance on the

---

9 SIMD (*https://oreil.ly/x0bLf*) is a type of data parallelism processing that performs the same instructions on multiple computational elements on different parts of the data.

Linux and Mac notebooks. Again, the use of threads and SIMD dramatically improve upon the performance of the WebGL-based backend.

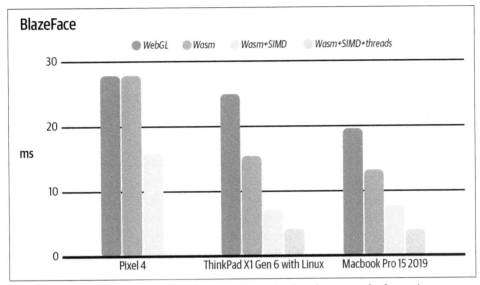

Figure 9-4. Relative performance of TensorFlow.js backends across platforms (source: https://oreil.ly/0Nq29)

At least for the time being, WebAssembly is not always going to be the fastest solution in every case. It is a relatively new platform, and it will be a while until all of the potential optimizations can be wrung out of what is there. However, given WebAssembly's young age, it is already changing the game about what is possible in a wide range of computational environments.

The key lessons of this chapter are that WebAssembly and its related technologies can offer us more choices, and in many cases better choices, for deploying high-performance software systems onto a largely varied computational surface. We will see many other uses as we go along, but now it is time to expand our options with respect to languages and WebAssembly.

## CHAPTER 10

Rust

There's talk on the street, it's there to remind you
Doesn't really matter which side you're on
You're walking away, and they're talking behind you
They will never forget you 'til somebody new comes along
— Eagles, "New Kid in Town"

For a period of my career I stopped caring about new programming languages. It seemed like there was always a new one right around the corner. Most of the time, they were not interesting in the slightest to me. These days a new programming language has to have sufficient advantage over what has come before to be able to capture our attention and be worth the effort to learn, invest in the toolchains, etc.

Around this time, I became aware of both Go and Rust and I put them in the same conceptual space: systems languages that provided roughly a similar speed to C and C++, but also contained language features that made them far safer. As I have always been a Unix nerd, I was drawn to Ken Thompson and Rob Pike's involvement in Go.[1] I was also excited to see some of the Plan 9 ideas gaining some traction. As a consequence, I put in some effort to learn Go and was happy that I did. I did not see the need to also learn Rust because I thought it was just more of the same.

And then I got interested in WebAssembly.

Once I heard that Rust was natively emitting WebAssembly on the backend, I knew I needed to dig in deeper. This is when I learned about the Rust language, its community, tools, and documentation and kind of fell in love. Don't get me wrong, I like the

---

[1] Ken Thompson was the creator the B programming language, which was a direct predecessor to C. He also invented and implemented much of the Unix operating system. Rob Pike is an author and programmer involved in the development of Unix and subsequent projects that influenced Go, such as Plan 9.

Go community and language as well, but the relationship between Rust and WebAssembly was such that the lion's share of my interest shifted and I have not looked back.

So far in this book, we have focused primarily on the relationship between C and C++ and WebAssembly. This is the first major step toward a different language. Rust is a modern language with a modern ethos. It provides good runtime performance with a safety net that would be nearly impossible to engender as an afterthought. Given the significant role C and C++ still play in the bugs, defects, and malware exploits we face on a daily basis, having a fast, safe systems language is a material improvement. After a long spell as darlings of the open source community, these benefits have started to become obvious to commercial developers, and interest in Rust is growing daily.

C and C++ obviously still play a significant role in our industry, but, if given the choice for new projects, I would reach for Rust instead. It really has become the new kid in town that everyone is talking about, so let's learn why before we look at the interplay between Rust and WebAssembly.

Introduction to Rust

Given the already massive scope of this book, I cannot teach you Rust with any kind of rigor. For that I encourage you to check out the free book by Steve Klabnik and Carol Nichols, *The Rust Programming Language* (*https://oreil.ly/VpzAo*), or the second edition or later of *Programming Rust* by Jim Blandy, Jason Orendorff, and Leonora F.S. Tindall (O'Reilly).

The high-level introduction to this new language is that it started as a side project by Graydon Hoare while at Mozilla but has morphed into an industry-changing language gaining traction at Google, Microsoft, Apple, and other leading technical companies. There are many reasons for their interest, but the main driver of adoption is that it is a fast, safe, modern language. Originally intended as a systems programming language for low-level libraries and operating system services, it has even started to find its way into Linux kernel extensions.

There are entire classes of bugs that are addressed by a fundamental series of design choices in the language. Issues that would have manifested as runtime errors in other languages become compile-time errors in Rust. Unfortunately, the language comes with a fairly steep learning curve. You will likely run into inexplicable edge cases that displease the Rust compiler and likely get rather frustrated initially. I have likened the experience to the maturation process teenagers go through.

Initially, there are not many expectations of you as a teenager, but slowly more is expected until you are suddenly an adult. The transition process can be painful and frustrating. As a developer, the Rust compiler expects you to communicate clearly and indicate your intentions so it can react accordingly. Languages like JavaScript make no such demands on you, so depending on your background, it may be a bit off-putting.

However, while you may chafe initially at the level of adulting the Rust compiler expects of you, it quickly becomes a language that people are passionate about. It has won several surveys of favorite languages over the last couple of years, so clearly moving past the steep learning curve is a rewarding experience.[2] Once teenagers become young adults, even with the extra expectations, few people ever long to go back to their younger selves.

Assuming you have installed Rust as detailed in the Appendix, we can easily handle a "Hello, World!" program such as Example 10-1.

Example 10-1. Rust "Hello, World!"

```
fn main() {
  println!("Hello, World!");
}
```

Here, we have a `main()` method and the ability to print strings to the console. While it may look like an emphatic name, the exclamation point simply marks this as a macro, a language feature we will not have time to explore.[3] For our purposes, just think of it as `printf()` in C or `System.out.println()` in Java. Compiling and running this simple program is as simple as writing the following commands:

```
brian@tweezer ~/g/w/s/ch10> rustc helloworld.rs
brian@tweezer ~/g/w/s/ch10> ./helloworld
Hello, World!
```

So far, no big deal, but it does not take long to run into a difference with Rust. Consider the basic example in Example 10-2.

Example 10-2. Rust immutable variables

```
fn main() {
  let s = "cool";
  s = "safe";

  println!("Rust is {}", s);
}
```

---

2 There are lots of places to read about Rust's popularity, but this article from *Nature* (*https://oreil.ly/ZAzfb*) is a cool one.

3 For the curious among you, you can find out more about macros in Rust online (*https://oreil.ly/iwqdz*).

We assign a string literal to variable s. Rust is pretty picky about types, but not unnecessarily so. When it can use type inference to figure out what type a variable should have, there is no reason to be verbose.[4] The Rust compiler can tell that a reference to a string is being assigned here. We then change our mind and overwrite the value with another string reference and then print out the new value. In almost any other programming language, this is a totally fine thing to do. In Rust…

```
brian@tweezer ~/g/w/s/ch10> rustc immutable.rs
warning: value assigned to `s` is never read
 --> immutable.rs:2:9
  |
2 |     let s = "cool";
  |         ^
  |
  = note: `#[warn(unused_assignments)]` on by default
  = help: maybe it is overwritten before being read?

error[E0384]: cannot assign twice to immutable variable `s`
 --> immutable.rs:3:5
  |
2 |     let s = "cool";
  |         -
  |         |
  |         first assignment to `s`
  |         help: make this binding mutable: `mut s`
3 |     s = "safe";
  |     ^^^^^^^^^^ cannot assign twice to immutable variable

error: aborting due to previous error; 1 warning emitted

For more information about this error, try `rustc --explain E0384`.
```

There is a lot going on in this error message. Because the Rust team is aware that the learning curve is steep, they put an inordinate amount of time into making sure that the error messages are helpful and informative.[5]

The first error message is simply saying that there is not much point to the first assignment because you immediately overwrite the value before it is ever read. This is just an observation indicating a potential code smell.[6] You can suppress this warning if you do not want to see it, but it is nice that it points these issues out by default.

---

4 Type inference (*https://oreil.ly/4dkVx*) is a quality of a program that allows a compiler or runtime to deduce the type of a value without being told what it is.

5 This will quickly become something you learn to love about the Rust compiler and the community that values developer experience so much.

6 Kent Beck popularized the evocative phrase *code smell* (*https://oreil.ly/EXkXV*) to suggest that you can sense a problem in code before you know it is there because of hints you pick up on. When food goes bad, you often smell it before you realize it. Same with code.

The real issue is that Rust variables are immutable by default. Once you assign a value, you cannot change it. That seems an odd policy, but it forces you to be clear when you want a variable value to change and when you do not. There is a large class of bugs that involve the unintentional overwriting of variables. You may not notice that you have done so until a test fails or there is a runtime issue.

Obviously, we need mutable variables in Rust; you just have to tell the compiler that is what you want, as you can see in Example 10-3.

Example 10-3. Mutable Rust variables

```
fn main() {
  let mut s = "cool";
  s = "safe";

  println!("Rust is {}", s);
}
```

Now, by recompiling (and suppressing the unused assignment warning) we end up in a happier place:

```
brian@tweezer ~/g/w/s/ch10> rustc -A unused_assignments immutable.rs
brian@tweezer ~/g/w/s/ch10> ./immutable
Rust is safe
```

It may annoy you at first that you have to communicate this clearly, but the Rust compiler is just teaching you how to be an adult, where communication is critical to well-being and success.

Let's look at another example of something that may trip you up when you start doing Rust. In Example 10-4, we have another simple program. We assign a string literal to a variable s and then reassign it to a variable t before printing both out.

Example 10-4. Using Rust variables

```
fn main() {
  let s = "Hello, world.";
  let t = s;
  println!("s: {}", s);
  println!("t: {}", t);
}
```

This is a perfectly reasonable thing to do, and we see that the Rust compiler has no issues with it:

```
brian@tweezer ~/g/w/s/ch10> rustc memcheck.rs
brian@tweezer ~/g/w/s/ch10> ./memcheck
s: Hello, world.
t: Hello, world.
```

With one minor change, however, we can break this, as seen in Example 10-5.

Example 10-5. Rust memory checker violation

```
fn main() {
  let s = "Hello, world.".to_string();
  let t = s;
  println!("s: {}", s);
  println!("t: {}", t);
}
```

The problem is helpfully highlighted in the error message from the Rust compiler:

```
brian@tweezer ~/g/w/s/ch10> rustc memcheck.rs
error[E0382]: borrow of moved value: `s`
 --> memcheck.rs:4:23
  |
2 |     let s = "Hello, world.".to_string();
  |         - move occurs because `s` has type `std::string::String`, which
  |           does not implement the `Copy` trait
3 |     let t = s;
  |             - value moved here
4 |     println!("s: {}", s);
  |                       ^ value borrowed here after move

error: aborting due to previous error

For more information about this error, try `rustc --explain E0382`.
```

It may not seem like much, but by adding the to_string() method call, we have vio-
lated Rust's memory checker. This is because we have turned a string literal into a
heap-allocated string. The stack is where short-term variables associated with the current function are allocated so they can easily be cleaned up when they go out of lexical scope (i.e., at the end of the function). Heap-allocated memory is allocated until it
no longer needs to be. In C and C++, you must generally manage this process yourself as a programmer. In Java and JavaScript environments, the runtime garbage collector does this for you.

Rust manages the lack of a runtime garbage collector by enforcing ownership of values. At any given time, only one variable can own the memory associated with a
heap-allocated value. In Example 10-5, we first assign ownership of the string to variable s. When we assign s to t, ownership transfers. At this point, s does not point to
anything valid anymore, so our attempt to use s in the println! macro is caught as a
violation.

Literal values and other structures may implement the Copy trait mentioned in the
error message above. This is a behavior that allows the associated bits to be copied
from variable to variable without inducing an ownership transfer. Because the Rust

string structure does not implement this trait, the ownership checking applies. Other cases where ownership transfer happens include when variables are passed into and out of functions, in loops, and in other lexical structures such as conditional clauses.

The good news is that, by being more explicit about our intentions, we can get around this problem without introducing new risk. The specific risk we are attempting to avoid is use before initialization, use-after-free, and other bugs that are common in languages such as C and C++. We can use references rather than direct access, which allows us to "borrow" a value. We can also have mutable references, but only one at a time. These function a bit like reader/writer locks in languages such as Java.

Once we are better communicators about our intentions, the Rust compiler can assist us with our goals rather than fighting us all the time. The net effect is that Rust moves several runtime errors to compile-time errors, which is a much better place to handle them. This eliminates even more classes of bugs and allows us to produce much higher-quality software, including fast, highly concurrent types of code useful in system development.

The experience of using Rust is not just about being hassled by the compiler, though. There are plenty of language features, tools, and aspects of the community that make it a joy to use once you get past the learning curve. The combination of Rust's speed, safety, and its being built on LLVM make it a great language to pair with WebAssembly.

Rust and WebAssembly

If you followed the instructions for installing Rust in the Appendix, then you already have the basics for doing WebAssembly with Rust available to you. As I mentioned earlier, it was Rust's native support for WebAssembly that initially piqued my curiosity about Rust.

You will recall that in Figure 5-1, you saw that LLVM provided a three-stage architecture. As Rust is an LLVM-based language, to support WebAssembly, it basically just needed a new backend. That is not entirely true, but for now it is a suitable fiction.

You can see which backends are installed by issuing the following command:

```
brian@tweezer ~/g/w/img> rustup target list | grep installed
wasm32-unknown-unknown (installed)
x86_64-apple-darwin (installed)
```

Rust backends are labeled as triples, indicating the instruction set architecture (ISA), the vendor, and the operating system. I ran that command on an Intel Mac so you can see the corresponding default backend. But you can also notice that the WebAssembly backend is installed. As it produces code targeting the WebAssembly stack machine, we are not talking about x86_64, aarch64, arm7, or riscv64. Because this code is portable, it does not matter which machine you plan to run it on, which is why the triple is filled out with *unknown-unknown*.

If you look to Example 10-6, you will see the code to add two numbers together (i32s in Rust) and a `main()` method to test the behavior.

Example 10-6. Rust function to add two integers

```
pub extern "C" fn add(x: i32, y: i32) -> i32 {
  x + y
}

fn main() {
  println!("2 + 3: {}", add(2,3));
}
```

Using the default backend, you can view the result of building and running a native Rust version of this code:

```
brian@tweezer ~/g/w/s/ch10> rustc add.rs
brian@tweezer ~/g/w/s/ch10> ./add
2 + 3: 5
```

Compiling the same code into a WebAssembly module is as straightforward as selecting the WebAssembly backend and indicating that we want to generate a C dynamic library. You can either remove the main function or add the compiler directive to suppress dead code complaints as follows:

```
brian@tweezer ~/g/w/s/ch10> rustc -A dead_code --target wasm32-unknown-unknown ↵
    -O --crate-type=cdylib add.rs -o add.wasm
```

We can use the wasm3 runtime to execute our function on the command:

```
brian@tweezer ~/g/w/s/ch10> wasm3 --func add add.wasm 2 3
Error: [Fatal] repl_call: function lookup failed
Error: function lookup failed ('add')
```

Err…or not:

```
brian@tweezer-2 ~/g/w/s/ch10> ls -laF add*
-rwxr-xr-x  1 brian  staff   334920 May  4 11:54 add*
-rw-r--r--  1 brian  staff      111 May  4 12:07 add.rs
-rwxr-xr-x  1 brian  staff  1501227 May  4 12:16 add.wasm*
```

Wow, that's a pretty big file compared to the native one. This is again because of expectations the Rust compiler has about what is necessary to execute this code in a WebAssembly environment. The native version can rely on native dynamic libraries to provide the needed functionality. By this point in the book, you should remember how to investigate the contents of a Wasm module:

```
brian@tweezer ~/g/w/s/ch10> wasm-objdump -x add.wasm
add.wasm:       file format wasm 0x1

Section Details:

Table[1]:
 - table[0] type=funcref initial=1 max=1
Memory[1]:
 - memory[0] pages: initial=16
Global[3]:
 - global[0] i32 mutable=1 - init i32=1048576
 - global[1] i32 mutable=0 <__data_end> - init i32=1048576
 - global[2] i32 mutable=0 <__heap_base> - init i32=1048576
Export[3]:
 - memory[0] -> "memory"
 - global[1] -> "__data_end"
 - global[2] -> "__heap_base"
Custom:
 - name: ".debug_info"
Custom:
 - name: ".debug_pubtypes"
Custom:
 - name: ".debug_ranges"
Custom:
 - name: ".debug_aranges"
Custom:
 - name: ".debug_abbrev"
Custom:
 - name: ".debug_line"
Custom:
 - name: ".debug_str"
Custom:
 - name: ".debug_pubnames"
Custom:
 - name: "producers"
```

OK, so we have a bunch of debugging information and exported memory and what-
not, but there is no add function exported. There is a compiler directive we can add to
the method definition that should solve this export issue, as shown in Example 10-7.

Example 10-7. Rust function to add two integers exported properly

```
#[no_mangle]
pub extern "C" fn add(x: i32, y: i32) -> i32 {
  x + y
}
```

Now, rebuild and check the results. You should see the add method in the Export
section. And we can invoke it on the command line:

```
brian@tweezer ~/g/w/s/ch10> wasm3 --func add add.wasm 2 3
Result: 5
```

As you might have guessed, we can also invoke our behavior through our typical HTML/JavaScript combo with almost no effort, as we do in Example 10-8.

Example 10-8. Invoking Rust functions from HTML

```html
<!doctype html>
<html lang="en">
  <head>
    <meta charset="utf-8">
    <link rel="stylesheet" href="bootstrap.min.css">
    <title>Rust and WebAssembly</title>
    <script src="utils.js"></script>
  </head>
  <body>
    <div class="container">
      <h1>Rust and WebAssembly</h1>
      2 + 3 = <span id="sum"></span>.
    </div>
    <script>
      fetchAndInstantiate('add.wasm').then(function(instance) {
        var add = instance.exports.add(2,3);
        var sumEl = document.getElementById('sum');
        sumEl.innerText=add;
      });
    </script>
  </body>
</html>
```

In Figure 10-1, you can see the now familiar outcome of invoking a function from JavaScript in the browser. The difference, of course, is that it was originally written in Rust instead of the C and C++ we have been using.

Figure 10-1. Invoking Rust from HTML

If that was all we had to talk about with Rust and WebAssembly, that would not be all that exciting. Fortunately, thanks to wasm-bindgen, things quickly get much more interesting.

wasm-bindgen

In subsequent chapters, I will introduce you to several features that will be unlocked by proposals drafted post–Minimum Viable Product (MVP). These include the ability to reference more complex structures such as strings and lists, threading support, multivalue return types, and more. Until then, wasm-bindgen will be a big help in bridging JavaScript and Rust at a high level so that you can pass data across the chasm beyond just numbers. The tool is not intended to be solely for Rust, but so far that has been where most of the benefits have been seen.

If you have installed wasm-bindgen and wasm-pack as described in the Appendix, you should have everything you need for the remainder of the chapter. The latter is not a requirement but it makes things easier, so we are going to start by using its bundling capabilities.

The "Hello, World!" for wasm-bindgen is invoking the `alert()` JavaScript method from Rust without having to import a method directly in WebAssembly. As you will quickly see, the full range of browser functionality will be unlocked and usable from Rust. Even more amazingly, it will do so looking as if it were all written in Rust from that perspective. Additionally, you will be able to share Rust code with JavaScript and have it appear as JavaScript. I have worked with several interlanguage bridge technologies in my day, and this is one of the better ones I have seen.

The first step is to create a Rust library project using the cargo build tool. This will establish the scaffolding for the basic project:

```
brian@tweezer ~/src> cargo new --lib hello-wasm-bindgen
    Created library `hello-wasm-bindgen` package
```

You can override the default code in the *src/lib.rs* file to be what is shown in Example 10-9.

Example 10-9. Our library for use with wasm-bindgen

```
use wasm_bindgen::prelude::*;

#[wasm_bindgen]
extern {
  pub fn alert(s: &str);
}

#[wasm_bindgen]
pub fn say_hello(name: &str, whom: &str) {
  alert(&format!("Hello, {} from {}!", name, whom));
}
```

This is slightly trickier Rust than we have seen so far, but not too bad. The first line imports the contents of the wasm_bindgen::prelude module so that we can use it in our Rust code. This includes some of the binding code that will connect us to the JavaScript runtime environment.

The next line is a Rust attribute name, #[wasm_bindgen]. This indicates that we plan on invoking an external function named alert(). This is among the functionality we imported with the aforementioned use statement from the prelude. If you think that this method sounds familiar, you would be right! This is ultimately going to invoke the method of the same name that you have probably called from JavaScript many times. Notice the signature, though. This is not a JavaScript function. From our perspective, we are just calling a Rust function from our Rust code. The bridge provided by wasm-bindgen is so seamless that we do not even have to think about another language at this point.

This "Hello, World!" instance is going to go the other way as well. From JavaScript, we are going to call into Rust. The next #[wasm_bindgen] attribute is applied to a Rust function defined in our library that takes two string slices. We use the Rust format! macro, which is equivalent to string-formatting functions in other languages. We take a reference to the returned string and pass it to the alert() function identified previously. This attribute is going to generate an equivalent JavaScript function to call from that side of the world. From its perspective it will be calling JavaScript, not Rust! The same attribute is keeping us in sync in either direction, which is rather remarkable.

The next step is to use wasm-pack to generate our support code. In order to do that, we will need to update our *Cargo.toml* to indicate that we want to generate a C dynamic library style output, and for that we need wasm-bindgen as a dependency, as shown in Example 10-10.

Example 10-10. Cargo.toml file

```
[package]
name = "hello-wasm-bindgen"
version = "0.1.0"
edition = "2018"

[lib]
crate-type = ["cdylib"]

[dependencies]
wasm-bindgen = "0.2.73"
```

Now we can use wasm-bindgen to generate a JavaScript module that wraps our Rust code. I have eliminated some warnings about missing attributes and *README* files as well as some cute little emojis that do not translate well:

```
brian@tweezer ~/s/hello-wasm-bindgen> wasm-pack build --target web
[INFO]:  Checking for the Wasm target...
[INFO]:  Compiling to Wasm...
   Compiling hello-wasm-bindgen v0.1.0 (/Users/brian/src/hello-wasm-bindgen)
    Finished release [optimized] target(s) in 0.26s
[INFO]: Optimizing wasm binaries with `wasm-opt`...
[INFO]:   Done in 0.73s
[INFO]:   Your wasm pkg is ready to publish at
[INFO]:   /Users/brian/src/hello-wasm-bindgen/pkg.
brian@tweezer ~/s/hello-wasm-bindgen> ls -laF pkg
total 72
drwxr-xr-x  8 brian  staff    256 May 10 17:20 ./
drwxr-xr-x  9 brian  staff    288 May 10 17:20 ../
-rw-r--r--  1 brian  staff      1 May 10 17:20 .gitignore
-rw-r--r--  1 brian  staff    861 May 10 17:20 hello_wasm_bindgen.d.ts
-rw-r--r--  1 brian  staff   4026 May 10 17:20 hello_wasm_bindgen.js
-rw-r--r--  1 brian  staff  15786 May 10 17:20 hello_wasm_bindgen_bg.wasm
-rw-r--r--  1 brian  staff    291 May 10 17:20 hello_wasm_bindgen_bg.wasm.d.ts
-rw-r--r--  1 brian  staff    266 May 10 17:20 package.json
```

We have used the `--target web` flag to indicate we would like our package to be loadable in a browser. Other options including using Webpack to bundle everything up or targeting Node.js or Deno, as we will see shortly. In the *pkg* directory, you will see the generated JavaScript, our Wasm module, and a *package.json* file. There are also TypeScript Declaration files for our code as well. If you use `wasm-objdump` and check out the `Export` section of our module, you will see the following:

```
Export[4]:
 - memory[0] -> "memory"
 - func[19] <say_hello> -> "say_hello"
 - func[34] <__wbindgen_malloc> -> "__wbindgen_malloc"
 - func[38] <__wbindgen_realloc> -> "__wbindgen_realloc"
```

This includes a `Memory` instance, our exported method, and some memory allocation functions.

The final step is to invoke the ES6 module from HTML and JavaScript, as seen in Example 10-11.

Example 10-11. Calling Rust from JavaScript

```
<!DOCTYPE html>
<html>
  <head>
    <meta charset="utf-8">
    <title>hello-wasm-bindgen Example</title>
  </head>
  <body>
    <script type="module">
      import init, {say_hello} from "./pkg/hello_wasm_bindgen.js";
      init()
```

```
        .then(() => {
          say_hello("Rust", "JavaScript");
        });
    </script>
  </body>
</html>
```

If you serve up the HTML file over HTTP as we have done previously, you should see the result shown in Figure 10-2. This is JavaScript calling into Rust through an exported function generated by wasm-bindgen, which in turn calls back into JavaScript through a generated Rust wrapper around JavaScript functionality in the browser also generated by wasm-bindgen.

Figure 10-2. Calling JavaScript from Rust from JavaScript

Despite the banality of the outcome, this is an incredibly satisfying result, as the bridge generated between these two languages looks natural from either side. It is so much easier just thinking about string slices in Rust rather than writing bytes into a memory instance, as we had to do previously.

OK, now that we have the basics down, let's try something more interesting. One of the features I really love about Rust is its pattern-matching support. Other languages do this as well, but I really like how Rust does it. Check out Example 10-12. The first thing you will see is a #[wasm_bindgen] attribute on a block of code indicating we would like to invoke a method called log() from JavaScript. Notice the second inner attribute with a js_namespace of console. This shows how we can directly invoke console.log() from Rust thanks to wasm-bindgen.

Example 10-12. Rust pattern matching in action

```
use wasm_bindgen::prelude::*;

#[wasm_bindgen]
extern "C" {
  #[wasm_bindgen(js_namespace = console)]
  fn log(s: &str);
```

```
}

#[wasm_bindgen]
pub fn describe_location( lat : f32, lon : f32 ) {
  let i_lat = lat as i32;
  let i_lon = lon as i32;

  use std::cmp::Ordering::*;

  let relative_position = match(i_lat.cmp(&38), i_lon.cmp(&-121)) {
    (Equal, Equal) => "very close!",
    (Equal, Greater) => "east of me",
    (Equal, Less) => "west of me",
    (Less, Equal) => "south of me",
    (Less, Greater) => "southeast of me",
    (Less, Less) => "southwest of me",
    (Greater, Equal) => "north of me",
    (Greater, Greater) => "northeast of me",
    (Greater, Less) => "northwest of me"
  };

  log(&format!("You are {}!", relative_position));
}
```

After the log() method is made available to us in Rust, we define a function called describe_location() that takes two f32s, which we will compare to my rough location at home. To simplify the comparison and not leak too many details about where I am, I only compare the integer portions of my current location (38N, –121W). To accommodate, I cast the incoming floats as integers and then import the functionality that allows me to compare integers. The truncated i_lat value is compared to my latitude and the i_lon value is compared to my longitude. The results are placed into a Rust tuple, which is like a Python tuple, a lightweight way to put one or more values into a single structure.

The values in the tuple are then matched against the various possibilities when another location is compared to mine. If the cmp() returns two Equal values, then the location is near me. If the latitudes are Equal but the longitudes are not, then the other position is either to the east or west of me. What we have here is an incredibly compact but readable way of handling nine separate cases. If this had been expressed as a bunch of nested if-then clauses, it would have been much more difficult to read.

Once we have generated the description of the relative position, we call the log function to print out the results. As this is ultimately the console.log() function, the result will print out in the developer console of your browser.

The next step is to build our package to import in HTML and JavaScript:

```
brian@tweezer ~/s/geo-example> wasm-pack build --target web
[INFO]: Checking for the Wasm target...
```

```
[INFO]:  Compiling to Wasm...
    Compiling geo-example v0.1.0 (/Users/brian/src/geo-example)
    Finished release [optimized] target(s) in 0.51s
[INFO]: Optimizing wasm binaries with `wasm-opt`...
[INFO]:  Done in 1.01s
[INFO]:  Your wasm pkg is ready to publish at /Users/brian/src/geo-example/pkg.
```

In Example 10-13, we see the HTML and JavaScript to invoke our behavior. We import the functions and then call a JavaScript function that tests for the availability of the `geolocation` object on the browser. If it is there, we request the current location, which triggers a pop-up for the user to approve. If given the location, the results are shown as the `innerText` of the placeholder paragraph element and we invoke our `describe_location()` method in Rust to do the pattern matching.

Example 10-13. Calling the Rust pattern matching from HTML

```html
<!DOCTYPE html>
<html>
  <head>
    <meta charset="utf-8">
    <title>parsing-example</title>
  </head>
  <body>
    <script type="module">
      import init, {describe_location} from "./pkg/parsing_example.js";
      init()
        .then(() => {
        getLocation();
        });

    var output = document.getElementById("output");

    function getLocation() {
      if (navigator.geolocation) {
        navigator.geolocation.getCurrentPosition(showPosition);
      } else {
        output.innerHTML = "This browser doesn't support Geolocation.";
      }
    }

    function showPosition(position) {
      output.innerHTML = "Your position:" +
        "<br>Latitude: " + position.coords.latitude +
        "<br>Longitude: " + position.coords.longitude;

      describe_location(position.coords.latitude, position.coords.longitude);
    }
    </script>

    <p>Open up your JavaScript console and allow the browser to see your location</p>
```

```
    <p id="output"></p>
  </body>
</html>
```

The results of executing this code are shown in Figure 10-3.

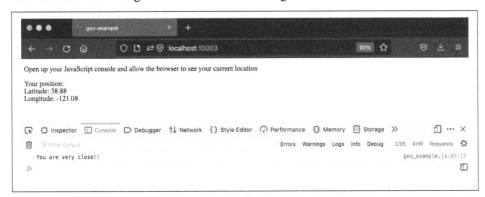

Figure 10-3. Pattern-matching geolocations from JavaScript in Rust

Designing Code for In and Out of the Browser

The final section I want to cover is another WebAssembly use case that I think is going to be increasingly popular. We have looked at using languages other than Java-Script to target the browser. We have also discussed the scenario of reusing existing code in a browser-based runtime. But what about code that is designed to run both inside and outside of the browser as a matter of course? I think once more people are comfortable with what WebAssembly provides, this is going to be an increasingly common scenario.

I had been expecting this kind of activity for as long as I have followed WebAssembly, but I was surprised at how far along Emil Ernerfeldt had gotten with his egui library (*https://oreil.ly/mbDo3*). He describes the project as "an easy-to-use immediate mode GUI in pure Rust."[7] Basically, it is a sophisticated user interface library that works both inside the browser and out.

We have mentioned several times in this chapter that Rust benefits from its LLVM heritage by allowing us to emit various backend targets. This is also what Emil is taking advantage of to make this work. But he has done so elegantly, and I think there is a lot that can be learned from where he has gone. The full details of how he makes it work are outside the scope of this chapter, but I want to draw attention to the project in case you are interested in doing something similar.

---

7 The GitHub repo explains why he is interested in an immediate mode approach.

First, let's see his app in action as a native application. If you are on Linux, you have to install a few more packages listed on the GitHub site, but after that, you simply have to run:

```
brian@tweezer ~/g/egui> cargo run --release -p egui_demo_app
```

The results should look something like what you see in Figure 10-4, depending on which options you click on. If you play around with the demo, you will see that it is an attractive, featureful user interface library. The Rust community is very much looking forward to more toolkits like this for building applications and games.

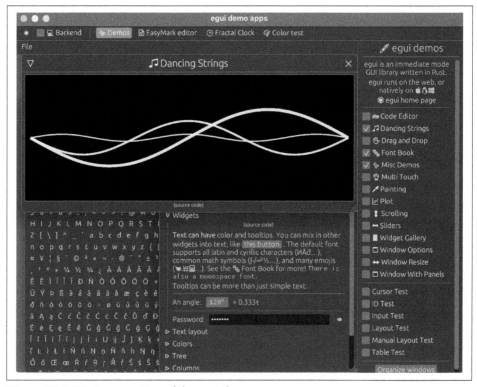

Figure 10-4. Native execution of the egui demo app

The code (*src/main.rs*) that executes when you run Emil's demo is shown in Example 10-14 (I have removed some configuration code to suppress warnings). Notice the main() method is only used when compiling natively.

Example 10-14. Main program for the egui demo app

```
// When compiling natively:
fn main() {
  let app = egui_demo_lib::WrapApp::default();
```

```
let options = eframe::NativeOptions {
    // Let's show off that we support transparent windows
    transparent: true,
      ..Default::default()
  };
  eframe::run_native(Box::new(app), options);
}
```

For native execution, the egui library has a pluggable backend that renders the components using the *egui_glium* library. This in turn presently uses a Rust wrapper around OpenGL called Glium.[8] The *egui_glium* library is part of the egui GitHub repo.

The file *src/lib.rs* shows another part of the story in Example 10-15 (I have removed some configuration code to suppress warnings here, too).

Example 10-15. The WebAssembly entry point for the egui demo app

```
#[cfg(target_arch = "wasm32")]
use eframe::wasm_bindgen::{self, prelude::*};

/// This is the entry-point for all the web-assembly.
/// This is called once from the HTML.
/// It loads the app, installs some callbacks, then returns.
/// You can add more callbacks like this if you want to call in to your code.
#[cfg(target_arch = "wasm32")]
#[wasm_bindgen]
pub fn start(canvas_id: &str) -> Result<(), wasm_bindgen::JsValue> {
  let app = egui_demo_lib::WrapApp::default();
  eframe::start_web(canvas_id, Box::new(app))
}
```

Notice the use of the `wasm_bindgen` annotation. The eframe library is also used as an abstraction to hide the details of running natively or in the browser. Compare the function used in Example 10-14 and the one used in Example 10-15.

For running the demo app in the web context, egui uses a library called *egui_web*. This relies on WebGL for rendering the components in an HTML 5 canvas via WebAssembly.

If you look in the *target/release* directory, you will see that the application is approximately 5.6 megabytes:

```
brian@tweezer ~/g/egui> ls -lah target/release
total 11736
drwxr-xr-x   13 brian  staff   416B Sep 29 15:56 .
```

---

8 The Glium library is not currently being maintained, so Emil is planning to replace it at some point.

```
drwxr-xr-x@    5 brian  staff   160B Aug 16 11:54 ..
drwxr-xr-x    57 brian  staff   1.8K Sep 29 15:55 build
drwxr-xr-x   394 brian  staff    12K Sep 29 15:56 deps
-rwxr-xr-x     2 brian  staff   5.6M Sep 29 15:56 egui_demo_app
-rw-r--r--     1 brian  staff   8.5K Sep 29 15:56 egui_demo_app.d
drwxr-xr-x     2 brian  staff    64B Aug 16 11:53 examples
drwxr-xr-x     2 brian  staff    64B Aug 16 11:53 incremental
-rw-r--r--     1 brian  staff   8.5K Sep 29 15:56 libegui_demo_app.d
-rwxr-xr-x     2 brian  staff    49K Sep 29 15:56 libegui_demo_app.dylib
-rw-r--r--     2 brian  staff   2.0K Sep 29 15:56 libegui_demo_app.rlib
```

If you look in the *docs* directory, you will see that a WebAssembly version of the application has also been built and is only 3.5 megabytes:

```
brian@tweezer ~/g/egui> ls -lah docs
total 7288
drwxr-xr-x    6 brian  staff   192B Sep 29 15:51 .
drwxr-xr-x   28 brian  staff   896B Sep 29 15:51 ..
-rw-r--r--    1 brian  staff    60K Sep 29 15:51 egui_demo_app.js
-rw-r--r--    1 brian  staff   3.5M Sep 29 15:51 egui_demo_app_bg.wasm
-rw-r--r--    1 brian  staff   222B Aug 16 11:51 example.html
-rw-r--r--    1 brian  staff   2.9K Aug 16 11:51 index.html
```

There is also an *index.html* file and some JavaScript to bootstrap the whole process. I have left most of the HTML out, but Example 10-16 highlights the important parts. The demo app is given the ID of the <canvas> element to render itself into.

Example 10-16. The HTML scaffolding for the egui demo app

```
<!-- this is the JS generated by the `wasm-bindgen` CLI tool -->
<script src="egui_demo_app.js"></script>

<script>
  // We'll defer our execution until the wasm is ready to go.
  // Here we tell bindgen the path to the wasm file so it can start
  // initialization and return to us a promise when it's done.
  wasm_bindgen("./egui_demo_app_bg.wasm")
    .then(on_wasm_loaded)
    .catch(console.error);

  function on_wasm_loaded() {
    // This call installs a bunch of callbacks and then returns.
    console.log("loaded wasm, starting egui app");
    wasm_bindgen.start("the_canvas_id");
  }
</script>
```

If you start up an HTTP server in the *docs* directory and point your browser to the port you choose, you can see the result in Figure 10-5.

```
brian@tweezer ~/g/e/docs> python -m http.server 10003
Serving HTTP on :: port 10003 (http://[::]:10003/) ...
```

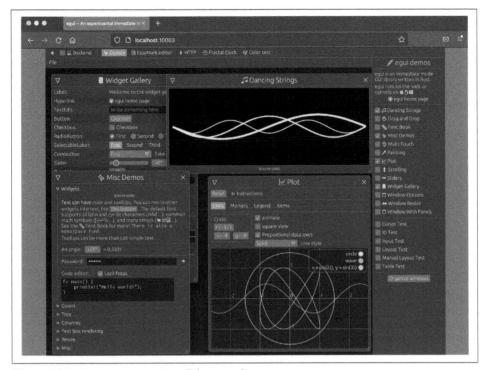

Figure 10-5. Browser execution of the egui demo app

If you are interested in how this all works, I encourage you to dig into the various libraries I have mentioned. There are helpful pointers and documents all over the place, including tips on creating your own custom widgets.

The demo app is quite sophisticated and overwhelming as a means of getting started, but to show you a bit about what the code looks like, please see Example 10-17, which is taken from the GitHub documentation.

Example 10-17. Code snippet for building a simple application

```
ui.heading("My egui Application");
ui.horizontal(|ui| {
  ui.label("Your name: ");
  ui.text_edit_singleline(&mut name);
});
ui.add(egui::Slider::new(&mut age, 0..=120).text("age"));
if ui.button("Click each year").clicked() {
  age += 1;
}
ui.label(format!("Hello '{}', age {}", name, age));
```

The results of this code sample are shown in Figure 10-6.

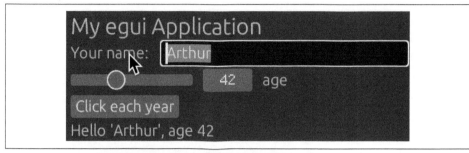

Figure 10-6. Rendered form of the sample code

If you are interested in building your own application using egui that will work either natively or in the browser, Emil has provided a working project template (*https://oreil.ly/UcboK*). Just fork the repo (or use the GitHub template to create your own repo) and follow the instructions to get up and running.

I hope you have fun playing around with this cool library and its related infrastructure. My larger point is that it represents the intentional design of software to target both native and browser-based application delivery. I expect to see much more of this approach before long.

The wasm-bindgen guidebook (*https://oreil.ly/I3j7b*) has many more exciting examples of things you can do to directly interact with browser functionality from Rust, including rendering to a <canvas> element, doing WebGL, and manipulating the DOM directly. There are also examples for calling JavaScript code from Rust from TypeScript in Deno (*https://oreil.ly/oJEZe*). We are going to look at how wasm-bindgen can be used to support threads in Rust in Chapter 12.

As you can see, Rust is a modern and exciting programming language in its own right. The fact that it can natively generate WebAssembly code is pretty cool too, but without the support of wasm-bindgen, it remains fairly tricky to build up anything significant. With this somewhat magical tool, however, Rust can drive the behavior of a browser in surprising and unexpected ways.

But now we must take a huge leap forward into a more general strategy of making WebAssembly applications more portable.

CHAPTER 11
WebAssembly System Interface (WASI)

I'm not in this world to live up to your expectations, and you're not in this world to live up to mine.

—Bruce Lee

There are some things that are unnecessarily difficult in WebAssembly as a consequence of the security and safety goals that are easier on other platforms. Reading from the filesystem, writing to the console, and manipulating strings in memory are all simple activities in a language like C, C++, or Rust. It is expected that an operating system will allow a user with sufficient privileges to do these things. There are not explicit, contextual boundaries.

Unfortunately, that is also the problem behind most modern cyber threats such as phishing attacks, privilege escalation, supply chain attacks, and more. If an attacker is able to convince a privileged user to run untrustworthy code, they can often steal access to other resources not otherwise due them. Sandboxed environments exist to prevent this, but they are often slow, cumbersome, and burdensome to developers. WebAssembly wants to solve this problem, and it does in many ways. Fundamentally, however, WebAssembly modules do not have access to anything that is not provided by their hosting environments.

The MVP and the tools that we have seen so far have largely been about making code portable. We are now going to learn how to make applications portable. The solution, as it turns out, is fundamentally about whether expectations can be met or not. This is not just a question of languages, but also of API availability, runtime environment configurations, security restrictions, and more. As a consequence, just like Bruce Lee's quotation, our host environments are not always here to meet the expectations of the code we are running. We can still be in control.

WebAssembly System Interface (WASI)

The cool demos and code samples you have seen so far, particularly the ones involving graphics, sound, video, and the like, are largely possible because they run in the browser. The browser is a piece of software designed to be a universal client, a host to other code. It is possible to extend the web by sending arbitrary programs down to the client for execution. It has built-in security restrictions, but it is actually quite a featureful programming environment these days, filled with APIs such as WebGL for 3D graphics, accelerated video, WebRTC for collaboration, and more. Emscripten provides implementations of standard APIs such as POSIX and OpenGL via what is available to the browser runtime environment so that standard C/C++ applications can simply compile and still work.

We have seen a mechanism for providing functions to module instances to invoke via objects they import. Remember, for example, passing in a JavaScript function that prints to the console rather than relying on the C standard library to provide access to `printf()`. This is a fundamentally unsatisfactory approach, though. Every WebAssembly module that needs to print to the console should just have a function to call, preferably the one it was already written against, whenever it needs it. This is about meeting expectations safely and performantly.

Because of security concerns, however, the other part of the Bruce Lee quotation is relevant. Just because a program wants to read or write to the filesystem does not mean it gets to. Our business-critical desktop computers are not in this world to meet the expectations of malicious software. We want to control the context in which applications get access to resources, if at all.

Another issue with respect to expectations is that runtime environments outside of the browser are a significant part of WebAssembly's potential execution surface. Many of these APIs are not available in the same way in environments like Node.js or Deno. There are not compatible Web IDL–defined interfaces exposing access to audio and video playback, 3D graphics, and the rest.[1] There are certainly other similar APIs available, but they are not directly compatible with what is inside of browsers, and applications would have to be rewritten to use them.

Normally, POSIX functions will be consistently defined across different operating systems and will map to lower-level kernel functions or platform-specific APIs such as Win32.[2] These are such crucial bits of reusable functionality that we want them to be fast and stable implementations. Arbitrary JavaScript wrapper functions provided

---

1 Web IDL (*https://oreil.ly/Lv1PY*) is the interface definition language (IDL) used to express the behavior provided by browsers as part of the standards process.

2 Known more generally as WinAPI (*https://oreil.ly/E2gDB*) these days, this was one of Microsoft's greatest strengths during the heyday of its operating system dominance.

---

by application developers are not likely to be fast or stable enough. Many of these extra-browser APIs do not have the same security guarantees of sandboxed-browser environments, so they are not directly available there either.

These are among the myriad of problems WebAssembly System Interface (WASI) is attempting to solve. It is a tall order and the effort is expanding and getting rather complicated at this point in time, but the fundamentals are fairly straightforward, so we will start there.

Ultimately, we want an ecosystem of functionality that programs permitted to access it can expect to be available. We want the functionality to work across language boundaries, which means we need ways to refer to high-level structures such as strings, lists, and arrays. We want protected but fast implementations. We want some manner of type safety and to not have to rely on too much feature testing in the code we write. We also want language features such as garbage collection and exception handling to be available from languages that support them without putting burdens on languages that do not. In order to meet these requirements, the WebAssembly platform needed to be extended. In Chapter 12 I will introduce some of these major extensions, but for now I want to stay above that discussion.

Let's revisit the Rust version of our famous example from Chapter 10 (shown in Example 11-1) one more time. We have established that the issue is that the println! macro is not available in a browser. Nor is the printf() function in the C version. We have seen various ways of getting around this, but these solutions have remained vexing.

Example 11-1. Rust "Hello, World!"

```
fn main() {
    println!("Hello, World!");
}
```

For reasons that will become clear momentarily, I am going to re-create the sample scaffolding of this basic Rust program and run it. The cargo new command will establish the directory structure of a project and fill in a simple application that is effectively the previous example:

```
brian@tweezer ~/g/w/s/ch11> cargo new --bin hello-world
    Created binary (application) `hello-world` package
brian@tweezer ~/g/w/s/ch11> cd hello-world/
brian@tweezer ~/g/w/s/c/hello-world> cargo build --release
    Finished release [optimized] target(s) in 0.03s
brian@tweezer ~/g/w/s/c/hello-world> cargo run --release
    Finished release [optimized] target(s) in 0.01s
     Running `target/release/hello-world`
Hello, world!
```

The cargo build tool created project scaffolding for us by placing a friendly program in *src/main.rs*. We built an optimized release version of this application and then ran the associated native executable. Remember, Rust is LLVM-based, so the default backend will be for whatever operating system you have installed the toolchain on.

We saw in Chapter 10 that we can use the WebAssembly backend to generate modules from Rust, but with all of the limitations involving strings, memory management, interacting with the operating system, etc., it does not work:

```
brian@tweezer ~/g/w/s/c/hello-world> cargo build ↵
  --target wasm32-unknown-unknown --release
   Compiling hello-world v0.1.0
       (/Users/brian/git-personal/wasm_tdg/src/ch11/hello-world)
    Finished release [optimized] target(s) in 0.89s
brian@tweezer ~/g/w/s/c/hello-world> ls -laF ↵
   target/wasm32-unknown-unknown/release/
total 3008
drwxr-xr-x  10 brian  staff      320 Jun 27 16:02 ./
drwxr-xr-x@  5 brian  staff      160 Jun 27 16:02 ../
drwxr-xr-x   2 brian  staff       64 Jun 27 16:02 build/
drwxr-xr-x   4 brian  staff      128 Jun 27 16:02 deps/
drwxr-xr-x   2 brian  staff       64 Jun 27 16:02 examples/
-rw-r--r--   1 brian  staff      228 Jun 27 16:02 hello-world.d
-rwxr-xr-x   2 brian  staff  1534049 Jun 27 16:02 hello-world.wasm*
drwxr-xr-x   2 brian  staff       64 Jun 27 16:02 incremental/
brian@tweezer ~/g/w/s/c/hello-world > wasm3 ↵
   target/wasm32-unknown-unknown/release/hello-world.wasm
Error: [Fatal] repl_call: function lookup failed
Error: function lookup failed ('_start')
```

A fundamental problem is that the basic module structure does not define the same type of application binary interface (ABI) that an executable program does.[3] It does not have the expected intialization function name. Developers think that main() is the starting point, but that is generally what is called by the very minimal C runtime environment from a method called start.

Another issue is that there is no direct way to write to the console or read and write files from a WebAssembly module. This would seem to be a pretty big obstacle for WebAssembly, but I encourage you not to give up hope just yet! What happens if we use a different backend? Rather than wasm32-unknown-unknown, we will use wasm32-wasi:

```
brian@tweezer ~/g/w/s/c/hello-world> cargo build --target wasm32-wasi --release
   Compiling hello-world v0.1.0
       (/Users/brian/git-personal/wasm_tdg/src/ch11/hello-world)
```

---

3 The application binary interface (*https://oreil.ly/DFwXK*) of an operating system defines how programs are linked and executed.

```
      Finished release [optimized] target(s) in 0.74s
brian@tweezer ~/g/w/s/c/hello-world> wasm3 ↵
    target/wasm32-wasi/release/hello-world.wasm
Hello, world!
```

Huh. Will you look at that?

Let's investigate the module:

```
brian@tweezer ~/g/w/s/c/hello-world > wasm-objdump ↵
    -x target/wasm32-wasi/release/hello-world.wasm
hello-world.wasm:       file format wasm 0x1

Section Details:

Type[18]:
 - type[0] () -> nil
 - type[1] (i32) -> nil
 - type[2] (i32) -> i64
 - type[3] (i32, i32) -> nil
 - type[4] (i32, i32) -> i32
 - type[5] (i32, i32) -> i64
 - type[6] (i32) -> i32
 - type[7] (i32, i32, i32) -> i32
 - type[8] (i32, i32, i32, i32) -> i32
 - type[9] () -> i32


...
Import[4]:
 - func[0] sig=8 <_ZN4wasi13lib_generated22wasi_snapshot_preview18fd_write>
     <- wasi_snapshot_preview1.fd_write
 - func[1] sig=1 <__wasi_proc_exit> <- wasi_snapshot_preview1.proc_exit
 - func[2] sig=4 <__wasi_environ_sizes_get>
     <- wasi_snapshot_preview1.environ_sizes_get
 - func[3] sig=4 <__wasi_environ_get> <- wasi_snapshot_preview1.environ_get
...

Export[5]:
 - memory[0] -> "memory"
 - global[1] -> "__heap_base"
 - global[2] -> "__data_end"
 - func[247] <_start.command_export> -> "_start"
 - func[248] <main.command_export> -> "main"


...
```

It is a WebAssembly module, but it also exports a known starting point so a WASI-aware environment such as *wasm3* knows how to initialize it and begin execution. There is much more to WASI than this bootstrap process, though. It also provides a convenient way for a module to import functionality that it needs to execute. This is essentially what the Rust *wasm32-wasi* backend is doing for us. It is emitting calls to a standard library implementation that will be provided by the host environment that our code will run in. Again, *wasm3* is at least a rudimentary WASI environment, so it provides those capabilities. It preceded WASI as an outside-the-browser WebAssembly engine, but it is actively supporting the evolving standards and newer proposals, which we will discuss in the next chapter.

If you follow the installation steps from the Appendix, you can install two more WASI environments, Wasmtime[4] and Wasmer.[5] Both are open source and independent initiatives:

```
brian@tweezer ~/g/w/s/c/hello-world> wasmtime ↵
    target/wasm32-wasi/release/hello-world.wasm
Hello, world!
brian@tweezer ~/g/w/s/c/hello-world> wasmer ↵
    target/wasm32-wasi/release/hello-world.wasm
Hello, world!
```

Finally, there is an extension to cargo itself that uses Wasmtime but helps make building, running, and testing Rust-based WASI applications even easier:

```
brian@tweezer ~/g/w/s/ch11 > cargo install cargo-wasi
    Updating crates.io index
    ...
brian@tweezer ~/g/w/s/c/hello-world> cargo wasi run
    Finished dev [unoptimized + debuginfo] target(s) in 0.03s
     Running `target/wasm32-wasi/debug/hello-world.wasm`
Hello, world!
```

The actual details of how this all works are more complicated than I want to get into at the moment, but to give you a bit of a peek behind the curtain, Example 11-2 is an example from the Wasmtime WASI tutorial (*https://oreil.ly/7CF3k*). It is working at a lower level than perhaps you have done before, but it is fairly typical systems programming.

Example 11-2. Invoking standard library behavior from Wat

```
;; Taken from the Wasmtime WASI Tutorial
(module
  ;; Import the required fd_write WASI function which will write the given io
  ;; vectors to stdout. The function signature for fd_write is:
  ;; (File Descriptor, *iovs, iovs_len, nwritten) -&gt; Returns # of bytes written
  (import "wasi_unstable" "fd_write"
    (func $fd_write (param i32 i32 i32 i32) (result i32)))

  (memory 1)
  (export "memory" (memory 0))
```

---

4 Wastime (*https://wasmtime.dev*) began as a Mozilla project but is now part of the Bytecode Alliance, which we will discuss soon.

5 Wasmer (*https://wasmer.io*) is the name of the company and the WebAssembly hosting environment.

```
;; Write 'hello world\n' to memory at an offset of 8 bytes
;; Note the trailing newline which is required for the text to appear
(data (i32.const 8) "hello world\n")

(func $main (export "_start")
  ;; Creating a new io vector within linear memory
  ;; iov.iov_base - This is a pointer to the start of the
  ;; 'hello world\n' string
  (i32.store (i32.const 0) (i32.const 8))
  ;; iov.iov_len - The length of the 'hello world\n' string
  (i32.store (i32.const 4) (i32.const 12))

  (call $fd_write
    (i32.const 1) ;; file_descriptor - 1 for stdout
    (i32.const 0) ;; *iovs - The pointer to the iov array at memory loc 0
    (i32.const 1) ;; iovs_len - We're printing 1 string
    (i32.const 20) ;; nwritten - Mem loc to store the # of bytes written
  )
  drop ;; Discard the number of bytes written from the top of the stack
  )
)
```

The Unix pipes-and-filters approach to tool composition allows you to redirect the output of one program to the input of another one.[6] Examples include using the less command to pause scrolling terminal messages or the grep command to find elements in the process table that match a certain pattern.

Files are the common abstraction in Unix for real files on disk as well as virtual files such as the input or output to a program. The ability to print to the console is managed by writing to a particular file descriptor. In this environment, file descriptor 0 in a program represents the standard input, or what was passed into the program. File descriptor 1 represents the standard output, or what the program logs out under normal circumstances. File descriptor 2 is the standard error, which is usually used for error messages.

It has been a few chapters since we messed around with Wat, and this is slightly more complicated than what we have seen so far, but I think you should be able to sort through it with some guidance.

The first thing we do is import a function called fd_write from the wasi_unstable namespace. This is where a WASI environment will meet our expectations if it wants to. If we are not provided with this behavior, we will not be able to execute.

---

6 This architectural style is one of the aspects of Unix (*https://oreil.ly/4LPOx*) that made it so powerful for publishers and productive for developers.

The fd_write function takes four parameters that indicate which file descriptor to use, where we have stored a string to write in memory, how long it is, and where to write the number of bytes written. As specified, this will be after our strings in memory.

We next define our module's Memory instance and export it. The function we just imported is going to want to interrogate this based on the parameters we send it. We use a data element to write the string "hello world" into our memory at byte 8. Finally, we export a method that ultimately calls all of this.

We write the numeric location of the base pointer to the string into the first four bytes and its length into the subsequent four bytes. The string itself will exist after these numbers. Finally, we call our imported fd_write function.

You will notice we do not even need to compile our Wat file back into a binary module. Our friendly little WASI environments can do that for us:

```
brian@tweezer ~/g/w/s/ch11> wasmtime hello.wat
hello world
brian@tweezer ~/g/w/s/ch11> wasmer hello.wat
hello world
```

Quite obviously, you are not going to want to write programs in Wat like this. I included this just to give you a sense of what is happening behind the scenes. You will write your programs in languages such as Rust or C and compile them with a WASI-aware toolchain. Speaking of C, we will now revisit our trusty "Hello, World!" program one final time in Example 11-3.

Example 11-3. C "Hello, World!" hopefully for the final time!

```
#include <stdio.h>

int main() {
  printf("Hello, World!\n");
  return 0;
}
```

We need to compile this to a WASI-friendly form. There are several ways to do that, but one of the easiest is to use the wasienv toolchain (*https://oreil.ly/Wg7wg*) from our friends at Wasmer. C compilation requires headers and libraries, but in this case, we also need a version of the standard library functionality that is WASI-aware.[7] Just as Emscripten has replacements for cc, c++, make, and configure, wasienv does too. I

---

7 I am presently trying to shield you from some of this complexity, but if you insist on knowing more, you can check out GitHub (*https://oreil.ly/SVB9f*).

have removed some compile warnings of no consequence, but otherwise you should start to get the picture of how powerful this all is:

```
brian@tweezer ~/g/w/s/ch11> wasicc -o hello hello.c
brian@tweezer ~/g/w/s/ch11> wasm3 hello.wasm
Hello, World!
brian@tweezer ~/g/w/s/ch11> wasmer hello.wasm
Hello, World!
brian@tweezer ~/g/w/s/ch11> wasmtime hello.wasm
Hello, World!
brian@tweezer ~/g/w/s/ch11> ./hello
Hello, World!
```

We have now used the same runtimes to run code compiled unmodified in both Rust and C. The same WASI form of the WebAssembly module will run on Linux or Windows too. As long as our expectations are being met by our WASI-enabled host, it should run anywhere WebAssembly does. Note that wasienv even went so far as to generate a standalone native application for us! You will learn more about what that entails in the next chapter.

As it turns out, Node.js and Deno both support WASI as well. There is even a JavaScript polyfill that will allow your WASI-enabled application to run in the browser! See Figure 11-1 for an example of the WASI polyfill (*https://wasi.dev/polyfill*) in action.

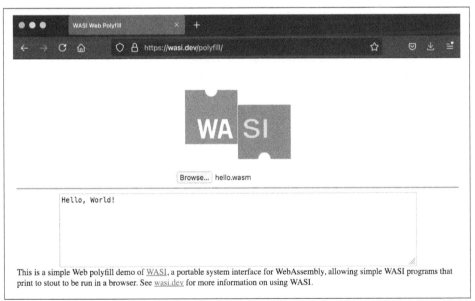

Figure 11-1. Running a WASI application in a polyfill in a browser

WebAssembly makes your code portable. WASI endeavors to make your application portable by satisfying its expectations when you want it to.

Capabilities-Based Security

There is another aspect to WASI that is crucial to the future of WebAssembly in this ubiquitous computational landscape. We want to be able to provide functionality to the applications we want to provide them to, but not to malicious software. As we often cannot tell which is which, we will probably have limited sandbox environments as the default.

From its inception, WASI has been envisioned as a means of enforcing capabilities-based security restrictions on the behavior it affords to hosted modules.[8]

The short version of what this means is that, just as WebAssembly does not give arbitrary code direct access to memory, WASI does not give it direct access to sensitive resources such as file handles, network sockets, or subprocess details. Instead, the resources will be exposed through unforgeable, opaque handles that provide the capability to the code. As this will require passing language-specific or perhaps OS-level structures to and from WebAssembly modules, we will need a way to make external references.

How and why this works is a complex moving target at the time this book is being written. I have struggled with how many of the details to focus on and have settled on the position that much of it will be a distraction at the moment. In part, this is because the proposals are being worked on. It is also because it is super complicated in some ways even as it bubbles up as an increasingly elegant design. I will expose you to more of the details in Chapter 12, but for now, let's focus on seeing the results.

In Example 11-4, we have a simple program written in Rust that writes a string out to a file and then reads it back in. From a programming perspective, it is quite simple. The big deal, of course, is access to the filesystem. If you are not yet a Rust guru, do not sweat the details; the flow of the program should still hopefully make sense.

Example 11-4. Rust program that uses the filesystem

```
use std::fs;
use std::io::{Read, Write};

fn main() {
  let greeting = "Hello, world!";
  let outfile = "hello.txt";
  let mut output_file = fs::File::create(outfile)
    .expect(&format!("Error creating {}", outfile));

  output_file.write_all(greeting.as_bytes())
```

---

8 It is outside of the scope of this book to provide you a meaningful discussion on the whole scope of capabilities-based security (*https://oreil.ly/mLml3*).

```
    .expect(&format!("Error writing: {}", outfile));

let mut input_file = fs::File::open(outfile)
    .expect(&format!("Error opening {}", outfile));

let mut input = String::new();
input_file.read_to_string(&mut input)
    .expect(&format!("Error reading: {} ", outfile));

println!("Read in from file: {}", input);
}
```

I have this code in another cargo-driven project, so generating a native executable is a piece of cake:

```
brian@tweezer ~/g/w/s/c/hello-fs> cargo build --release
    Finished release [optimized] target(s) in 0.01s
brian@tweezer ~/g/w/s/c/hello-fs> cargo run --release
    Finished release [optimized] target(s) in 0.01s
     Running `target/release/hello-fs`
Read in from file: Hello, world!
brian@tweezer ~/g/w/s/c/hello-fs> ls -alF
total 32
drwxr-xr-x  10 brian  staff  320 Jun 27 13:18 ./
drwxr-xr-x  10 brian  staff  320 Jun 27 18:42 ../
-rw-r--r--   1 brian  staff  177 Jun 27 12:18 Cargo.toml
-rw-r--r--   1 brian  staff   13 Jun 27 18:47 hello.txt
drwxr-xr-x   3 brian  staff   96 Jun 27 13:18 src/
drwxr-xr-x@  7 brian  staff  224 Jun 27 18:42 target/
brian@tweezer ~/g/w/s/c/hello-fs> cat hello.txt
Hello, world!
```

As you see, we can build and run the program. The file is created and read back into a string that we print out to the console. This is possible because, as the main user and administrator of this machine, I have permission to do these things.

What if I downloaded a random program from the internet and ran it, though? That's probably not a good idea. The permissions I am afforded are conferred to the random code through a scenario we call the *confused deputy problem*.[9] If it is a malicious application, it could delete files, steal my Bitcoin private keys,[10] or encrypt my hard drive to extract a ransom.

However, let's recompile the application targeting WASI and try to run it in Wasmtime:

---

9 When permissions are intermingled, it gets hard to sort out who is allowed to do what (*https://oreil.ly/jO0dC*).

10 And thus any Bitcoin I had, which, as I started paying attention in 2008, would have been substantial if I had actually, you know, mined and stuff. Sigh.

```
brian@tweezer ~/g/w/s/c/hello-fs> cargo build --target wasm32-wasi --release
    Finished release [optimized] target(s) in 0.01s
brian@tweezer ~/g/w/s/c/hello-fs> wasmtime ↵
    target/wasm32-wasi/release/hello-fs.wasm
thread 'main' panicked at 'error creating hello.txt
note: run with `RUST_BACKTRACE=1` environment variable to display a backtrace
Error: failed to run main module `target/wasm32-wasi/release/hello-fs.wasm`

Caused by:
    0: failed to invoke command default
    1: wasm trap: unreachable
       wasm backtrace:
           0: 0x838a - <unknown>!__rust_start_panic
           1: 0x7fd5 - <unknown>!rust_panic
           2: 0x7c42 - <unknown>!std::panicking::rust_panic_with_hook
           3: 0x7190 - <unknown>!std::panicking::begin_panic_handler::{{closure}}
           4: 0x70d1 - <unknown>!std::sys_common::__rust_end_short_backtrace
           5: 0x7790 - <unknown>!rust_begin_unwind
           6: 0xdc62 - <unknown>!core::panicking::panic_fmt::h79dd662186e4ad97
           7: 0xebb2 - <unknown>!core::result::unwrap_failed::hc8762c9cd74198d4
           8:  0xce3 - <unknown>!hello_fs::main::h13132a06338f22dc
           9:  0x73d - <unknown>!std::sys_common::__rust_begin_short_backtrace
          10:  0xe02 - <unknown>!std::rt::lang_start::{{closure}}
          11: 0x8139 - <unknown>!std::rt::lang_start_internal::hb132ad43e5d53599
          12:  0xdc9 - <unknown>!__original_main
          13:  0x44d - <unknown>!_start
          14: 0x11bff - <unknown>!_start.command_export
       note: run with `WASMTIME_BACKTRACE_DETAILS=1` environment variable to
             display more information
```

Well, that didn't work. There is quite a lot of noise, but the salient point is that we don't have the capability to do what we are trying to do because the WASI host has not given it to us in the form of an unforgeable handle (called a "preopened file descriptor" in the previous example).

Relaunching the executable but invoking the command-line argument that allows for directory access solves the problem:

```
brian@tweezer ~/g/w/s/c/hello-fs> wasmtime --dir=. ↵
    target/wasm32-wasi/release/hello-fs.wasm
Read in from file: Hello, world!
```

Wasmer frames the message slightly differently, but it is the same issue:

```
brian@tweezer ~/g/w/s/c/hello-fs> wasmer target/wasm32-wasi/release/hello-fs.wasm
thread 'main' panicked at 'error creating hello.txt: Os
note: run with `RUST_BACKTRACE=1` environment variable to display a backtrace
error: failed to run `target/wasm32-wasi/release/hello-fs.wasm`
│   1: WASI execution failed
│   2: failed to run WASI `_start` function
│   3: RuntimeError: unreachable
            at __rust_start_panic (hello-fs.wasm[171]:0x838a)
            at rust_panic (hello-fs.wasm[163]:0x7fd5)
```

```
    at std::panicking::rust_panic_with_hook (hello-fs.wasm[156]:0x7c42)
    at std::panicking::{{closure}} (hello-fs.wasm[145]:0x7190)
    at std::sys_common (hello-fs.wasm[144]:0x70d1)
    at rust_begin_unwind (hello-fs.wasm[155]:0x7790)
    at core::panicking::panic_fmt (hello-fs.wasm[239]:0xdc62)
    at core::result::unwrap_failed (hello-fs.wasm[262]:0xebb2)
    at hello_fs::main::h13132a06338f22dc (hello-fs.wasm[17]:0xce3)
    at std::sys_common (hello-fs.wasm[12]:0x73d)
    at std::rt::lang_start::{{closure}} (hello-fs.wasm[20]:0xe02)
    at std::rt::lang_start_internal:: (hello-fs.wasm[164]:0x8139)
    at __original_main (hello-fs.wasm[18]:0xdc9)
    at _start (hello-fs.wasm[10]:0x44d)
    at _start.command_export (hello-fs.wasm[310]:0x11bff)
  ╰─> 4: unreachable
```

And the solution is the same:

```
brian@tweezer ~/g/w/s/c/hello-fs> wasmer --dir=. ↵
    target/wasm32-wasi/release/hello-fs.wasm
Read in from file: Hello, world!
```

Adding a command-line option to the executable instance does not seem like the most robust security mechanism, but that misses the larger point. You may certainly use Wasmer or Wasmtime to launch your applications, but it is not required. In the next chapter you will learn how to write WASI-enabled code of your own, in which case you could use whatever mechanism you would like to enable or disable behavior.

With that, let's regroup and take a broader view on WASI to wrap up this chapter.

The Bigger Picture

The full vision of WebAssembly is way more expansive than most people have realized. There is a decent awareness about the capabilities of the MVP out there, but for most people that is where it ends. The idea of being able to use languages other than JavaScript to deploy code to the browser is kind of cool but not a strict necessity, given the advancements in the language and the JavaScript runtime engines.

To me, the more important part of the vision is that we will be able to write code in whatever language we want and use it in just about any environment we want. This allows us to leverage existing software in new environments without having to rewrite it. And that allows us to pick a language that is appropriate to a problem and not require a new runtime. If an organization had the Java Virtual Machine (JVM) deployed in production, the move to Ruby on Rails or a Python-based solution would probably require the installation of their respective environments.[11]

---

11 Yes, yes, I know about Jython and JRuby.

It is in no way an all-or-nothing prospect. Sometimes we will want to run code natively for performance reasons, sometimes we will want the benefit of the zero-installation aspects of the web. Sometimes we will want to run in a sandbox, sometimes we will not. Consider all the variables that would go into bringing this vision into existence, and it would be nearly impossible to design from the ground up.

But what you have hopefully started to see in this chapter is how this vision is coming into reality because of the deliberate choices that the WebAssembly designers have been making. They have tried to walk a line to avoid over- or underengineering things. The MVP left out language features that not every language supported, like threads, garbage collection, and exceptions. There are technical proposals and working examples of all of these things, but it would have been too much up front.

Clearly, there are limitations in the platform as it is. A steady stream of proposals are being published to extend the capabilities of the platform where and when it makes sense to do so. WASI has emerged as a focal point in allowing these proposals to emerge independently and to be adopted by platforms such as Wasmtime, Wasmer, and Wasm3 incrementally. Admittedly, this makes it very confusing to track what has been added where, but through procedural mechanisms they are starting to sort that out as well.

In order to facilitate a significant amount of the desired behavior, the WASI designers realized that there was a need to standardize how modules linked to each other. We needed a solution that allows us to refer to the unforgeable handles in memory without revealing the underlying structures. We also needed a way to refer to types such as strings, lists, and records. There became a dependency to the proposals design and implementation that would unlock some of this additional behavior. Some of these proposals will be introduced in the next chapter, but Wasmtime, Wasmer, and Wasm3 have started implementing several of these fundamental proposals already.

This process will continue and new WASI modules will be designed. While the initial behavior focused on files and console access, there are already proposals for a range of features, including cryptographic functions, cryptocurrency contracts, 2D and 3D graphics, networking, and neural network systems. There will not be a single WASI namespace, but as many as there is value in having. Not every application will need every module. Not every environment will provide full implementations of these modules. They can be contextually restricted, virtualized, or shared across multiple modules with the same dependencies. To this end, WASI may never be "done."

In Figure 11-2, you can see the basic contours of what all of this means and approximately how we get there. In Chapter 12 and subsequent chapters, I will elaborate on some of these points, but for now I think the vision is a suitable goal.

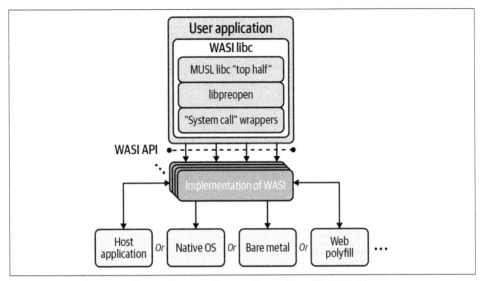

Figure 11-2. The WASI layered vision (source: https://oreil.ly/9jS4h)

At the top of the software layering, we have our applications. This is obviously the majority of what we write, including standalone executables, Web applications, frameworks, libraries, microservices, serverless functions, and more. Those are going to represent the lion's share of the business value we create. When we make poor technology choices, that business value gets locked up into silos. It is hard to extract functionality, so often our only real choice is to reimplement, which is generally the opposite of adding business value. Even if we make good technology choices, however, our industry does not sit idle, and reuse has a generally finite scope.

In this vision, however, we can imagine the emergence of a generalized framework for expressing expectations about the environments our software runs in. We have started to see how we get language independence from WebAssembly by writing to an intermediate, portable representation. That leaves us with often unmet expectations in the environments we hope to expand to fill. Now we are starting to see how the host environments can be modular, virtualizable, swappable, and more to provide functionality that meets our interface expectations. Code running in a browser but expecting filesystem access can be given an abstraction that meets the needs but uses local storage or something else. You can even imagine a scenario where the "filesystem" abstraction is a userland filesystem such as Fuse backed by a cloud storage provider transparently.[12]

---

12 Fuse (*https://oreil.ly/0v9M2*) provides the basis of many virtual filesystems.

The point is that our code does not have to be rewritten necessarily to float between these environments, whether they are fully privileged native applications, virtualized, hosted, in-browser, or embedded. Leveraging modular compiler architectures such as LLVM gives us the ability to add a backend that will express our expectations in a flexible manner. We can implement code sharing and dynamic linking strategies as it makes sense to.

The flip side is that we have a snowballing security hellscape unfolding around us with malicious software, phishing attacks, and ransomware. If we have the ability to run code from anywhere in any language in sandboxed environments, this could go a long way toward strengthening our default security postures.

The vision of a safe, portable, and fast computational ecosystem is so powerful that the Bytecode Alliance (*https://oreil.ly/mElS2*) was formed to carry it forward. The early members include Mozilla, Intel, Microsoft, Fastly, and more. They are striking a balance between safe, protected environments and performance. Rather than big, heavyweight communication processes between isolated modules, they are creating a "nanoprocess" mechanism that is bringing the many varied requirements into being. They are imagining a brighter future for our industry that is able to develop high-performance, secure code that meets the needs of modern systems and to capture business value for longer than we currently can. That is an idea we can all get behind.

## CHAPTER 12

Extending the WebAssembly Platform

He picks up scraps of information
He's adept at adaptation
'Cause for strangers and arrangers
Constant change is here to stay
  —Rush, "Digital Man"

The MVP (*https://oreil.ly/0ZDqB*) definition of WebAssembly put a stake in the ground but was never intended as a comprehensive solution for all uses. It primarily focused on language features that are ubiquitous and runtimes that do not require the complexities of threading, garbage collection, and exception handling. There were several other limitations that we have seen throughout the book. While it is impressive that people have found ways around these shortcomings, the MVP was never the end state. It was the beginning.

The designers of the WebAssembly platform have taken a surgical approach to its decisions. While it may be confusing from the outside, there is an internal consistency that takes into consideration several of the larger and longer-term goals. Many of the motivations for these decisions are documented alongside the specifications themselves. Rather than lumping shoehorned solutions to the omissions into the next big release, the designers have created a series of follow-on proposals that are tracked independently. Several of these proposals are interdependent, so there is an order to which they have been submitted and adopted.

Because the post-MVP world is evolving this way, it gets a little tricky to keep track of which features are available in which distribution. I fully expect there to be tools and libraries to assist with this, but hopefully the burden on the developers will be minimized. Some of these complexities are not super interesting or useful, so I do not want to spend a lot of time on them, but it is somewhat illuminating to see how things like the multivalue and Reference Type proposals will help enable the heavier-weight Interface Types proposal.

For our purposes, we will consider them as a collection of follow-on features that are not fully supported yet but are representative of where the WebAssembly platform is going beyond its modest beginnings. I will not comprehensively cover the proposals, as many are more esoteric or have not developed fully yet. Just be aware that there are several attempts to improve the experience of targeting WebAssembly to make our code more widely usable, safe, fast, and portable.

WASI Runtimes

In Chapter 11, we introduced the main ideas behind WASI. It has become one of the major vectors for adding new capabilities to the platform. There is a process for introducing a proposed extension (*https://oreil.ly/HYt02*), which will then go through a series of phases on its way to adoption and standardization. As we indicated in the last chapter, not every runtime will support every proposal. Even if one supports a proposal under some circumstances, for security reasons, it may not in others. We saw some basic command-line usage with the Wasmer and Wasmtime engines, but the more interesting reality is that you will be able to execute arbitrary functionality from your own applications using WASI-based mechanisms.

This will allow you to securely build and deploy plug-in mechanisms, serverless functions, hot swap replacements, data filters, retail promotions, Kubernetes nodes, blockchain engines, and extension points that can be written in arbitrary languages. The combination of freedom of language, performance, and sandboxed isolation has pushed many projects and companies to already start doing this.

Edge computing companies such as Fastly and Cloudflare are allowing customers to geographically distribute microservices and serverless functions for low-latency access in multitenant environments. Istio and Envoy are allowing their users to create filters and support new protocols with WebAssembly-based mechanisms. Second State's WasmEdge environment is, among other uses, targeting blockchains and software-defined vehicles. WasmCloud is providing a distributed system infrastructure based upon the actor model. Even *Microsoft Flight Simulator* (*https://oreil.ly/XYcJ8*) is moving away from dynamic link library–based plug-ins for WebAssembly modules. We will discuss some of these other projects in Chapter 15.

For now I will show you the basics of using WebAssembly and WASI with some simple modules. Once you are comfortable with the concepts and sequence of events, we will introduce some of the new proposals that are supported by our WASI-based frameworks to see how the platform is evolving to fill in some of the MVP omissions.

First, create a Rust binary project:

```
brian@tweezer ~/g/w/s/ch12> cargo new --bin hello-wasi
    Created binary (application) `hello-wasi` package
brian@tweezer ~/g/w/s/ch12> cd hello-wasi
```

We need to add a dependency on the Wasmtime crate so we have access to the run-time structures that allow us to instantiate modules and execute code. Edit the *Cargo.toml* file in the *hello-wasi* directory to look like Example 12-1. Keep in mind that by the time you read this, the version numbers may be different, but it should still work.

Example 12-1. Cargo.toml file

```
[package]
name = "hello-wasi"
version = "0.1.0"
edition = "2018"

[dependencies]
wasmtime = "0.28.0"
```

We are going to use the Rust version of the libraries, but there are similar structures for other languages such as C and Python. We will look at the .NET and Assembly-Script versions in subsequent chapters. It is even possible to use the command-line version of Wasmtime with bash, as you can see in Example 12-2.

Example 12-2. Calling our function from bash

```
#!/bin/sh
# Based on https://docs.wasmtime.dev/lang-bash.html
function how_old() {
  local x=$(($1))
  local y=$(($2))
  local result=$(wasmtime hello.wat --invoke how_old $x $y 2>/dev/null)
  echo "$result"
}

for num in "2021 2000" "2021 1980" "2021 1960"; do
  set -- $num
  echo "how_old($1, $2) = $(how_old "$1" "$2")"
done
```

```
brian@tweezer-2 ~/g/w/s/c/hello-wasi> chmod ogu+rx hello.sh
brian@tweezer-2 ~/g/w/s/c/hello-wasi> ./hello.sh
how_old(2021, 2000) = 21
how_old(2021, 1980) = 41
how_old(2021, 1960) = 61
```

We have greater control over the life cycle when we use the libraries, classes, and structures in the supported development languages. First, we will use our age-calculating module from Chapter 2 as something to call. You can refresh your memory by checking out Example 12-3.

Example 12-3. Our age-calculating Wasm module

```
(module
  (func $how_old (param $year_now i32) (param $year_born i32) (result i32)
    get_local $year_now
    get_local $year_born
    i32.sub)

  (export "how_old" (func $how_old))
)
```

Now we will create a standalone Rust application that invokes the behavior through the Wasmtime libraries. Keep in mind that Wasmer, Wasm3, and other environments will have their strategies for doing this as well, and we will demonstrate some of them over the remainder of the book. I will walk you through the details, but take a look at Example 12-4.

Example 12-4. Minimal Wasmtime WASI integration in Rust

```
use std::error::Error;
use wasmtime::*;

fn main() -> Result<(), Box<dyn Error>> {
  let engine = Engine::default();
  let mut store = Store::new(&engine, ());
  let module = Module::from_file(&engine, "hello.wat")?;
  let instance = Instance::new(&mut store, &module, &[])?;

  let how_old =
    instance.get_typed_func::<(i32,i32), (i32), _>(&mut store, "how_old")?;
  let age : i32 = how_old.call(&mut store, (2021i32, 2000i32))?;

  println!("You are {}", age);

  Ok(())
}
```

After importing prelude definitions of the various features we are using, we begin to use the structures as defined by Wasmtime's Rust library. Consult Table 12-1 for a description of these types.

Table 12-1. Wasmtime structures

Name	Description
Engine	A global context for configuration values intended to be shared across threads
Store	A collection of WebAssembly objects including instances, globals, memories, and tables
Module	The compiled form of a WebAssembly module
Instance	An instance of the compiled module

The `Engine` contains any special configuration details. As you see in Example 12-4, we are just using a default configuration. This is used to create the `Store`. This provides a context for the WebAssembly functionality and is thus a unit of isolation. Different WebAssembly structures created in a `Store` cannot be shared or accessed from other `Store` instances. In the Rust version of the Wasmtime API, mutable references to the `Store` instances are passed into the functions, which precludes sharing them across threads.

The `Engine` is next used to initialize and compile the `Module` instance. There are a variety of mechanisms for retrieving the underlying bytes, but for our purposes, we are just reading in the *.wat* file from the filesystem. Keep in mind we are building a native Rust application here, not a WASI application, so it will therefore be allowed to access the filesystem.

Once the `Module` has been compiled, we can create a new `Instance` of it. In this case we are not providing any import objects, but in a moment we will see examples of sharing functions from the Rust host environment to a module. From the `Instance` we are able to retrieve a reference to an exported function wrapper so that it can be invoked almost as if it were a regular Rust function. We use the type-safe `get_typed_func`, which here takes two `i32` parameters and returns an `i32` result.

Finally, we invoke our function with the values `2021i32` and `2000i32`, which represent Rust 32-bit integer type literals for the numbers 2021 and 2000. The result is captured in a Rust `i32` variable and then printed to the console.

I have removed extraneous build output below, but I wanted to demonstrate that it is just a regular Rust `cargo build` command using the native OS backend to generate the application invoking the WebAssembly behavior:

```
brian@tweezer ~/g/w/s/c/hello-wasi> cargo build --release
    Finished release [optimized] target(s) in 3m 22s
brian@tweezer ~/g/w/s/c/hello-wasi> cargo run --release
    Finished release [optimized] target(s) in 0.38s
     Running `target/release/hello-wasi`
You are 21
```

Now that you have seen the basics, we will investigate some of the new proposals that Wasmtime supports as a runtime. As this book is being written, this is definitely a moving target, so by the time you read it, there could be more support added. At this point in your WebAssembly career, it is my opinion that you need not dwell on the details of the proposals themselves, although I will link to them where relevant. Instead, I think it is more important for you to see tangible examples of how the WebAssembly platform is evolving. Consequently, I am only going to focus on the proposals that are available in a WASI environment, but will hint at what else is coming when we wrap up the chapter.

Multi-Value Return

The MVP settled on some fairly basic semantics for invoking functions. While they may take any number of parameters, functions are only able to produce a single result. For many situations, this is obviously fine, but it is easy to imagine scenarios where this would be overly limiting.

Consider some of our earlier examples involving strings. Because we are using a linear Memory instance to allocate the strings, we need a reference to the base address of the string as well as the length of the string. There is no easy way to do that without relying on a trick, like we did where we wrote the length of the string first and then had the sequence of characters.

What about a language that supports tuples, such as Python or Rust? This allows a developer to easily package several values into a single structure to return from a function, but a client from another language may want to unbox or destructure them into a different representation to be more idiomatic for that language.

Even something as simple as swapping a pair of values or sorting an array becomes problematic. It would have to be done in place in the linear memory block. Several arithmetic functions also can return multiple values if you consider modular operations, carry bits, and the like.

Beyond function return values, another limitation in the MVP is that instruction sequences such as conditional blocks and loops are unable to consume values or return more than one result. It could equally be interesting to swap values, conduct arithmetic with overflow, or have a multivalue tuple response there too.

If you recall from Chapter 2, the result of a WebAssembly function is found at the top of the stack. There is no real reason the top several elements of the stack could not be interpreted as multiple return values. So, both as an improvement to the platform and to facilitate other extensions, the Multi-Value Return type exension was an important next step.[1] At this point it has been merged into the main specification and is implemented in many WebAssembly environments.

The proposal introduces new instructions such as the aforementioned arithmetic functions. This includes `i32.divmod`, which accepts a numerator and divisor and returns the quotient and the remainder. It also allows multiple values to remain on the stack and not have to be copied into the linear memory instance. This is both faster and more memory-efficient.

Because Wasmtime supports the Multi-Value Proposal already, we can easily demonstrate how useful it is. In Example 12-5, you see a Wat file that provides the structure we will use. The first line imports a function that takes two parameters and returns two parameters from the Rust environment. As you can see, it is no big deal to extend the `result` syntactically to support more than one value. Implementing it is obviously more complicated, but as I mentioned, the results come from the top of the stack, so it is not exactly rocket surgery. We call our new function `swap` because that is what the function we will pass in will do.

Example 12-5. A simple Wat file demonstrating Multi-Value Return types

```
(module
  (func $swap (import "" "swap") (param i32 i32) (result i32 i32))

  (func $myfunc (export "myfunc") (param i32 i32) (result i32 i32)
    (call $swap (local.get 0) (local.get 1))
  )
)
```

The next line defines an exported function called `myfunc` that calls our `swap` function. Keep in mind that the parameters sent to the function are addressable as local variables in position 0 and 1. We call the instructions to push those values to the stack and then directly call our imported function. We do not have to do anything special in our function definition other than to indicate that we return two `i32` values as our result. These should be at the top of the stack once `swap` returns. Those behind-the-scenes details are what the Wasmtime team had to implement, but the impact on the Wat syntax is quite low.

In Example 12-6, you see the host application that is going to call our Wat functions. The majority of the application is quite similar to what you saw in Example 12-4.

---

1 As it represents a fundamental change to the WebAssembly platform, the Multi-Value Proposal has been merged into the WebAssembly standard itself.

Example 12-6. Exercising Multi-Value Return types with Wasmtime Rust libraries

```rust
use std::error::Error;
use wasmtime::*;

fn main() -> Result<(), Box<dyn Error>> {
  let engine = Engine::default();
  let mut store = Store::new(&engine, ());
  let module = Module::from_file(&engine, "mvr.wat")?;

  let callback_func = Func::wrap(&mut store, |a: i32, b: i32| -> (i32, i32) {
    (b, a)
  });

  let instance = Instance::new(&mut store, &module, &[callback_func.into()])?;

  let myfunc =
    instance.get_typed_func::<(i32,i32), (i32, i32), _>(&mut store, "myfunc")?;
  let (a, b) = myfunc.call(&mut store, (13, 43))?;

  println!("Swapping {} and {} produces {} and {}.", 13, 43, a, b);

  Ok(())
}
```

What is new is that we are defining a callback function by calling `Func::wrap`. This takes a mutable reference to our `Store` instance and a Rust closure that takes two `i32` parameters and returns a tuple of two `i32` parameters. We are using idiomatic Rust to express the functionality, which is pretty cool! The closure implementation is quite trivial. We just return a tuple with the parameters in the opposite order.

Now that we have our callback, notice we pass it to the import context when we create the module `Instance`. After this we fetch a wrapper to the `myfunc` function exported from our WebAssembly module and call it with a tuple value. This is again idiomatic Rust and a natural way of passing in two parameters. These will be destructured behind the scenes into the two parameters our function is expecting. The result of calling the exported function is captured as a tuple, which we then destructure and print out the results:

```
brian@tweezer ~/g/w/s/c/hello-mvr> cargo build --release
    Compiling hello-mvr v0.1.0
        (/Users/brian/git-personal/wasm_tdg/src/ch12/hello-mvr)
     Finished release [optimized] target(s) in 3.17s
brian@tweezer ~/g/w/s/c/hello-mvr> cargo run --release
     Finished release [optimized] target(s) in 0.22s
      Running `target/release/hello-mvr`
Swapping 13 and 43 produces 43 and 13.
```

Reference Types

Having the ability to specify multiple return values is a necessary precursor to some of the additional proposals. Another enabling proposal is the ability to specify references to opaque handles. This is going to be crucial for adding garbage collection, having typed references, using exception handling, and more, but it is also key to having the host environments be able to pass in opaque references referring to resources we do not want the WebAssembly modules to necessarily have raw access to. Keep in mind that we are talking about being able to pass in arbitrary references to arbitrary structures in arbitrary languages on arbitrary operating systems. Trying to be both this flexible and this performant is no easy task!

We have been able to make references previously, but only to functions and only in `Table` instances that we could not manipulate once they were created. This was in part to disallow the modules from manipulating sensitive details in memory or being able to change which function was in which slot. Recall from Chapter 7 that we had to make indirect calls to the function references rather than the more common direct calls to other functions.

This new proposal affords us the ability to manipulate `Table` members, grow the `Table` instance size, and pass `externref` references back and forth between WebAssembly modules and their host environments.[2]

Wasmtime supports the ability to make `externref` references, so let's create another sample application using their APIs. To be clear, any WASI environment will have to support these fundamental proposals, but we're focusing on Wasmtime:

```
brian@tweezer ~/g/w/s/ch12> cargo new --bin hello-extref
        Created binary (application) `hello-extref` package
```

This is another relatively simple change to the syntax of our Wat files. A quick check of Example 12-7 will show you that we may store `externref` elements in a `Table` or pass them in as parameters or return them as function results. This is a simplified version of the Wasmtime example on these reference types. I am not focusing on them here, but it is also possible to make global variable references to `externref` elements.

Example 12-7. A Wat file with externref parameters, Table elements, and results

```
(module
  (table $table (export "table") 10 externref)
```

---

2 You can read the Reference Types proposals on GitHub (*https://oreil.ly/xUwx0*) if you are into that kind of thing.

```
    (func (export "func") (param externref) (result externref)
      local.get 0
    )
  )
)
```

Our module exports a Table with the space for 10 references. We also have a function that simply returns its parameter. Unfortunately, the Rust code in Example 12-8 is substantially more complicated than other examples we have looked at, because we are wrapping these references, cloning them, deferencing them, and extracting the wrapped data as needed. I will walk you through it, though, so we can focus on what is new.

Example 12-8. A Wasmtime Rust application that uses externref elements

```
use std::error::Error;
use wasmtime::*;

fn main() -> Result<(), Box<dyn Error>> {
  let mut config = Config::new();
  config.wasm_reference_types(true);

  let engine = Engine::new(&config)?;
  let mut store = Store::new(&engine, ());
  let module = Module::from_file(&engine, "extref.wat")?;

  let instance = Instance::new(&mut store, &module, &[])?;

  let eref = ExternRef::new("secret key");
  let arr : [u8; 4] = [1, 2, 3, 4];

  let eref2 = ExternRef::new(arr);

  let table = instance.get_table(&mut store, "table").unwrap();
  table.set(&mut store, 3, Some(eref.clone()).into())?;
  table.set(&mut store, 4, Some(eref2.clone()).into())?;

  let ret = table.get(&mut store, 3)
    .unwrap()
    .unwrap_externref()
    .unwrap();

  let ret2 = table.get(&mut store, 4)
    .unwrap()
    .unwrap_externref()
    .unwrap();

  let str = *ret.data().downcast_ref::<&'static str>().unwrap();
  let arr2 = *ret2.data().downcast_ref::<[u8; 4]>().unwrap();

  println!("Retrieved external reference: {} from table slot {}", str, 3);
```

```
    println!("Retrieved external reference: {:?} from table slot {}", arr2, 4);

    let func = instance.get_typed_func::<Option<ExternRef>, Option<ExternRef>, _>
        (&mut store, "func")?;

    let ret = func.call(&mut store, Some(eref.clone()))?;

    let str2 = *(ret.unwrap()).data().downcast_ref::<&'static str>().unwrap();

    println!("Received {} back from calling extern-ref aware function.", str2);

    Ok(())
}
```

The first thing you will see is the introduction of a Config instance. We have been using default configurations for our Engine instances previously, but we need to turn on support for the external references and then configure our Engine accordingly. From then on things should look familiar from a setup perspective.

To demonstrate the flexibility we have with respect to the references, we create two instances of the ExternRef structure from the Wasmtime API. One might be an unforgeable bearer token or something that could be passed back when the module makes shared function calls. For our purposes, I just have a string slice that says "secret key." The other reference is to an array of bytes. As the ExternRef structure is a parameterized type, it is able to wrap both data types.

After we create the references, we retrieve the exported Table from the module and store clones of our references in slots 3 and 4. We use Some wrappers so that it makes it easier to tell when a reference is . there or not. If nothing is there, we might get a None instance. This is via a structure called an Option (*https://oreil.ly/aZatk*) in Rust. As the Table stores externref elements, there is no way for the module to look at the details. When we retrieve them back out, however, they still represent the structures we put in them. Other programming languages will have different mechanisms for this procedure depending on static typing and memory management details, but it will look basically the same.

Pulling the references out looks a little strange, but the first unwrap() function determines whether we have made an index reference within the boundaries of the Table instance or not. It then extracts the externref and verifies it is an instance of that type (as opposed to some other reference type). The final unwrap() makes sure that it did not produce a null reference, which is another addition this proposal brings to the WebAssembly platform.

The next steps are perhaps even stranger still, but we are deferencing our references, extracting the data, and casting them to our expected types, in this case a string slice with a static lifetime (also known as a *string literal*) and a four-element u8 array.

Assuming these downcasts are successful, we print out the element values we have pulled back out of the module instance.

Our final step fetches a reference to the module's exported function, which takes an Option-wrapped ExternRef and returns an Option-wrapped ExternRef. Recall from Example 12-7 that our function simply returns its parameter. We call our function with a cloned copy of our ExternRef, capture the return value, and go through the same downcasting to extract the value.

Now that everything has been explained, we can execute the example as per usual:

```
brian@tweezer ~/g/w/s/c/hello-extref> cargo run --release
    Finished release [optimized] target(s) in 0.36s
     Running `target/release/hello-extref`
Retrieved external reference: secret key from table slot 3
Retrieved external reference: [1, 2, 3, 4] from table slot 4
Received secret key back from calling extern-ref aware function.
```

This is admittedly not the most exciting example in the world, but this proposal, like the Multi-Value Proposal, is more about what it enables, rather than being something you would use in and of itself.

Module Linking

The final proposal that we will cover briefly in this chapter is the Module-Linking Proposal.[3] The scope of this proposal is quite large, but it is ultimately about allowing modules themselves to be imported through a variety of mechanisms and styles.

Consider the fundamentals of the WASI standard library. We want to have a dependency on a module that will provide this behavior without having to import individual methods one by one. That approach would be fragile, annoying, and ultimately would perform poorly if every function invocation had to go through a JavaScript wrapper or something similar. We do, however, like the idea of virtualizing the implementations so that filesystem access might be approximated by the use of local storage in a browser while other APIs might behave as expected (e.g., printing to the JavaScript console through fd_write). We also want the benefit of shared nothing architectures, such as the Unix pipes-and-filters strategy we have discussed previously, without performance penalties there either. And we want to be able to have shared instances of widely used modules to save on memory. What we need is the ability to describe types of modules and allow different implementations to satisfy those types.

---

3 The Module-Linking Proposal (*https://oreil.ly/CoZWT*) is fairly complicated and requires the support of several of the more fundamental proposals to be supported first.

Because there are complicated requirements, it is a complicated proposal. To keep things simple for now, we are going to demonstrate a simple example, but the full implications are going to be huge for the resilience and convenience of large, complicated module dependency trees in our WebAssembly systems. There is even a new textual format for describing these interfaces based on Wat. It only allows interface definitions, however, so it has an extension of *.wit* to differentiate the type.

In Example 12-9, we see a sample module as defined in the Module-Linking Proposal.

Example 12-9. A Wat file for a sample module

```
(module
  (memory (import "a") 1 2)
  (func (import "b") (param i32))
  (table (export "c") 1 funcref)
  (func $notImportedOrExported (result i64)
    i64.const 0
  )
  (func (export "d") (result f32)
    f32.const 0
  )
)
```

In Example 12-10, we see the corresponding interface file (*.wit*), which has no implementation details but still defines the "type" of the module based upon the elements it imports and exports. This is ultimately going to give us the ability to link modules more cleanly, flexibly, and performantly.

Example 12-10. A Wit file for the same module

```
(module
  (memory (import "a") 1 2)
  (func (import "b") (param i32))
  (table (export "c") 1 funcref)
  (func (export "d") (result f32))
)
```

For convenience's sake, I am just going to show the module-linking example from the Wasmtime examples (*https://oreil.ly/pNbAD*). We have two modules, one that depends on the other and one that depends on having a WASI capability of writing to the console.

Our *Cargo.toml* file shown in Example 12-11 has a few more dependencies than we have seen so far. The most important one, however, is the `wasmtime-wasi` dependency. This is an implementation of the standard WASI functionality that we are going to link against in the following example.

Example 12-11. A Cargo.toml file for our module-linking example

```
[package]
name = "hello-modlink"
version = "0.1.0"
edition = "2018"

[dependencies]
wasmtime = "0.28.0"
wasmtime-wasi = "0.28.0"
anyhow = "1.0.19"
```

In the first module shown in Example 12-12, we import a function called `double` that will take an `i32`, double it, and return an `i32`. We are also importing a convenience function called `log` that will print a string in a `Memory` at the given offset and of the given length. We will also import a `Memory` instance to use and a global variable representing an offset to use as the location of our activity.

Our exported `run` function loads the constant 2 to the stack and then calls the `double` function. Remember that the top of the stack will contain the parameter, so we expect this to produce the value 4. We do not do anything with the output, but you can feel free to convince yourself that it does work. The point is mainly that our call to an imported function did actually work.

After doubling the value, we call the `log` function to print out "Hello, World!" Notice we write our string into memory with a `data` element at the location specified by the global variable.

Example 12-12. A module that we will link against that depends on another module

```
(module
  (import "linking2" "double" (func $double (param i32) (result i32)))
  (import "linking2" "log" (func $log (param i32 i32)))
  (import "linking2" "memory" (memory 1))
  (import "linking2" "memory_offset" (global $offset i32))

  (func (export "run")
    ;; Call into the other module to double our number, and we could print it
    ;; here but for now we just drop it
    i32.const 2
    call $double
    drop

    ;; Our `data` segment initialized our imported memory, so let's print the
    ;; string there now.
    global.get $offset
    i32.const 14
    call $log
  )
```

```
  (data (global.get $offset) "Hello, world!\n")
)
```

The second module is shown in Example 12-13. It defines a type for a function that takes four i32 parameters and returns an i32. This type will correspond to the fd_write method that we will import from the WASI namespace wasi_snapshot_pre view1. This method, as we saw in Chapter 11, takes parameters for the file description, where the string vectors start, how many there are, and where it should write the return value representing the number of bytes written.

There is also a simple function called double that loads the i32 parameter sent in to the stack, follows up with the constant 2, and then invokes the i32.mul instruction, which will pop off the top two stack values, multiply them, and write the result back to the top of the stack.

Our exported log function calls the imported fd_write after setting up the details. Notice many modules might import the fd_write functionality, but here we have a reusable function that hides most of the details. Other modules can import our function definition and pass in a memory pointer and length to achieve the same results.

Finally, our module exports a Memory instance and a global variable indicating the current offset to write values into. This is a (potentially fragile) way to allow the memory used to be managed by this module while allowing other modules to write into unused space.

Example 12-13. A second module that our first module depends upon

```
(module
  (type $fd_write_ty (func (param i32 i32 i32 i32) (result i32)))
  (import "wasi_snapshot_preview1" "fd_write" (func $fd_write (type $fd_write_ty)))

  (func (export "double") (param i32) (result i32)
    local.get 0
    i32.const 2
    i32.mul
  )

  (func (export "log") (param i32 i32)
    ;; store the pointer in the first iovec field
    i32.const 4
    local.get 0
    i32.store

    ;; store the length in the first iovec field
    i32.const 4
    local.get 1
    i32.store offset=4
```

```
    ;; call the `fd_write` import
    i32.const 1      ;; stdout fd
    i32.const 4      ;; iovs start
    i32.const 1      ;; number of iovs
    i32.const 0      ;; where to write nwritten bytes
    call $fd_write
    drop
  )

  (memory (export "memory") 2)
  (global (export "memory_offset") i32 (i32.const 65536))
)
```

The Rust code in Example 12-14 introduces a few more features of the Wasmtime APIs. The first is the concept of a Linker. This is a tool that will help link modules together based upon their import and export configurations. Because the WASI functionality is widely used, it is available as the separate dependency we saw in Example 12-11. We basically add details of this module to our Linker so they are available to be linked to modules that depend on this behavior.

After this we instantiate our two modules, configure the WASI instance, and add the details to our Store so that they will be contextually available at runtime.

We register our second module with the Linker instance because we are going to want to make it available to our first module. Keep in mind that the whole idea here is about balancing reuse, swappability, performance, isolation, and the other requirements.

Example 12-14. A module that we will link against that depends on another module

```
use anyhow::Result;
use wasmtime::*;
use wasmtime_wasi::sync::WasiCtxBuilder;

fn main() -> Result<()> {
  let engine = Engine::default();

  // First set up our linker, which is going to be linking modules together. We
  // want our linker to have wasi available, so we set that up here as well.
  let mut linker = Linker::new(&engine);
  wasmtime_wasi::add_to_linker(&mut linker, |s| s)?;

  // Load and compile our two modules
  let linking1 = Module::from_file(&engine, "linking1.wat")?;
  let linking2 = Module::from_file(&engine, "linking2.wat")?;

  // Configure WASI and insert it into a `Store`
  let wasi = WasiCtxBuilder::new()
```

```
    .inherit_stdio()
    .inherit_args()?
    .build();
  let mut store = Store::new(&engine, wasi);

  // Instantiate our first module, which only uses WASI, then register that
  // instance with the linker since the next linking will use it.
  let linking2 = linker.instantiate(&mut store, &linking2)?;
  linker.instance(&mut store, "linking2", linking2)?;

  // And with that we can perform the final link and execute the module.
  let linking1 = linker.instantiate(&mut store, &linking1)?;
  let run = linking1.get_typed_func::<(), (), _>(&mut store, "run")?;
  run.call(&mut store, ())?;
  Ok(())
}
```

Finally, we link our first module to our second module, fetch the run function, and invoke it:

```
brian@tweezer ~/g/w/s/c/hello-modlink> cargo run --release
   Compiling hello-modlink v0.1.0
      (/Users/brian/git-personal/wasm_tdg/src/ch12/hello-modlink)
    Finished release [optimized] target(s) in 21.49s
     Running `target/release/hello-modlink`
Hello, world!
```

Feature Testing

One of the ways you can navigate this topsy-turvy world of partial support for numerous proposals is to use a library from Google called *wasm-feature-detect* (*https://oreil.ly/aHPO0*). It's not just a clever name. That is what it does.

It is quite straightforward and easily extensible with plug-in tests. They solicit input from developers who want to add checks for new proposal features they do not yet test for. Contributions involve a *.wat* file that provides the use of one of the new proposals to see if it works. The module will be compiled by wabt.js.[4]

In Example 12-15, you can see the test for the Multi-Value return proposal.

---

4 wabt.js (*https://oreil.ly/hy9ti*) is a port of the functionality of the WebAssembly Binary Toolkit (WABT) that we introduced early in this book.

Example 12-15. A wasm-feature-detect detector for Multi-Value return support

```
;; Name: Multi-value
;; Proposal: https://github.com/WebAssembly/multi-value
;; Features: multi_value

(module
  (func (result i32 i32)
    i32.const 0
    i32.const 0
  )
)
```

Using the library to test for certain features is straightforward as well. In Example 12-16, I have a simple test that goes through most of the available tests and indicates whether they are supported by the current browser or not.

Example 12-16. A test document to see which of the new proposals a browser supports

```
<!doctype html>
<html lang="en">
  <head>
    <meta charset="utf-8">
    <script type="module">
      import {
        bigInt,
        bulkMemory,
        exceptions,
        multiValue,
        mutableGlobals,
        referenceTypes,
        saturatedFloatToInt,
        signExtensions,
        simd,
        tailCall
      } from "https://unpkg.com/wasm-feature-detect?module";

      function test(test, promise) {
        promise().then( supported => {
          console.log("Test: " + test + " is " + supported);
        });
      }

      test("BIGINT", bigInt);
      test("BULK MEMORY", bulkMemory);
      test("EXCEPTIONS", exceptions);
      test("MULTIVALUE", multiValue);
      test("MUTABLEGLOBALS", mutableGlobals);
      test("REFERENCETYPES", referenceTypes);
```

```
        test("NONTRAPPING F-to-I", saturatedFloatToInt);
        test("SIGN EXTENSIONS", signExtensions);
        test("SIMD",  simd);
        test("TAIL CALL", tailCall);
      </script>
    </head>
    <body>
    </body>
</html>
```

In Figure 12-1, you can see the results of loading this test HTML in Safari. At the time
of this writing, this is Safari 15.0, which was recently released with more support for
WebAssembly. Notably lacking is support for the SIMD proposal.

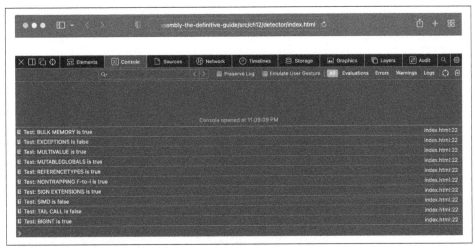

Figure 12-1. Testing WebAssembly features in Safari

In Figure 12-2, you can see the results of loading this test HTML in Firefox. It has
always been one of the browsers with the strongest WebAssembly support, so it is not
surprising that the coverage is so good.

In Figure 12-3, you can see the results of loading this test HTML in Chrome. Since it
is also a browser with strong WebAssembly support, I was surprised by the lack of
support for reference types, but I imagine that will appear soon enough.

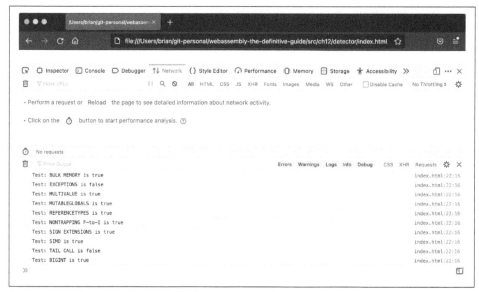

Figure 12-2. Testing WebAssembly features in Firefox

Figure 12-3. Testing WebAssembly features in Chrome

Other Proposals

There are many other proposals (*https://oreil.ly/vjob5*) coming to the WebAssembly platform. There are probably going to be new ones all the time. This is one of the primary methods that the WebAssembly platform designers are using to extend the platform incrementally over time.

Each proposal is considered on its own merits and its potential impact on the text and binary formats of modules, the parsing and validation of modules, dependencies on or for other proposals, and more. What you have heard about the making of laws and sausages[5] is true for the standards process as well. These proposals use precise and formal language to describe the details so there is no error from difference in interpretation by implementors.

Some of the proposals are fundamental, such as the ability to add garbage collection, higher-level interface types, threads, vectorized math, and more. Others are more subtle or are designed to enable other new features but must be designed and implemented first. There are not a lot of developer-friendly descriptions of most of these yet, but I believe Wasmtime, Wasmer, Wasm3, and other environments are going to be the best place for you to learn about them as they add support over time.

If the whole process seems a little hodgepodge, well, that is a fair criticism, which is why there is a proposal to add feature detection to the WebAssembly platform—so that it is easier to detect which features are enabled and which are not. Direct access is going to be the best bet, but there may be opportunities for shims, polyfills, and other fallback positions in case they are not. Ideally, we will not have the need for an excessive amount of feature detection, as that complicates testing strategies and portability, but it is inevitable that there will be some of it.

For now, this is enough of a peek at what is coming and how WebAssembly will evolve over time. Now it is time to learn about how we can use this platform from the .NET world.

---

5 Although it is often attributed to Otto von Bismarck, evidence suggests that it was John Godfrey Saxe who said that laws were like sausages. If you like either, you should not watch them be made.

## CHAPTER 13

WebAssembly and .NET

I think foosball[1] is a combination of soccer and shish kabobs.
—Mitch Hedberg

Throughout my career I have had a respectfully indifferent relationship with .NET. I have nothing against it; I just have almost never needed it and have spent little time working on anything Windows-specific, which for many years it was.

Back in the early 2000s, I did help initiate a .NET-based project with some coworkers to visualize scenarios simulating attacks on buildings. The idea was that by using real physics models of explosions, we could marry visualization with possible outcomes based upon various protective measures. Security planners could consider different locations for physical barriers and run tests for their facilities involving explosives-laden vehicles. If they could only get so close, what kind of an impact on the building or people standing just inside the entrance might they have?[2] Windows was the target platform and clearly we needed some computational speed, so we chose a Managed C++ basis for the core libraries and C# for the application. I was not on the project long, but it was successful enough in the end.

Other than that, I have done what I have needed to do with Java, C++, JavaScript, Rust, Python, and other languages and environments. I know a lot of people who love .NET and the tools that surround it, but it has just never mattered much to my career.

---

1 If you are not familiar with the name, foosball (*https://oreil.ly/Gxwzk*) is a popular game in many homes and recreation facilities where humans manipulate soccer players on metal rods.

2 Fortunately, I was not part of the project that blew up cadavers in the desert to determine the impact on bodies.

That being said, I have always been intrigued by initiatives like Mono, so I keep somewhat aware of what is happening in that world.[3] Plus, many of my friends are experts and champions of the space, so they let me know what is going on there too. One of the exciting shifts for its advocates is that the Microsoft development tools and .NET frameworks are now real solutions for cross-platform development.

I was still surprised when I started to learn about some of the .NET and WebAssembly initiatives that were gaining steam. They initially felt like combinations of soccer and shish kabobs—strange and anachronistic pairings. The more I thought about it, though, I realized that there are some compelling and consequential aspects located at the integration of these technologies that are worth exploring.

.NET and Wasmtime

As you are no doubt starting to realize, there are quite a few different use cases for WebAssembly beyond the straightforward approaches engendered by the MVP. We will start with an integration that isn't overly .NET-specific, along the lines of what we have seen in previous chapters. The Wasmtime platform supports .NET integrations through its NuGet package.[4] This example supports the idea of extending .NET applications with WebAssembly modules, libraries, and plug-ins.

You will need to install the .NET Core SDK before you can attempt the following. Please consult the Appendix for instructions to help you accomplish this. Once the tools are available, we will create a new directory and initialize a project. The dotnet command-line tool is able to create structures based on existing templates. One of the simplest ones is the console template, so we will use that:

```
brian@tweezer ~/g/w/s> mkdir wasmtime-dotnet
brian@tweezer ~/g/w/s> cd wasmtime-dotnet
brian@tweezer ~/g/w/s/wasmtime-dotnet> dotnet new console
The template "Console Application" was created successfully.

Processing post-creation actions...
Running 'dotnet restore' on
    /Users/brian/src/wasmtime-dotnet/wasmtime-dotnet.csproj...
  Determining projects to restore...
  Restored /Users/brian/src/wasmtime-dotnet/wasmtime-dotnet.csproj (in 58 ms).
Restore succeeded.
```

Once the project structure is initialized, we will need to add a dependency to the Wasmtime NuGet package. As of the time of writing, 0.28.0-preview1 is the latest version. You may want or need to use a newer version:

---

3 Mono (*https://oreil.ly/nJcy4*) is an open source, cross-platform .NET framework.

4 NuGet is a package management system for managing code dependencies à la NPM. The Wasmtime NuGet package is available online (*https://oreil.ly/6SHin*).

```
brian@tweezer ~/g/w/s/wasmtime-dotnet> dotnet add package ↵
  --version 0.28.0-preview1 wasmtime
  Determining projects to restore...
  Writing /var/folders/mn/4kd_fxdj3lxbpljfhjyp5sw40000gn/T/tmp5A8L0B.tmp
  .
  .
  .
```

At this point, there should be a generated console application in your project called *Program.cs*, which should look like Example 13-1.

Example 13-1. Generated C# console application

```
using System;

namespace wasmtime_dotnet
{
  class Program
  {
    static void Main(string[] args)
    {
      Console.WriteLine("Hello World!");
    }
  }
}
```

Double-check that everything is set up correctly by executing the following command:

```
brian@tweezer ~/g/w/s/wasmtime-dotnet> dotnet run
Hello World!
```

If you see our usual friendly greeting, we can move on. To keep things simple, we will just use our existing howold function for consistency. For reference, please make sure the module shown in Example 13-2 is in a file called *hello.wat* in your project directory (e.g., *wasmtime-dotnet* if you followed my command earlier).

Example 13-2. Our age-calculating Wasm module

```
(module
  (func $how_old (param $year_now i32) (param $year_born i32) (result i32)
    get_local $year_now
    get_local $year_born
    i32.sub)

  (export "how_old" (func $how_old))
)
```

Unsurprisingly, the Wasmtime classes will be named similarly to what we have seen in Rust even though we are now going to be using C# as the basis of our integration. If you change the *Program.cs* file to what you see in Example 13-3, we are back in business with Wasi support.[5]

Example 13-3. Using Wasmtime to execute WebAssembly in C#

```
using System;
using Wasmtime;

namespace wasmtime_dotnet
{
  class Program
  {
    static void Main(string[] args)
    {
      using var engine = new Engine();
      using var module = Module.FromTextFile(engine, "hello.wat");
      using var linker = new Linker(engine);
      using var store = new Store(engine);

      var instance = linker.Instantiate(store, module);
      var howOld = instance.GetFunction(store, "how_old");

      Console.WriteLine($"You are {howOld.Invoke(store, 2021, 2000)}");
    }
  }
}
```

Executing the code obviously does what you expect:

```
brian@tweezer ~/g/w/s/wasmtime-dotnet> dotnet run
You are 21
```

Of course, we have great support for the other kinds of things you want to do when crossing the boundary between host and WebAssembly module. In Example 13-4, we have an example of an imported function from our .NET host being invoked.

Example 13-4. Calling a function passed in from the host environment

```
(module
  (type $voidfunc (func))
  (import "hello" "world" (func $hello.world (type $voidfunc)))
  (func $exec
    call $hello.world
  )
  (export "exec" (func $exec))
)
```

---

5 The next two examples are based upon the Wasmtime .NET library examples (*https://oreil.ly/BRKrQ*).

The code to set up the module and share the function to invoke is highlighted in Example 13-5. Notice we can use a C# closure as the basis of the function we store in the Store instance. We retrieve the exported exec function from the module and call it, which turns around and calls the hello.world namespaced function we provided.

Example 13-5. Our host environment providing a C# closure to invoke

```
using System;
using Wasmtime;

namespace wasmtime_dotnet
{
  class Program
  {
    static void Main(string[] args)
    {
      using var engine = new Engine();
      using var module = Module.FromTextFile(engine, "hello.wat");
      using var linker = new Linker(engine);
      using var store = new Store(engine);

      linker.Define(
        "hello",
        "world",
        Function.FromCallback(store,
          () => Console.WriteLine("I like soccer and shishkabobs.")));
      );

      var instance = linker.Instantiate(store, module);
      var exec = instance.GetFunction(store, "exec");
      exec.Invoke(store);
    }
  }
}
```

Running the dotnet command-line tool will show us what you expect:

```
brian@tweezer ~/g/w/s/wasmtime-dotnet> dotnet run
I like soccer and shishkabobs.
```

There are plenty of additional examples on GitHub (*https://oreil.ly/BRKrQ*), including other examples of Wasi integration. There are similar examples available for using .NET with the Wasmer runtime as well. The main point is that WebAssembly can easily be invoked from and interact with a .NET environment. The next use case is a bit of a departure but is still an up-and-coming combination of these technologies.

Blazor

Microsoft has another vision of WebAssembly that aligns with its renewed interest in providing tools and frameworks for developers on all major platforms. The Blazor framework (*https://oreil.ly/13YL1*) allows developers to target the web with interactive components and applications written in C#. Development can be done with a variety of tools on Windows, macOS, and Linux.

Blazor uses the Razor syntax, which is a mashup markup language of HTML and C#. If you think that sounds a bit like soccer and shish kabobs, I agree, but we will see some working examples shortly. The main benefit is that it allows developers to build user interfaces using existing tools and .NET libraries rather than relying on JavaScript user interface frameworks. While those are popular with JavaScript developers, the learning curve is pretty steep compared to a more conventional object-oriented user interface experience.

The applications written with this framework have the option of being deployed either on the server or in the browser. Both modes allow the user interface to be rendered in the browser, but in the first scenario, the main logic is executed on the server. Communication of user interface updates is managed through a SignalR connection (*https://oreil.ly/YJpal*). This is a remote procedure call (RPC) method that allows the server to invoke behavior in JavaScript in the browser via WebSockets, Server-Sent Events, or Long Polling techniques. This is not the use case we will focus on, but it is connected to the larger point I would like to make with respect to this use case. I will return to it soon. This deployment model is visualized in Figure 13-1.

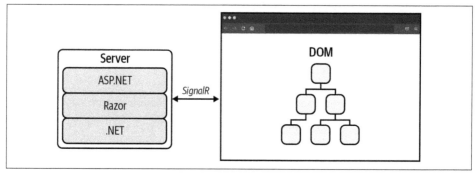

Figure 13-1. Blazor server deployment model

The more relevant scenario is the in-browser deployment model called Blazor WebAssembly. In this scenario the C# and Razor files are compiled into .NET assemblies, which are then downloaded to the browser. The produced artifact is a single-page application (SPA) that runs in the browser and can make changes to what is being displayed locally. Obviously, for this to work the .NET runtime must also be available in the browser, so it too must be downloaded. Local user interface updates

---

are able to affect the DOM directly through JavaScript interoperability. This deployment model is shown in Figure 13-2.

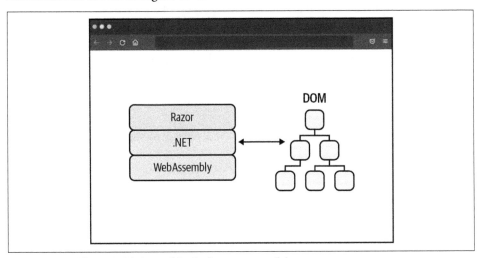

Figure 13-2. Blazor WebAssembly deployment model

It may not be clear how this works, but look no further than the Mono platform mentioned previously. It has been compiled to WebAssembly, therefore code artifacts that run on top of it should work in any environment it does. The size of the .NET runtime is a potential concern for smaller profile devices such as phones and embedded devices, but in general this is a penalty you will pay infrequently, as it is just a dependent web resource and can have cache controls put on it so that it's not a constant bandwidth burden.

We will build a sample application shortly, but for now, consider the Blazor WebAssembly demo site shown in Figure 13-3. This shows a simple stateful counter and a button to manipulate it, as well as some routable components on the left to display other panels in the SPA.

Figure 13-3. Blazor WebAssembly demo website

To get a sense of how this might possibly work, consider the details shown in Figure 13-4. The Mono platform is shown as *mono.wasm*. It is initialized by a companion JavaScript file called *mono.js*, which will look like a variety of bootstrapping JavaScript we have seen throughout the book. Toward the bottom of the image you will see console log details about this bootstrapping process. Even though many of the .NET assemblies are tens to hundreds of kilobytes in size, you will note they are all cached from previous sessions, so they will not need to be refetched.

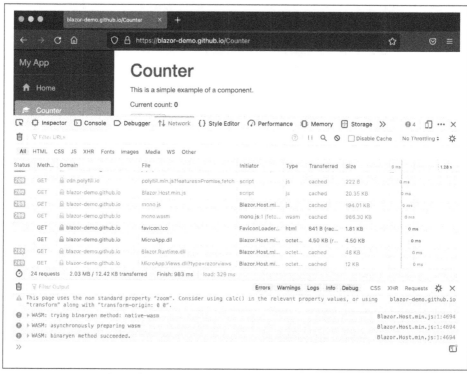

Figure 13-4. Network traffic around the Blazor demo website

Both deployment strategies have their pros and cons. The Blazor server model does not burden the client with downloading a large binary runtime, but it does have the issue of latency in the interactions between the backend and frontend user interface components. That could potentially be problematic on slow and flaky networks or remote clients. The Blazor WebAssembly model does not generally have access to the complete .NET platform to make the runtime download a manageable size. Debugging is also an issue with Blazor WebAssembly for the time being, but that is clearly an issue Microsoft should be able to address given its attitude toward giving developers good tools.

For now, let's generate the Blazor WebAssembly demo scaffolding. Fortunately, we do not need to install anything beyond what we have already used in the previous examples. However, we will be referencing a new template called blazorwasm, which will set us up for this deployment model. If you wanted to create a server-hosted model, you would use blazorserver as your template name:

```
brian@tweezer ~/g/w/s> dotnet new blazorwasm -o blazor-web
The template "Blazor WebAssembly App" was created successfully.
This template contains technologies from parties other than Microsoft,
see https://aka.ms/aspnetcore/5.0-third-party-notices for details.

Processing postcreation actions...
Running 'dotnet restore' on /Users/brian/src/blazor-web/blazor-web.csproj...
  Determining projects to restore...
  Restored /Users/brian/src/blazor-web/blazor-web.csproj (in 4.83 sec).
Restore succeeded.
```

At this point, we have a working application available to us. If we investigate the directory structure, we will see that we are indeed standing on the shoulders of giants. There is an overwhelming amount of code at play behind the scenes to make an otherwise simple application work. The tree command below produces 700 lines of files and directories. Granted, the typical JavaScript framework pulls in an overwhelming amount of dependencies too. You can decide for yourself if the trade-off is worth it, but clearly many organizations will come to the conclusion that it is.

I have removed extraneous lines from the following example to focus on the main files you care about, but if you are feeling adventurous and have tree installed, give it a try.

What remains is a fairly straightforward project. The files that end in *.razor* are the component files. There are several configuration files strewn throughout the directory structure. Several components have custom Cascading Style Sheet (CSS) files to define their styles:

```
brian@tweezer ~/g/w/s/c/blazor-web> tree .
.
├── App.razor
├── Pages
│   ├── Counter.razor
│   ├── FetchData.razor
│   └── Index.razor
├── Program.cs
├── Properties
│   └── launchSettings.json
├── Shared
│   ├── MainLayout.razor
│   ├── MainLayout.razor.css
│   ├── NavMenu.razor
│   ├── NavMenu.razor.css
│   └── SurveyPrompt.razor
```

```
├── _Imports.razor
├── bin
... <======= A bunch of .NET dependencies removed
├── blazor-web.csproj
├── obj
... <======= A bunch of .NET dependencies removed
└── wwwroot
    ├── css
    │   ├── app.css
    │   ├── bootstrap
    │   │   ├── bootstrap.min.css
    │   │   └── bootstrap.min.css.map
    │   └── open-iconic
    │       ├── FONT-LICENSE
    │       ├── ICON-LICENSE
    │       ├── README.md
    │       └── font
    │           ├── css
    │           │   └── open-iconic-bootstrap.min.css
    │           └── fonts
    │               ├── open-iconic.eot
    │               ├── open-iconic.otf
    │               ├── open-iconic.svg
    │               ├── open-iconic.ttf
    │               └── open-iconic.woff
    ├── favicon.ico
    ├── index.html
    └── sample-data
        └── weather.json
```

After the application-specific files and a metric ton of .NET dependencies, we see a directory called *wwwroot*, which represents various assets and resources that will need to be served up to complete the application. This includes fonts, some sample JSON data, and a minimized Bootstrap base for the application.[6]

I cannot give a detailed tutorial on Razor components and everything that goes into them, but I want to walk through the basics of the application to allow you to thread the needle with respect to its functionality. The main views are stored in the *Pages* directory. Shared layouts are stored in the *Shared* directory. The main application file shown in Example 13-6 is in *App.razor* in the main project directory.

Example 13-6. The top-level application component defined in Razor

```
<Router AppAssembly="@typeof(Program).Assembly" PreferExactMatches="@true">
  <Found Context="routeData">
    <RouteView RouteData="@routeData" DefaultLayout="@typeof(MainLayout)" />
```

---

6 Bootstrap (*https://getbootstrap.com*) is an open source stylesheet system that is widely used to produce responsive, mobile-first applications.

```
    </Found>
    <NotFound>
      <LayoutView Layout="@typeof(MainLayout)">
        <p>Sorry, there's nothing at this address.</p>
      </LayoutView>
    </NotFound>
  </Router>
```

This represents high-level details of the application, including the default layout identified as a `MainLayout`. If it is unable to find a working layout, notice it has a default message. This is an SPA we are expecting to be served over HTTP, so we do need a mechanism for routing endpoints to pages. We will see those details shortly.

In Example 13-7, we have the default layout from *Shared/MainLayout.razor*. We can see that it inherits behavior from a `LayoutComponentBase` and has a `NavMenu` in a side bar `<div>` element on the left. This highlights that Razor components mix C# object interactions and HTML layouts. It is a bit of a funky syntax, but once you get used to it, it is not especially onerous.

Example 13-7. The default layout is a shared template

```
@inherits LayoutComponentBase

<div class="page">
  <div class="sidebar">
    <NavMenu />
  </div>

  <div class="main">
    <div class="top-row px-4">
      <a href="http://blazor.net" target="_blank" class="ml-md-auto">About</a>
    </div>

    <div class="content px-4">
      @Body
    </div>
  </div>
</div>
```

By convention, the file *Index.razor* holds the landing page, just like most websites are defined by a file called *index.html*. In Example 13-8, the body of this component will be inserted into the `@Body` location in the `MainLayout` when the default route is invoked.

Example 13-8. The default route points to Index.razor in the Pages directory

```
@page "/"

<h1>Hello, world!</h1>

Welcome to your new app.

<SurveyPrompt Title="How is Blazor working for you?" />
```

We see our first `@page` directive here, which indicates to the main application that default HTTP requests to "/" should point to this rendered page. We see our typical friendly greeting rendered as HTML as well as an embedded component for a survey.

As this page and its assets do need to be served over HTTP, we will start it up using the following command:

```
brian@tweezer ~/g/w/s/blazor-web> dotnet run
Building...
info: Microsoft.Hosting.Lifetime[0]
      Now listening on: https://localhost:5001
info: Microsoft.Hosting.Lifetime[0]
      Now listening on: http://localhost:5000
info: Microsoft.Hosting.Lifetime[0]
      Application started. Press Ctrl+C to shut down.
info: Microsoft.Hosting.Lifetime[0]
      Hosting environment: Development
info: Microsoft.Hosting.Lifetime[0]
      Content root path: /Users/brian/src/blazor-web
```

In Figure 13-5, you will see the generated output if you point your browser to *http://localhost:5000*. If you wish to see all of the .NET assemblies and the runtime loaded, make sure to open up the network view first. Note that if you click on the survey link, it will take you to an actual SurveyMonkey survey!

Routing to a read-only rendered HTML snippet is cool and all, but how about maintaining some state and using nondefault routes? The Counter link on the left in the sidebar will take you to a view rendered from the *Pages/Counter.razor* file shown in Example 13-9.

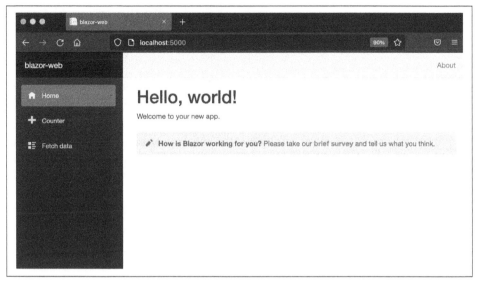

Figure 13-5. Generated Blazor WebAssembly application in action

Example 13-9. A page with stateful fields and interactive UI elements

```
@page "/counter"

<h1>Counter</h1>

<p>Current count: @currentCount</p>

<button class="btn btn-primary" @onclick="IncrementCount">Click me</button>

@code {
  private int currentCount = 0;

  private void IncrementCount()
  {
    currentCount++;
  }
}
```

We see some more interesting behavior in this code sample. First, you will notice the @page directive points to a location other than the default route, so you can imagine setting up multiple views for your SPA. You see some more of the funky syntax, but this time we define a <button> element and the behavior we wish to invoke when the user presses it. In this case, the @onclick hint tells us we want to call a function called IncrementCount on our component. This is defined in the @code block further down, as is the state the component will maintain in a field called currentCount. This is initialized to 0 but is incremented every time the button is pressed.

While you may not choose to embed your components directly in the *.razor* files like this, it is at least possible to do so and makes for a pretty simple effort to get state maintained and reflected in the view. Click on the Counter link and see it in action. Stop the server and try printing out a message to the console using `Console.Write Line` every time the button is pressed. Spend a minute marveling at how far you have come in this book, given our early laments about WebAssembly not supporting strings.

The final thing I want to point out here is the contents of the *Pages/FetchData.razor* file shown in Example 13-10. This includes a bunch of details that you would need to handle for a more useful SPA such as fetching remote data, using conditional logic in the view, and iterating over the data that you have fetched.

Example 13-10. A more sophisticated page with a dependency-injected `HttpClient`

```
@page "/fetchdata"
@inject HttpClient Http

<h1>Weather forecast</h1>

<p>This component demonstrates fetching data from the server.</p>

@if (forecasts == null)
{
  <p><em>Loading...</em></p>
}
else
{
  <table class="table">
    <thead>
      <tr>
        <th>Date</th>
        <th>Temp. (C)</th>
        <th>Temp. (F)</th>
        <th>Summary</th>
      </tr>
    </thead>
    <tbody>
      @foreach (var forecast in forecasts)
      {
        <tr>
          <td>@forecast.Date.ToShortDateString()</td>
          <td>@forecast.TemperatureC</td>
          <td>@forecast.TemperatureF</td>
          <td>@forecast.Summary</td>
        </tr>
      }
    </tbody>
  </table>
```

```
}
@code {
  private WeatherForecast[] forecasts;

  protected override async Task OnInitializedAsync()
  {
    forecasts = await
        Http.GetFromJsonAsync<WeatherForecast[]>("sample-data/weather.json");
  }

  public class WeatherForecast
  {
    public DateTime Date { get; set; }

    public int TemperatureC { get; set; }

    public string Summary { get; set; }

    public int TemperatureF => 32 + (int)(TemperatureC / 0.5556);
  }
}
```

Most of this sample should be pretty clear to developers familiar with C# and .NET functionality. We have handling for an empty initial data set. The code includes a function that returns an asynchronous Task that will be used to fetch the JSON data stored in the *wwwroot/sample-data/weather.json* file. Again, this is technically not part of the application, so it will not be compiled into the assemblies but will instead be served up similarly to the other HTTP resources.

You have seen enough to know that we could import a JavaScript function that would allow us to use an XMLHttpRequest or fetch request to retrieve data. One of the nice things about this use case for integrating WebAssembly, the web, and a platform like .NET is that the platform provides this functionality directly in a convenient mechanism.

Notice the second directive at the top of Example 13-10. This is a dependency injection directive. If you are familiar with container-based frameworks like Spring, you will know this is a declarative way to request an object of the right type be made available on our component. It may not be clear where this object instance is going to come from. If you take a gander at Example 13-11, this is our main program that will initiate the whole process. We highlight where the HttpClient is added to our component.

Example 13-11. The main program for our project

```
using System;
using System.Net.Http;
using System.Collections.Generic;
using System.Threading.Tasks;
using System.Text;
using Microsoft.AspNetCore.Components.WebAssembly.Hosting;
using Microsoft.Extensions.Configuration;
using Microsoft.Extensions.DependencyInjection;
using Microsoft.Extensions.Logging;

namespace blazor_web
{
  public class Program
  {
    public static async Task Main(string[] args)
    {
      var builder = WebAssemblyHostBuilder.CreateDefault(args);
      builder.RootComponents.Add<App>("#app");

      builder.Services.AddScoped(sp
        => new HttpClient {
          BaseAddress = new Uri(builder.HostEnvironment.BaseAddress)
        }); ❶

      await builder.Build().RunAsync();
    }
  }
}
```

❶ The HttpClient instance is added as a scoped component grounded in our deployed context.

As you can see on the indicated line, an instance of the System.Net .Http.HttpClient object is added as a scoped component that is available to be injected into our pages. This way our page component does not need to worry about the life cycle or configuration for this object, we get to reuse the functionality, and we do not have to perform additional configuration to pass an imported function into our code at all.

Even though we have only looked at the scaffolding project generated by the command-line dotnet tool based on a Blazor WebAssembly project, I hope you have a good idea what this use case does for us. We essentially have an environment that benefits from WebAssembly without having to expose it as a prominent feature of the development runtime if you do not want to. The application we are building upon reuses .NET frameworks and components, the Razor syntax, and, as we saw, a bunch of other functionality.

On the one hand, this will give C# developers entrée to a simple way to develop applications that can be deployed to the browser. As one of the optional constraints detailed in Dr. Roy Fielding's thesis, this is a very useful way to extend the behavior of our "universal client."[7]

Developers using .NET have clearly had ways of building web applications, but, like other platforms, they are a mixture of C# (or another .NET language on the backend) and then JavaScript in the browser. We have now opened up a path toward a fairly significant amount of reuse between desktop enterprise applications and those that can now run in a browser. It is not a direct path, but I imagine it will get even better over time, to where you can simply recompile a codebase to target other platforms.

That is when I think this WebAssembly use case will perhaps make an even bigger splash. If the bosses realize that they can have significant reuse from their codebases and help their C# developers have an easier time building web pages, I think there will be a dramatic shift in the frontend technologies used for enterprise applications back to .NET.

Uno Platform

One final use case for WebAssembly and .NET integration deserves mention because it has, surprisingly, even broader reach than the previous example. The Uno Platform (*https://platform.uno*) is a multiplatform development framework for building pixel-perfect applications with C# and WinUI. From a single codebase, you can target Windows, iOS, macOS, Android, Linux, and now, thanks to WebAssembly, the web. This is a radically different prospect than what Blazor promises, even though Blazor-based applications should run in many of these environments in browsers.

The difference is that Uno is targeting native applications as well and making them look identical in every environment. This has been one of the hobgoblins of cross-platform development for my entire career. You either have multiple codebases and target native applications that look suitable for the operating system (e.g., an application looks like a macOS application when running there), or you have a single codebase that looks the same everywhere, and therefore not like a native application. Neither is an ideal situation. You do not want your application to behave differently than the ones users are comfortable with on their main desktop environment, but you also do not want to rebuild an application multiple times.

---

7 While it is incorrect to say Dr. Fielding "invented" REST, his thesis (*https://oreil.ly/hDMxD*) gave formal definitions to many of the ideas that had already been implemented in early web infrastructure. His thesis was an analysis of architectural styles, of which REST is one. It's a very readable thesis and worth your time.

There have been innumerable solutions to the common look-and-feel approach, but most of them look and feel terrible. The ones that are passably attractive and useful are limited to native applications, not running in the browser. This is for reasons that I hope are pretty clear by now. The native libraries that provide the common look and feel are not available in the browser. Even if it were worth the time to emulate using Canvas graphics and WebGL or something similar, the codebases would have to be JavaScript and not C, C++, or C# like the other codebases.

This is what is so compelling about the Uno Platform. Its developers really seem like they have cracked this nut with some solid engineering and abstractions. .NET deserves a big portion of the credit, but WebAssembly is the final piece of the puzzle.

Elsewhere in this book, we have used WebAssembly as the prominent vision for developing our applications. This includes the benefits and limitations that it provides. We have seen a variety of solutions around these limitations with additional tooling, infrastructure, new proposals to extend the platform, and more. With both Blazor WebAssembly and now also with the Uno Platform, WebAssembly is simply a convenient implementation detail. With Blazor, whether you are hosting on the server or in the browser does not materially affect the development style. Both use Razor components and JavaScript interoperability. The server model just uses more of a separation and an independent communication model.

With the Uno Platform, the dominant style, codebase, and abstractions are built around Xamarin, an open source platform that provides cross-platform development targeting Android, iOS, macOS, Linux, or anywhere there is a .NET runtime available.[8] Given the portability of the Mono platform, this is the means of ubiquitous native support.

Xamarin includes a user interface technology called Xamarin.Forms that builds upon XAML component binding. Uno does not use this part of Xamarin, but instead focuses on WinUI-based applications. WinUI is a modern user interface toolkit also built upon XAML that provides Fluent Design,[9] accessible applications, and other modern application development techniques.

In Figure 13-6, you can see the high-level architecture of the Uno Platform. On Windows, it is understandably a native platform for these technologies. When targeting iOS, Android, and macOS, the Uno Platform uses Xamarin native libraries with WinUI, a combination supported by the .NET 5 and .NET 6 platforms. On Linux, it does something cool with the Skia library,[10] which is also WebAssembly-friendly

---

8 Xamarin (*https://oreil.ly/rHApx*) is a cool platform in and of itself, but without WebAssembly, it cannot target the browser in the same way.

9 Fluent Design is a design language from Microsoft introduced in 2017 to target modern UI systems.

10 Skia (*https://skia.org*) is a nice cross-platform, open source, 2D graphics library.

(*https://oreil.ly/6gCyO*). And, finally, because the Mono runtime has been compiled to WebAssembly and is available in-browser as you have seen, it is the basis of the strategy to target browsers.

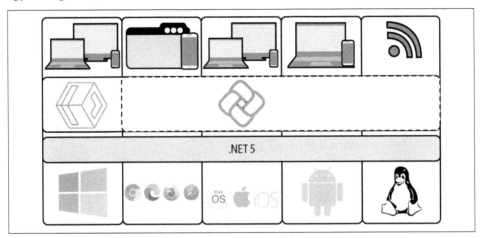

Figure 13-6. The Uno Platform architecture

Once again, there is a tremendous amount of engineering that has gone into providing a pixel-perfect cross-platform solution with this remarkable scope. My main interest is to let you know about this use case and let you investigate it for your own needs, so I will leave it to you to explore the Uno Platform. As incentive, however, I want to point out some examples of it in action that I think will underscore the value proposition.

First, the NuGet Package Explorer (NPE), originally a .NET 6–based Windows Presentation Foundation (WPF) application, has been ported to a Progressive Web Application (PWA) on the WebAssembly target. This is an application that had been downloaded hundreds of thousands of times as a native application. It is now not only available as a web application, but it also runs with a consistent look and feel across all the various platforms Uno supports. You can see the NPE in action in Figure 13-7 and give it a shot yourself (*https://nuget.info*).

The Uno Platform Playground (*https://oreil.ly/olc6U*) is another great way to get more comfortable with the combination of technologies and how they come together. There are a significant number of examples for you to explore via the snippets menu. Figure 13-8 shows the Cards example, which includes a ListView XAML element populated by elegant-looking cards.

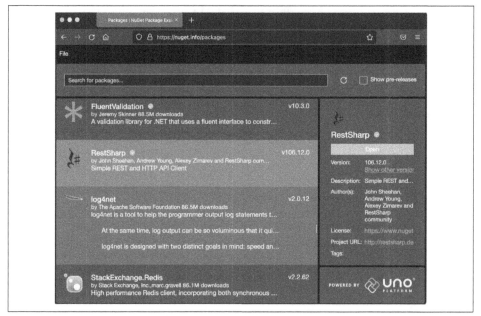

Figure 13-7. The NuGet Package Explorer running in Firefox on macOS

Figure 13-8. The Uno Platform Playground

Finally, Figure 13-9 shows a more complicated example of a Uno-based ray tracer and the rendered output. Not only is it a more sophisticated application that produces slick results, but it is also a way of comparing the relative performance for ray tracing in different languages and runtime environments.[11]

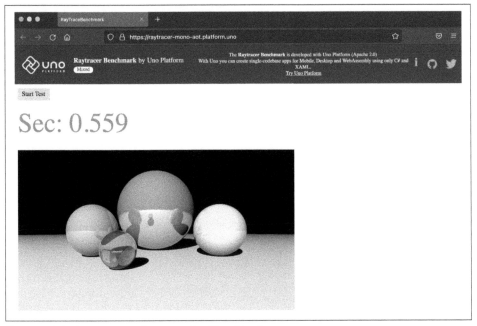

Figure 13-9. A ray tracer demo on the Uno Platform

There is clearly a lot more that could be said about the integration of the two independent but powerful platforms of .NET and WebAssembly. There are some new books emerging on the topic that I encourage you to check out, but I have also tried to provide you with several places to find working projects and code examples for your own explorations.

In this chapter, we have seen exciting results that I think portend coming shifts in our industry. At a minimum, it shows how C# developers can stick with the language they know and love and be effective at building applications that run in a variety of places without having to rely solely on JavaScript in the frontend. In the next chapter, we will see a way to make it easier for JavaScript and TypeScript developers to benefit from WebAssembly as well.

---

11 The RayTracer app (*https://oreil.ly/LHpnv*) and GitHub repo (*https://oreil.ly/giGAc*) are both available online.

## CHAPTER 14

Using AssemblyScript and WebAssembly

There's something strange going on tonight
There's something going on that's not quite right
Joey's nervous and the lights are bright
There's something going on that's not quite right
    —Wire, "Strange"

It is getting harder for me to make cultural references that the general populace gets. There is a good chance that many of the people reading this book will not recognize this song, but it is still important to reference the classics. For those of you cultured enough[1] to recognize the aforementioned song as an R.E.M. song on the *Document* album,[2] you may be surprised to learn it is a cover. The original was done by the band Wire. If you listen to the original, your reaction to this might be that something strange is going on, just like the song says. It is both familiar and not at the same time.

In this chapter, I am going to introduce a language called AssemblyScript that might prompt the same reaction. It is a Binaryen-based compiler that turns a subset of TypeScript into WebAssembly. It is obviously similar to TypeScript (which is, in turn, similar to JavaScript), but upon closer inspection, something strange is going on here, too. Still, it fits a different use case for WebAssembly and shows you how versatile this platform can be.

---

1 Also known as old.

2 Seriously, this is a classic album.

TypeScript is a popular superset of JavaScript that transpiles[3] to regular JavaScript so that it will run anywhere JavaScript will. Its main purpose is to express your intent using a strongly typed language to minimize the kind of annoying and rampant type errors that fill the average JavaScript codebase. As such, even though it uses a compiler, its goal is more about safety than performance.

If you have not used a strongly typed language before, the idea may seem to be more of a burden than a benefit. To be fair, some developers do feel that way. However, a type system–focused language defines the meaning and operations that apply to different types. A compiler enforces that you only attempt to invoke operations on the types that define them so you do not end up with runtime errors. Consequently, strongly typed systems help you produce software that is more correct, immutable, encapsulated, composable, and, often, readable. This is not to say that you cannot do the same with loosely typed systems, you just have less assistance when you try to do so.

TypeScript was developed at Microsoft as a response to its increased use of browsers to deliver its office application suites and other business systems. While individual applications in JavaScript can be easily developed, complex, high-performance suites of applications present challenges once they grow past a certain size. TypeScript was an attempt to solve some of those growth issues while still staying within the vibrant JavaScript ecosystem.

As a simple example, Example 14-1 shows us a TypeScript snippet that defines a function. Notice that the parameter is typed as a `string`. Idiomatically, it is used just like a piece of regular JavaScript.

Example 14-1. Basic TypeScript example

```
// src/greeter.ts
function greeter(person: string) {
  return "Hello, " + person;
}
let user = "Mannequin Skywalker";
document.body.textContent = greeter(user);
```

Browsers and host environments such as Node.js and Deno do not execute TypeScript, however. The compiler will transpile it into regular JavaScript:

```
brian@tweezer ~/s/t/hello-ts> tsc src/greeter.ts
brian@tweezer ~/s/t/hello-ts> ls -alF src
total 32
drwxr-xr-x  6 brian  staff  192 Jan 14 17:17 ./
```

---

3 Transpilation (*https://oreil.ly/8ObGO*) is the process of translating one source codebase into another codebase, as opposed to a binary executable (compilation).

```
drwxr-xr-x  8 brian  staff  256 Jan 14 16:55 ../
-rw-r--r--  1 brian  staff  125 Jan 14 17:19 greeter.js
-rw-r--r--  1 brian  staff  135 Jan 14 17:19 greeter.ts
```

You will have to look a little closely at the generated JavaScript to tell the difference. In Example 14-2, you can see that all that has really happened is that the type has been removed.

Example 14-2. JavaScript generated from TypeScript

```
// src/greeter.js
function greeter(person) {
  return "Hello, " + person;
}
var user = "Mannequin Skywalker";
document.body.textContent = greeter(user);
```

So, what is the big deal? Why do we put the type there just to take it away? The benefit of adding the type is that the compiler can catch errors. By ensuring your code is not used wrongly (to the best of its ability), the overall correctness and quality of the software should improve. We see such an error in Example 14-3, which would not be detected until runtime in JavaScript.

Example 14-3. A type error in TypeScript

```
// src/greeter.ts
function greeter(person: string) {
  return "Hello, " + person;
}
let user = [0, 1, 2];
document.body.textContent = greeter(user);
```

The TypeScript compiler is easily able to stop this mistake from happening at compile time, a much better time to find errors!

```
brian@tweezer ~/s/t/hello-ts> tsc src/greeter.ts
src/greeter.ts:7:37 - error TS2345: Argument of type 'number[]' is not assignable
to parameter of type 'string'.
7 document.body.textContent = greeter(user);
                                      ~~~~
Found 1 error.
```

Even better, TypeScript-aware development environments will be able to flag the error as soon as you enter the code. VS Code from Microsoft and other popular IDEs have nice support for developer assistance using this language.

"Definitely Not a TypeScript to WebAssembly Compiler"

This section header is a direct quotation from the AssemblyScript GitHub page. It is part of an attempt to be clear about the role it plays and that it will not be possible to simply compile a typical TypeScript codebase to WebAssembly. That being said, AssemblyScript is an attempt to provide a JavaScript-like (and, more to the point, TypeScript-like) experience but with the performance and security WebAssembly offers. It is largely considered a useful way of building higher-performance Web-based applications without having to rely on C, C++, or Rust. It should be a relatively straightforward transition for existing Web developers to move into and benefit from this platform.

First of all, AssemblyScript does not run as JavaScript; it runs as WebAssembly. The compiler generates WebAssembly modules, which should effectively work like other modules we have seen. There are some cool features that you will see shortly, however, for allocating memory in your module's `Memory` instances, passing strings back and forth between JavaScript host environments and Wasm modules, and more.

Unfortunately, while I did attempt to teach you some C in the C-based chapters and Rust in the Rust-based chapters, I do not really have the space to teach you much TypeScript and then tell you how AssemblyScript is different. So, I will assume that you know TypeScript and will tell you briefly how AssemblyScript differs before showing some basic examples.[4]

First, while TypeScript does enforce types, it has `any` and `undefined` for better compatibility with untyped JavaScript. AssemblyScript does not support either of these types. Another difference is the lack of `union` types, one of my favorite features of TypeScript.

Because AssemblyScript is compiled into Wasm, it has no ability to do anything with network connections, filesystem access, or DOM manipulation, just like any other module. Those have to be provided through import objects or through WASI, as you will see momentarily.

AssemblyScript lives close to the WebAssembly instruction set we have seen throughout the book. The numeric types are basically what you would imagine them to be, including `i32`, `i64`, `f32`, `f64`, and `usize`, which is used for indexing memory. As the MVP version of WebAssembly supports 32-bit addressing, that currently corresponds with the `i32` type.

---

4 There are several great tutorials and walkthroughs for learning TypeScript on its website (*https://www.type scriptlang.org*).

In addition, there is currently no support for implementing interfaces, closures, exceptions, or access modifiers for classes (public, private, or protected). The good news is that most of these limitations will be overcome eventually. Some of them can be addressed directly by future versions of the AssemblyScript compiler, while others will rely on the WebAssembly platform to evolve.

There are additional differences, but rather than spending any more time focusing on how they are different (there are better documentation resources online), let's see something positive and look at AssemblyScript in action.

Simple Example

By now you should not be surprised that our first example will be to add two numbers together. It is usually the simplest thing we can show in WebAssembly before things get weird. You will see just such a starter example in Example 14-4.

Example 14-4. The ubiquitous code to add two integers together

```
export function add(a: i32, b: i32): i32 {
 return a + b;
}
```

If you have installed the AssemblyScript compiler as detailed in the Appendix, then you should be able to run the following command:

```
brian@tweezer ~/g/w/s/ch14> asc hello.ts -b hello.wasm
brian@tweezer ~/g/w/s/ch14> ls -alF
total 98560
drwxr-xr-x   7 brian  staff       224 Jul 18 15:39 ./
drwxr-xr-x  13 brian  staff       416 Jul 14 11:52 ../
-rw-r--r--   1 brian  staff        62 Jul 18 15:39 hello.ts
-rw-r--r--   1 brian  staff        91 Jul 18 15:39 hello.wasm
```

One of the things that should jump out at you is how small the Wasm module is. Obviously there is not a ton of functionality there yet, but there is also very little overhead. Calling on the services of our exploratory tools shows us what else is going on:

```
brian@tweezer ~/g/w/s/ch14> wasm-objdump -x hello.wasm

hello.wasm:     file format wasm 0x1

Section Details:

Type[1]:
 - type[0] (i32, i32) -> i32
Function[1]:
 - func[0] sig=0 <add>
Table[1]:
```

```
  - table[0] type=funcref initial=1
Memory[1]:
  - memory[0] pages: initial=0
Global[3]:
  - global[0] i32 mutable=0 - init i32=8
  - global[1] i32 mutable=1 - init i32=16392
  - global[2] i32 mutable=0 - init i32=16392
Export[2]:
  - func[0] <add> -> "add"
  - memory[0] -> "memory"
Elem[1]:
  - segment[0] flags=0 table=0 count=0 - init i32=1
Code[1]:
  - func[0] size=7 <add>
```

Unless you tell it otherwise, the AssemblyScript compiler will generate a Memory instance and export it for you automatically. Notice that the compiler has also exported our function just by adorning the function with the keyword export. This makes it easy to use these compiled functions from JavaScript.

If we use our simple *utils.js* file from before and a simple HTML scaffolding like Example 14-5, we should see what we expect to see in the JavaScript console. There are good tools for generating more elaborate scaffolding for AssemblyScript projects, but I want to keep things simple for the time being.

Example 14-5. Simple HTML to load our AssemblyScript-based Wasm module

```
<!doctype html>
<html lang="en">
  <head>
    <meta charset="utf-8">
    <link rel="stylesheet" href="bootstrap.min.css">
    <title>Basic AssemblyScript</title>
    <script src="utils.js"></script>
  </head>
  <body>
    <script>
      fetchAndInstantiate('hello.wasm').then(function(instance) {
          console.log(instance.exports.add(12, 30));
      });
    </script>
  </body>
</html>
```

In addition to making it easier to export functions from Wasm modules, Assembly-Script also makes it easy to import functionality for the module to call into its Java-Script environment. In Example 14-6, you can see we are expressing an intent to import a function called log() by using the declare keyword.

Example 14-6. Declaring functions for import to AssemblyScript

```
declare function log(num: i32): void;

export function addAndLog(a: i32, b: i32): void {
  log(a + b);
}
```

You still have to provide the expected function as a function on an imported object as per usual, but the syntax for declaring it is much simpler. Note the namespace convention in Example 14-7.

Example 14-7. HTML that provides our expected imported function

```
<!doctype html>
<html lang="en">
  <head>
    <meta charset="utf-8">
    <link rel="stylesheet" href="bootstrap.min.css">
    <title>Importing JavaScript Functions to AssemblyScript</title>
    <script src="utils.js"></script>
  </head>
  <body>
    <script>
      var importObject = {
        hello: {
          log: value => console.log(value)
        }
      };

      fetchAndInstantiate('hello.wasm', importObject).then(function(instance) {
        instance.exports.addAndLog(12, 30);
      });
    </script>
  </body>
</html>
```

An AssemblyScript module named `hello.wasm` will expect a namespace of `hello` to be available in the imported object. You can verify this by checking out what the module expresses in its `Import` section:

```
brian@tweezer ~/g/w/s/c/hello-imp> wasm-objdump -x hello.wasm
hello.wasm:     file format wasm 0x1

Section Details:

Type[2]:
 - type[0] (i32) -> nil
 - type[1] (i32, i32) -> nil
Import[1]:
```

```
 - func[0] sig=0 <hello.log> <- hello.log
Function[1]:
 - func[1] sig=1 <addAndLog>
Table[1]:
 - table[0] type=funcref initial=1
Memory[1]:
 - memory[0] pages: initial=0
Global[3]:
 - global[0] i32 mutable=0 - init i32=8
 - global[1] i32 mutable=1 - init i32=16392
 - global[2] i32 mutable=0 - init i32=16392
Export[2]:
 - func[1] <addAndLog> -> "addAndLog"
 - memory[0] -> "memory"
Elem[1]:
 - segment[0] flags=0 table=0 count=0 - init i32=1
Code[1]:
 - func[1] size=9 <addAndLog>
```

One final thing that the AssemblyScript compiler does is to make it pretty easy to work with a module's Memory instance.[5] As I mentioned previously, unless you tell it not to, the compiler will create a Memory instance for your module. In Example 14-8, we grow this memory by a page to make sure we have 64K of memory to play with (although we will not need anywhere near that much, it is the minimum size we can request).

Example 14-8. AssemblyScript and Memory instance manipulation

```
memory.grow(1);

store<u8>(0, 100);

export function whereToStore(): i32 {
  let basePtr = load<u8>(0);
  return basePtr;
}

export function readFromLocation(loc: i32): i32 {
  let value = load<u8>(loc);
  return value;
}
```

After we guarantee some space to use, we write a location into the 0th position. We then have two functions exported to our JavaScript host environment. One reports the current location to write to, while the other gives you the ability to read from a

---

5 This example and others were inspired by the website (*https://oreil.ly/AxavX*) by Aaron Turner (@torch2424), who is a talented, generous developer and a badass DJ too. Check him out.

specified location. The methods load<T>() and store<T>() are convenient wrappers around the actual low-level WebAssembly instructions that provide similar behavior.

As you know and will see again shortly, we could manipulate the memory buffer directly. I just wanted to show you some options on both sides. A more sophisticated example might give the ability to write memory to the next available location and autoincrement the location.

There is an example of using this functionality from JavaScript in Example 14-9.

Example 14-9. Interacting with Memory

```
<!doctype html>
<html lang="en">
  <head>
    <meta charset="utf-8">
    <title>AssemblyScript and Wasm Memory</title>
    <script src="utils.js"></script>
  </head>
  <body>
    <script>
      fetchAndInstantiate('mem.wasm').then(function(instance) {
        var mem = instance.exports.memory;
        var u8Arr = new Uint8Array(mem.buffer);

        let location = instance.exports.whereToStore();
        u8Arr[location] = 123;

        let value = instance.exports.readFromLocation(location);
        console.log("Round-tripped value: " + value);
      });
    </script>
  </body>
</html>
```

We do wrap the Memory instance's buffer with a typed array. We invoke the whereTo Store() function and then write into our Uint8Array at that location. Next we pass that location into the readFromLocation() function exported from our module, which loads the value stored at the default location. Happily, when printed to the console, the value is what we expect, 123.

Garbage Collection and the AssemblyScript Runtime

One of the big holes in the WebAssembly MVP platform is a garbage collection capability. Languages like C/C++ and Rust do not need it, but other higher languages will. There is a proposal working its way through the standards process, but until it is available through the platform, various projects are creating shims and add-on support.[6]

If you are unfamiliar with the concept of garbage collection, it is the automated cleanup of allocated resources when they are no longer necessary. C and C++ require you to call `malloc()` and `free()` (or `new()` and `delete()`), so there is nothing really automated about the process. Rust has strict memory ownership guidelines, as you saw in Chapter 10, so that it knows when values go out of scope lexically and can then clean things up. These two approaches represent trade-offs of low overhead, but they are dangerous if you mess them up or heavy-handed but safe. Python uses reference counting to know when memory can be freed. Other languages such as Java and JavaScript use garbage collection and track memory references through a variety of sophisticated but time-consuming algorithms. Part of what has kept Java as a bit player in the embedded computing space is that these algorithms can kick in unpredictably and block other processing from happening. This is unacceptable for high-precision devices used for medical or industrial safety purposes. As always, there are trade-offs everywhere.

AssemblyScript added a garbage collection capability as of version 0.18. I will demonstrate a more convenient way of interacting with it in a later section via the Loader. But for now I just want to mention it because you can use it directly if you tell the AssemblyScript compiler to export access to the runtime with the `--exportRuntime` directive. Not only that, you have the option of controlling the behavior of the runtime by using the `--runtime` parameter. This allows you to specify whether it should use an incremental, minimal, stub, or even a custom pluggable implementation.

I think a deep introduction to this process is outside of the scope of this chapter, but could be useful depending on what you attempt to do with AssemblyScript.[7]

I did want you to know about its existence, though, and to make you aware that it is possible to allocate memory from a module's exported `Memory` instance, as well as pin and unpin references that point into it so that they will or will not be collected by other processes. We will see some examples of using these abilities next.

AssemblyScript Standard Library

Another nice addition to AssemblyScript's ecosystem is a standard library of structures and functionality that you would expect from a modern programming infrastructure. As we have seen, WebAssembly requires these common functions to

---

6 This proposal requires the completion of several other proposals first, as indicated in Chapter 12, but you can read more about it on GitHub (*https://oreil.ly/cFJ8f*).

7 You can find more details about what is provided with the AssemblyScript Garbage Collector support online (*https://oreil.ly/3zb1s*).

---

be provided by the host environment through import objects or more generally through WASI capabilities. This library (*https://oreil.ly/i1gJP*) has support for math functions, dates, string manipulation, and more.

As a simple example, we will build a set of functions for calculating details of a circle based on its radius. In Example 14-10, we have three exported functions for calculating the diameter (2r), circumference (2πr), and area (πr²).[8] Because AssemblyScript defaults to f64 numbers, we cast them to f32 numbers before returning the values from the functions.

Example 14-10. AssemblyScript that uses the Standard Library

```
export function diameter(radius: f32): f32 {
  let diam = <f32>(2.0 * radius);
  return diam;
}

export function circumference(radius: f32): f32 {
  let circ = <f32>(2.0 * Math.PI * radius);
  return circ;
}

export function area(radius: f32): f32 {
  let area = <f32>(Math.PI * Math.pow(radius, 2));
  return area;
}
```

In Example 14-11, we instantiate our module and invoke the functionality. While it would obviously be faster to just do this simple math in JavaScript, more sophisticated calculations benefit from having this functionality available within the module definition so that we do not have to manually request such functionality from within our AssemblyScript algorithms.

Example 14-11. Invoking AssemblyScript that uses the Standard Library from JavaScript

```
<!doctype html>
<html lang="en">
  <head>
    <meta charset="utf-8">
    <title>AssemblyScript Standard Library</title>
    <script src="utils.js"></script>
  </head>
  <body>
    <script>
      fetchAndInstantiate('stdlib.wasm').then(function(instance) {
```

---

8 While it is commonly believed that π are squared, it isn't true. π are round. Cornbread are squared.

```
        let diameter = instance.exports.diameter(2.0);
        console.log("Diameter of a circle for a radius 2.0: " + diameter);
        let circumference = instance.exports.circumference(2.0);
        console.log("Circumference of a circle for a radius of 2.0: "
          + circumference);
        let area = instance.exports.area(2.0);
        console.log("Area of a circle for a radius of 2.0: " + area);
      });
    </script>
  </body>
</html>
```

If everything is as it should be, you should see the following printed out to your Java-Script console when you serve the HTML to the browser over HTTP:

```
Diameter of a circle for a radius 2.0: 4
Circumference of a circle for a radius of 2.0: 12.566370964050293
Area of a circle for a radius of 2.0: 12.566370964050293
```

AssemblyScript Loader

To move beyond the basics, we are going to rely on an existing example from the AssemblyScript Examples GitHub repo. It provides many of the talking points I wish to wrap up with, so I figured it was just as easy to use it as the basis of the next couple of examples.

To start off with, clone the repository. We are going to focus on the *loader* directory, but please check out the other examples, which include fun uses of graphics, N-body simulators, and more:

```
brian@tweezer ~/git-others> git clone ↵
    https://github.com/AssemblyScript/examples.git as-examples
Cloning into 'as-examples'...
remote: Enumerating objects: 261, done.
remote: Counting objects: 100% (261/261), done.
remote: Compressing objects: 100% (163/163), done.
remote: Total 261 (delta 110), reused 215 (delta 72), pack-reused 0
Receiving objects: 100% (261/261), 553.00 KiB | 3.87 MiB/s, done.
Resolving deltas: 100% (110/110), done.
brian@tweezer ~/git-others> cd as-examples/
brian@tweezer ~/g/as-examples> ls
LICENSE      game-of-life interference loader      n-body      transform
README.md    i64          libm         mandelbrot  sdk
brian@tweezer ~/g/as-examples> cd loader
```

Once you are in the *loader* directory, install the dependencies and then run the *asbuild* script (defined in the *packages.json* file). This will create both optimized and unoptimized, debuggable versions of the AssemblyScript code we will focus on with support for the runtime (because of the --exportRuntime directive):

```
brian@tweezer ~/g/a/loader> npm install

added 4 packages, and audited 5 packages in 1s

1 package is looking for funding
  run `npm fund` for details

found 0 vulnerabilities
brian@tweezer ~/g/a/loader> npm run asbuild

> @assemblyscript/loader-example@1.0.0 asbuild
> npm run asbuild:untouched && npm run asbuild:optimized

> @assemblyscript/loader-example@1.0.0 asbuild:untouched
> asc assembly/index.ts -b build/untouched.wasm -t build/untouched.wat
    --exportRuntime --sourceMap --debug

> @assemblyscript/loader-example@1.0.0 asbuild:optimized
> asc assembly/index.ts -b build/optimized.wasm -t build/optimized.wat
    --exportRuntime --sourceMap --optimize
```

The AssemblyScript code is located in the *assembly/index.ts* file. To keep things manageable here, I will only show you some of the important snippets. Example 14-12 shows us a surprisingly trivial way of sharing strings back and forth between WebAssembly and a JavaScript host environment. We are not going to be running in the browser, but there are similar mechanisms for making this work too.

Example 14-12. AssemblyScript that uses WebAssembly strings

```
// see: tests/index.js "Test for Example 1"

export function getHello(): string {
  return "Hello world (I am a WebAssembly string)";
}
```

Pause and consider what is going on. AssemblyScript is defining a string as a literal. This string will be allocated and initialized in WebAssembly linear memory. All those details we puzzled over in Chapter 4 seem like a distant memory at this point.

Example 14-13 is taken from *test/index.js*. At the top of this file we load in the modules and then extract elements of the exported runtime. This includes the ability to initialize strings and arrays, pin the pointers so they will not be garbage collected, and pass values back and forth. I hinted at this capability in the previous discussion about garbage collection.

Example 14-13. Setting up the use of WebAssembly strings in JavaScript

```
// Load the node module exporting our WebAssembly module
const myModule = require("../index");

// Obtain the runtime helpers for
const {
  // memory management
  __newString, __newArray,
  // garbage collection
  __pin, __unpin,
  // and interop
  __getString, __getArray, __getArrayView
} = myModule;
```

Example 14-14 finally represents the first test. The string returned from our module's getHello() method will be allocated in our module's Memory instance. The location of this string in memory is managed by the runtime, but we are able to pin it to keep it from being garbage collected. The __getString() method will go through the motions of wrapping the underlying buffer and converting the string into a usable JavaScript string.

Example 14-14. Using the exported runtime for working with WebAssembly strings

```
// Test for Example 1: Passing a string from WebAssembly to JavaScript.
{
  console.log("Example 1:");

  // Obtain a pointer to our string in the module's memory.
  const ptr = __pin(myModule.getHello());

  // Print its contents
  console.log("  " + __getString(ptr));

  __unpin(ptr); // it is ok if the string becomes garbage collected now
}
```

If you have a strong stomach and a bold spirit, you can investigate the loader's implementation details (briefly shown in Example 14-15), including this function, by checking out the file *node_modules/@assemblyscript/loader/index.js*. It may surprise you, but you should be mostly comfortable with what is going on, given where we have been so far in this book.

Example 14-15. Window into the details of the AssemblyScript loader

...

```
/** Reads a string from the module's memory by its pointer. */
function __getString(ptr) {
  if (!ptr) return null;
  const buffer = memory.buffer;
  const id = new Uint32Array(buffer)[ptr + ID_OFFSET >>> 2];
  if (id !== STRING_ID) throw Error(`not a string: ${ptr}`);
  return getStringImpl(buffer, ptr);
}

extendedExports.__getString = __getString;
...
```

AssemblyScript decodes these strings into UTF-16 strings through functions like get
StringImpl(), shown in Example 14-16. It is slightly above the __getString()
method in the *index.js* file. It, in turn, uses elements of the AssemblyScript Standard
Library for string manipulation.

*Example 14-16. Decoding Memory references using UTF-16 and AssemblyScript's
Standard Library*

```
...
/** Gets a string from memory. */
function getStringImpl(buffer, ptr) {
  let len = new Uint32Array(buffer)[ptr + SIZE_OFFSET >>> 2] >>> 1;
  const wtf16 = new Uint16Array(buffer, ptr, len);
  if (len <= STRING_SMALLSIZE) return String.fromCharCode(...wtf16);
  try {
    return utf16.decode(wtf16);
  } catch {
    let str = "", off = 0;
    while (len - off > STRING_CHUNKSIZE) {
      str += String.fromCharCode(...wtf16.subarray(off, off += STRING_CHUNKSIZE));
    }
    return str + String.fromCharCode(...wtf16.subarray(off));
  }
}
...
```

I am not going to show you all of the details, but I wanted to show you a little bit
about what was going on behind the curtain. First of all, you have been exposed to a
lot of these details. Secondly, AssemblyScript, the compiler, and the Loader shield you
from a lot of this complexity so you can just focus on the expression of your code.
WebAssembly has some fairly primitive instructions, but relying on high-level tools

can keep us from having to deal with the annoying fiddly bits that we started off with in the earlier chapters.

If you run the tests, you will see the first output from Example 14-14 in the output. Test 2 does something similar but from the other direction, passing JavaScript strings in so they are converted into WebAssembly strings. There is another neat trick at play in the file *myConsole.ts* that allows us to log back to the JavaScript console seamlessly. I will let you dig into the details on your own:

```
Example 1:
  Hello world (I am a WebAssembly string)
```

The other tests and examples do similar round trips for arrays and classes. Overall, these examples highlight the sweet spot that AssemblyScript fills. There is no single use case that makes WebAssembly make sense. We have talked about reusing existing libraries and writing low-level code in portable ways using Rust or C for performance reasons.

If you have mostly been a JavaScript developer all of your professional life, it is going to be a tall order to suddenly learn a language like that. AssemblyScript brings a slightly strange but still much more familiar language that you largely already know. It allows you to compile it down to potentially higher-performance code. That is a nice additional use case indeed.

## CHAPTER 15

Applied WebAssembly: In the Cloud and on the Edge

I've looked at clouds from both sides now
From up and down and still somehow
It's cloud illusions I recall
I really don't know clouds at all
    —Joni Mitchell, "Both Sides Now"

Given the popularity and ubiquity of cloud computing initiatives these days, it may seem odd to start this chapter with a quotation about not understanding clouds. If we are being honest, I think that it is fair to say that a lot of people do not understand the full scope of cloud computing. There is the obvious speed improvement and ease of spinning up instances, in contrast to the often untenable scenario of procuring physical hardware systems. But having everything in the cloud is just as silly of a strategy as having nothing in the cloud.

The real driver of your thinking about cloud strategy should not just be procurement and developer productivity, even though those are important considerations. A more general idea is to consider the cost of computation. This is a more complex calculation than it may seem, though, in terms of what I mean by both "cost" and "computation." In this chapter, I am going to focus on how where we run our computation is changing rapidly and why WebAssembly is going to be a key part of that.

A Short, Personal Detour

Earlier in my career, I was one of the first employees at a company called Parabon.[1] We built an internet-distributed computing platform to aggregate idle time on computers all over the world. Keep in mind this was pre-cloud. In addition to porting our engine with its Java-based core for safety to eight platforms, we also built the client APIs, the server infrastructure for scheduling the work, and a half-dozen or more vertical applications to use it. The kind of jobs we ran included gene sequence comparisons that scaled linearly, genetic algorithm-based feature selection for exhaustive regression searches, and a Monte Carlo–based rendering system.

The whole point of this initiative was to find arbitrage opportunities in computational capacity. Organizations did not buy enough computing power for their peak needs, and therefore there were ceilings on what they could tackle computationally. We gave them an elastic capability for one class of problem known as "embarrassingly parallel" problems (*https://oreil.ly/wfSA0*). Customers could ask for as many or as few computational resources as they needed to solve a particular problem. This gave them a knob to turn to incur marginal costs based on their needs.

When doing exhaustive searches, that allowed them to include more features than they normally had the resources to analyze. This was helpful in one case to a pharmaceutical company to find out why a certain therapy only worked for some patients and not others. Another example of a good match was a NASA consultant who was able to speed up his simulations from taking nine months on equipment he had access to under normal circumstances to four or five hours on our platform. In order to achieve the portability across the various operating systems and the protection we promised to our computation providers, he had to port his code from Fortran to Java. While Fortran could run circles around the upstart language from Sun at the time in a direct competition, we would make it up with parallelization.

Even with the limitation of the embarrassingly parallel problem constraint, given where things were with broadband rollout at the time, data-intensive tasks such as the digital rendering were not good fits for our platform. The compute-to-data ratio was too low. It cost too much in terms of time and bandwidth to get the data where it needed to be. What we were fundamentally offering was a form of computational intermediation. Even at the time, I felt like more was needed to really provide the most value, but cloud computing had not emerged yet to give us a fuller vision of resource virtualization.

---

[1] These days, Parabon (*https://oreil.ly/sYyvr*) focuses on the intersection of computation and DNA for next-generation therapies and forensic tools, such as those used for solving cold cases. There was a popular television show based on its work with CeCe Moore called *The Genetic Detective*.

Another work experience that drove my thinking was my time in the video game industry. I worked on a game that was based on another game that had 40 million users, so we were pretty sure we were going to need to scale up. Putting everything into the cloud would have been cost prohibitive, however, so we ran a mix of data center equipment that we purchased and set up and then used cloud services as an elastic spillover. Again, we were able to use the extra resources only when we needed them and did not have to pay for them to be running all the time.

Our Industry Evolves

With that background in place, when I talk about the "cost" of computation, I mean the time cost, the money cost, the opportunity cost of not having elastic supply, the power consumption cost, and the latency cost. These are all costs that we are trying to minimize these days. Cloud computing is one part of the strategy, but so are architectural designs such as microservices and serverless functions. Apple's M1 designs are another. There are two CPUs in the M1 chip, one that is more performance-oriented and one that is more power consumption–oriented. Researchers are analyzing sophisticated approaches for using machine learning strategies to order LLVM optimizations to either maximize performance or minimize power consumption. The application code does not change, just its compiled form.

Where and how we engage computational elements to solve problems has become one of the most important aspects of a successful IT strategy. This includes advanced and custom hardware such as vectorizing CPU instructions,[2] graphics processing units (GPUs), field-programmable gate arrays (FPGAs),[3] application-specific integrated circuits (ASICs),[4] and Tensor Processing Units (TPUs).[5] Each of these types of hardware has different capabilities, instructions, costs, and performance characteristics. Mapping workloads to these elements is going to be a big part of getting computation done in ways that minimize a range of costs.

Physical location is another element of cost, because latency is, as you know, something we cannot discount.[6] If you are familiar with the concept of cloud regions or the use of a content delivery network (CDN) to serve up static resources, you will understand the benefit of getting things closer to where your users are. Domain Name

---

2 This includes technologies such as Advanced Vector Extensions (AVX) (*https://oreil.ly/k9QE7*) and Streaming SIMD Extensions (SSE) (*https://oreil.ly/KvLtD*).

3 FPGAs (*https://oreil.ly/sf55T*) allow software programs to be written to the hardware as needed.

4 ASICs (*https://oreil.ly/ZHn2P*) represent high-performance, low-energy, single-use computing elements.

5 Google developed TPUs (*https://oreil.ly/qwDSE*) to be deployed as needed with consumer-facing applications that need performance boosts.

6 The fallacies of distributed computing (*https://oreil.ly/IRUp0*) are worth memorizing.

System (DNS) trickery allows an endpoint to be selected dynamically based upon the geographic region a user is coming from.

Edge computing is an emerging service offering that takes these ideas a step further to mix together the ideas of distributed computing (à la Parabon), cloud hosting, and geographically distributed resources. The difference is that we are no longer simply talking about static resources, but executable code. The web architecture allows us to push things all the way into the browser. As you have seen, WebAssembly has a prominent role in this use case. Sometimes you would like to go in browser or on device for privacy reasons, low-latency user experiences, and more. At other times, you may not want to run proprietary code on the user's device, but will still want to get close. This is the realm of edge computing. It is a continuum of deployment localities that spans centralized data centers, regional boundaries, service provider access point boundaries, on-premise systems, local access points, and on device. To say things have gotten a little complicated would be an accomplished exercise in understatement.

Implicit in this range of localities is a variety of hardware architectures, privacy models, access to potentially sensitive information, and computational capabilities. The demand we put on the NASA researcher I mentioned previously (i.e., porting his code to Java) is unlikely to be a reasonable request these days. These environments will need to give customers the freedom to choose their languages but also provide the protection to avoid them stepping on each other in a multitenant system.

A snapshot view of this continuum of locations can be seen in Figure 15-1. Developers will want to be able to deploy software artifacts across this landscape for different reasons. There is value in doing large model training and data analysis in the cloud. The results may not be well suited to running on mobile devices or embedded systems. Some services can be located closer to the users for low-latency, better experiences. For intellectual property protection reasons, you may not want to send some behavior all the way down to the device. In other cases, privacy regulations such as Payment Card Industry (PCI), Health Insurance Portability and Accountability Act (HIPAA), and General Data Protection Regulation (GDPR) will encourage or require you to.

We have strategies for deploying scalable infrastructure in the cloud via containers-based environments and Kubernetes-driven infrastructure. The vast majority of things that would do well in that space would be completely useless in a mobile device or embedded system.

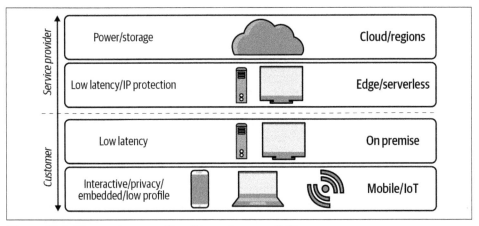

Figure 15-1. The continuum of locality and responsibility

WebAssembly and WASI provide a good story to offer coverage across all of this variance. I think they are going to shine in this realm and catch fire beyond the promising uses we have seen so far. I would like to introduce you to some of the leading projects at the time of writing, but fully expect these to expand dramatically in the near future.

In a 2021 talk (*https://oreil.ly/spQjM*), Liam Randall from Cosmonic and the wasmCloud project highlighted the continuum I have been discussing. Take a look at Figure 15-2, which is based on an image he showed.

What we see is how our industry has changed over time. What developers need to be responsible for has been shrinking. What we can rely on our runtime environments to provide has grown. Initially, we had to manage everything. We had to buy the hardware, install the operating systems and patches, and add any dependent libraries or applications. Keeping these systems patched was a full-time job and could often introduce incompatibilities with what our systems were built against.

Open source operating systems such as Linux and FreeBSD changed the industry. What previously involved expensive licenses for proprietary operating systems became free. We could have as many copies as we wanted, but the effort to set up and configure them on various hardware configurations remained an expensive activity ripe for innovation.

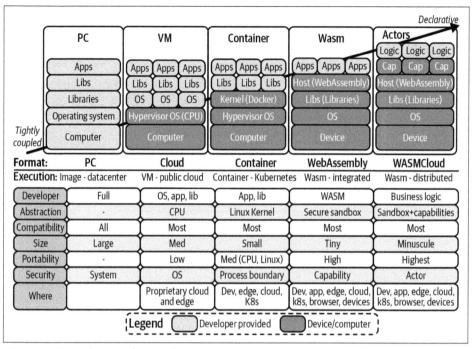

Format:	PC	Cloud	Container	WebAssembly	WASMCloud
Execution:	Image - datacenter	VM - public cloud	Container - Kubernetes	Wasm - integrated	Wasm - distributed
Developer	Full	OS, app, lib	App, lib	WASM	Business logic
Abstraction	-	CPU	Linux Kernel	Secure sandbox	Sandbox+capabilities
Compatibility	All	Most	Most	Most	Most
Size	Large	Med	Small	Tiny	Minuscule
Portability	-	Low	Med (CPU, Linux)	High	Highest
Security	System	OS	Process boundary	Capability	Actor
Where		Proprietary cloud and edge	Dev, edge, cloud, K8s	Dev, app, edge, cloud, k8s, browser, devices	Dev, app, edge, cloud, k8s, browser, devices

Figure 15-2. Evolution of our industry

The cloud explosion introduced a virtualization layer where we could be protected from the details of the hardware. This gave us the ability to have shared access to physical systems with time-sliced usage. Spinning up predefined images of various operating system configurations made it easy to meet demand and move quickly from a known starting point. These virtual machine images were large, cumbersome, and overkill for a variety of uses. There was still a significant burden for the application developer to manage dependencies, but it was progress.

Container systems as we know them can be traced to seeds in the 1970s with the addition of the *chroot* system.[7] In 2000, FreeBSD's Jail system (*https://oreil.ly/sur6P*) emerged as a way of allowing multitenant hosts to further separate what was shared and what was unique to each user. This drove interest and development in Linux control groups many years later, leading to the development of Linux Containers (LXC) in 2008. Google and CloudFoundry had some offerings along the way, but it was ultimately Docker being released in 2013 that really got the ball rolling.

---

7 The *chroot* (*https://oreil.ly/1LFzQ*) system helped isolate processes by changing the root directory for them and their children.

Overall, this containerization approach allowed finer-level granularity around the virtualization than the heavier-weight images of the previous generation. More of the infrastructure could be predefined, so we could focus on installing the right versions of our shared libraries and applications.

WebAssembly introduced a new version of the idea of safe, stable, portable code, as you have seen. API availability remains an issue, but WASI helps with that. The concept of sandboxed code has become increasingly important in environments like this not just because of the supply chain attacks we discussed in Chapter 8, but also because we wish to deploy code at the various layers of Figure 15-1 in multitenant systems. As Liam Randall mentions in his talk linked earlier, this is a trend you can probably expect to continue as capabilities-based security systems are gaining traction.

In several recent chapters we explored applications loading and executing reusable WebAssembly modules through the Wasmtime and Wasmer APIs. Ultimately, this is the basis for the final transition to where we find ourselves. This use case helps define a new layer of application hosts that will provide options for supporting plug-ins, modules, extensions, and even basic functionality. The code requires approved capabilities to do anything outside of basic execution, such as reading from the filesystem, spawning threads, or opening up a network connection. This approach will facilitate a wide range of uses such as long-running applications with plug-in proxies and filters written in different languages, microservices, and serverless functions.

In addition to this flexible computational style, the overhead of these approaches is even smaller and the security tighter than that provided even by the container models that everyone is currently so excited about. This is going to allow us to reach into the entire range of our computational landscape highlighted in Figure 15-1. To reinforce the potential impact we are discussing, Solomon Hykes, a Docker cofounder, is often quoted in these discussions: "If WASM+WASI existed in 2008, we wouldn't have needed to create Docker. That's how important it is. Webassembly on the server is the future of computing."[8] As he acknowledges subsequently, this does not necessarily mean Docker is going away, but rather that we are talking about something of equal significance. The two technologies will likely find ways to work together.

Let's see how these ideas come together in various ways to lay the foundation for our heterogeneous and expansive computational future. We are going to explore a handful of commercial and open source offerings as examples of what is being considered now. There will undoubtedly be more before we know it.

---

[8] He said this on Twitter (*https://oreil.ly/3Lxvp*).

Fastly Compute@Edge

Fastly has been a successful CDN provider for the last decade. It is a founding member of the Bytecode Alliance and has recently hired many of the engineers focused on WebAssembly and WASI from Mozilla. It is moving well beyond serving up static content and into this new world we are imagining with its Compute@Edge platform.

At the core of this offering is the Lucet WebAssembly compiler and runtime that is being merged with the Mozilla Wasmtime project we mentioned in Chapter 11. In open sourcing it and contributing it to the Bytecode Alliance, Fastly hopes to make both runtimes richer by capitalizing on their strengths. Both are built around the Cranelift project (*https://oreil.ly/nBvjI*), and when combined with WASI, will facilitate customers being able to push functionality written in a variety of programming languages safely into Fastly's Edge@Compute environment.

One of the defining characteristics of the Lucet runtime is its ability to instantiate WebAssembly modules in under 50 microseconds, compared to V8's 5 milliseconds to do the same thing.[9] In addition to this speed advantage, it can also do so with a low memory overhead, measured in kilobytes rather than tens of megabytes.

Interacting with the Compute@Edge platform works about as you would imagine. You register an account and get access to the API, which is protected by tokens.[10] There is a command-line tool for initiating projects and deploying them into the ecosystem with dynamic DNS entries. Code can presently be written in Rust, AssemblyScript, or JavaScript. Many of the features are in beta at the moment, but they are moving quickly and are heavily involved in the development and stewardship of the related technologies and standards.

While there are registration requirements for deploying arbitrary code to Fastly's systems, its Terrarium platform is easily explorable in a browser due to its WebAssembly basis. It is built around WebAssembly Studio (*https://webassembly.studio*) and provides a simple way to experience the ease of deploying functionality to its platform.

Start by going to *https://wasm.fastlylabs.com*. You should see a site with a pop-up that allows you to choose a variety of projects. There are empty projects oriented toward C, TypeScript, and basic Wat codebases. There are also C and Rust examples that do real work like submitting DNS queries over HTTPS, image processing, a weather app that fetches remote data, a GraphQL example that communicates with GitHub, and a throttling proxy example.

---

9 Fastly's announcement about open source Lucet (*https://oreil.ly/N4Ywk*) can be found online.

10 Given the registration process, I will not be showing working examples, but you can find more details online (*https://oreil.ly/DBooJ*) if you are interested.

Once you select one of the project types, the browser will fill in its associated structure. In this case, I have chosen the image processing example in C. Each of the files is available to explore and edit, but I have simply clicked on the Build & Deploy button toward the top in Figure 15-3. Notice that it generates a random DNS name for the hosted app as a convenience.

Figure 15-3. C image processing example compiled and deployed

If you follow the generated domain name, you will see the HTML generated by the selected file *main.c.* This is shown just for thoroughness in Figure 15-4.

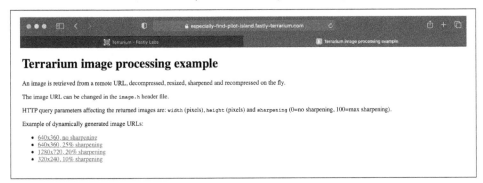

Figure 15-4. Accessing the deployed image processing example via a browser

Finally, if you click on the link to sharpen the larger image by 20%, you will see something like the cat picture shown in Figure 15-5. The exciting thing is not that you can publish an application to the web and invoke it through a browser. It is that you can pick your language, including eminently unsafe languages such as C, and deploy it into a hybrid architecture in someone else's infrastructure (with the possibility of geo-graphic replication for low-latency interactions) without concern.

Figure 15-5. Cat image sharpened by 20%

On the continuum of deployment localities, we are mainly looking at edge comput-ing, as is indicated by the name. Next we will look at a solution that will help develop-ers deploy WebAssembly modules to their existing Kubernetes clusters.

Krustlet

While Docker containers provide the isolation and behavior dependency mecha-nisms, Kubernetes has become one of the primary environments for orchestrating these containers into automated deployments of sophisticated applications and work-flows. The two technologies have really fed off of each other's strengths. So much so that they are quite tightly coupled as engines of deployment. While this is not an issue in large cloud deployments, it becomes a problem when we want to target smaller-profile platforms. Ultimately, we are going to seek a mechanism that will allow com-position of behavior expressed in lighter structures. But finding a way to integrate WebAssembly with Kubernetes directly is a reasonable goal. This is exactly what Microsoft's DeisLabs team has been experimenting with over the last several years.[11]

---

11 The DeisLabs team (*https://deislabs.io*) is largely made up of people who worked on Helm, the Kubernetes package manager.

The team has identified WebAssembly as an alternate way to deploy safe, fast, secure software. They consider it easier to start from a secure basis like this rather than having to lock down the container instances, which is tricky to get right. They have developed Krustlet (*https://krustlet.dev*), a Rust-based Kubelet (thus the name). Other noted benefits of this approach are faster startup and shutdown times and smaller deployment elements than conventional containers. This creates new opportunities for use with IoT sensors and devices, embedded systems, and other constrained environments, as well as being compatible with existing Kubernetes environments.

The DeisLabs team does not think existing applications are going to suddenly be repackaged as composed WebAssembly modules, however, so this is in no way intended to replace Docker. Instead, it is a minimally functional Kubelet that interacts with Kubernetes basically "as is." Rather than using only Open Container Initiative (OCI) containers, you can mix and match the functionality with WebAssembly and a runtime environment. These runtime layers are not fixed, but Krustlet has historically worked with Wasmtime and the predecessor to the wasmCloud project. By breaking the coupling between Kubernetes and containers, we expect cool things to come from efforts such as this. Notably, Krustlet has been adopted by the Cloud Native Computing Foundation (CNCF) as a sandbox project.

Keep in mind, this is largely a way of extending the status quo with WebAssembly. It will ultimately allow for a wider range of engines and computational localities in concert with a container and Kubernetes-based strategy. It also highlights that we have options in terms of our orchestration strategies and application host providers, which we will discuss next.

Suborbital

The Suborbital project (*https://suborbital.dev*) grew out of a similar interest in decoupling the composition, orchestration, and scheduling of behavior from containers. The team had originally considered Docker containers as a basis of their workflow but found them cumbersome, slow, and hard to secure. WebAssembly was a better overall fit, so let's see how it comes together.

There are several parts to the Suborbital platform. The first is a Go-based development environment for expressing API services called Vektor. This allows simple expressions of complex behavior including establishing and configuring servers. The Vektor guide includes Example 15-1, a way of demonstrating starting a server configured with a Let's Encrypt–backed certificate and registering and mounting simple handlers.

Example 15-1. Sample Vektor server

```
import "github.com/suborbital/vektor/vk"

server := vk.New(vk.UseAppName("Vektor API Server"),
 vk.UseDomain("vektor.example.com"))

server.GET("/ping", HandlePing)

if err := server.Start(); err != nil {
  log.Fatal(err)
}

func HandlePing(r *http.Request, ctx *vk.Ctx) (interface{}, error) {
  return "pong", nil
}
```

The next element is a Go-based runtime scheduling function and runnable behavior called Reactr. It can be a standalone application or run as a service and accept work through HTTPS connections to provide a function-as-a-service (FaaS) environment. It handles memory management, the capabilities security system, and can schedule runnable work written in Rust, AssemblyScript, and Swift. The functions can be scheduled synchronously, asynchronously, or chained together to provide a Unix pipes-and-filters-style functional composition model.

The Grav environment is a Go-based distributed messaging mesh for scaling communication between the managed components. It is designed to have low overhead, high resilience, support a variety of messaging styles (e.g., request/reply and broadcast) and both in-memory and interprocess messaging models. It has a specific intended use, however, and is not intended to replace more established, general-purpose environments such as RabbitMQ or Kafka.

A comprehensive and consistent command-line tool called *subo* allows you to interact with the Suborbital environment and hides many of the details over particular language build systems, container structures, and more. Deployed artifacts can be bundled in a variety of ways and can be hot-swapped incrementally at runtime.

Atmo is the final piece that ties it all together. It is a server-side API framework for declaratively managing the deployed functionality. Developers can focus on the functionality and rely on the infrastructure to scale out based on needs. While Atmo is not tied to Kubernetes per se, it can be used to assist in the autoscaling infrastructure if it is configured to do so. Atmo is configured via YAML Directive files to define how the runnable functions should be deployed and bundled. This includes managing routes, business logic, and state management.

Suborbital is still in beta, but it provides a compelling vision of the kind of runtime environment that is suggested by the final column in Figure 15-2. There is even a headless version of Atmo coming called Flight Deck that will allow software as a service (SaaS) vendors to extend their applications naturally with APIs and functionality managed by this ecosystem.

WasmEdge

The next project I want to highlight is the WasmEdge project from Second State (*https://www.secondstate.io*). It is a secure and high-performance WebAssembly runtime that has been adopted by the CNCF as an official sandbox project. It is also imagined as the target runtime across the spectrum of locations we have been discussing so far in this chapter.

In addition to the typical host features we have seen, WasmEdge has a mechanism for measuring the consumption of execution time that will be useful in an attempt to monetize serverless FaaS environments and blockchain-based systems. Wasmtime also has this ability, as we will see in Chapter 16.

The WasmEdge team is a big advocate for the concept of the Jamstack (*https://jamstack.org*), a technology suite that includes Javascript, APIs, and Markup. The basic idea is that frontends are converted into optimized, static single pages and assets during the build process. This allows their runtime performance to have reduced complexity and load burdens. While the frontends may be converted into static resources, they maintain dynamic behavior by interacting with backend APIs and hypermedia systems.

The backend is cleanly queryable using standard HTTP clients such as browsers or command-line tools such as HTTPie.[12]

To execute a deployed function to the FaaS is as simple as the following, but be careful. I have elided the bytes of the compiled WebAssembly code:

```
brian@tweezer ~> http https://rpc.ssvm.secondstate.io:8081/api/executables/1
{
  "wasm_id": 1,
  "wasm_sha256": "0xfb413547a8aba56d0349603a7989e269f3846245e51804932b3e02bc0",
  "wasm_description": "Function as a Service (FaaS)",
  "wasm_as_buffer": {
    "type": "Buffer",
    "data": [
      48,
      44,
      57,
```

---

12 Visit the HTTPie website (*https://httpie.org*) to learn why it is my favorite command-line HTTP client.

```
        55,
        .
        .
        .
      ]
    },
    "wasm_state": "{}",
    "wasm_callback_object": "{}"
  }
```

As you can see, new endpoints can be defined by manipulating resources. To invoke the behavior of an endpoint to issue a friendly, parameterized greeting, you can issue the following:

```
brian@tweezer ~> echo "from the future" | http ↵
    -f POST https://rpc.ssvm.secondstate.io:8081/api/run/161/say ↵
    Content-Type:text/plain
HTTP/1.1 200 OK
Access-Control-Allow-Origin: *
Connection: keep-alive
Content-Length: 22
...
Content-Type: text/html; charset=utf-8
Date: Tue, 17 Aug 2021 18:48:13 GMT
ETag: W/"16-kf3Sg+1nPhqMOp7M01tMU9CkSVk"
...

hello from the future
```

Other features provided by WasmEdge include capabilities-based security, a RockDB-backed storage mechanism, WASI integration, TensorFlow functionality, and more.

An example that uses this functionality is described on the Second State website (*https://oreil.ly/bmtkx*). This example uses a Multi-task Cascaded Convolutional Network (MTCNN) model trained off of the FaceNet dataset (*https://oreil.ly/gWLJK*).

The example includes a link to the GitHub repository with the actual code, as well as a description of the process of building, deploying, and calling this capability via command-line tools and from a browser. The result of submitting a famous picture from the 1927 Solvay Conference is shown in Figure 15-6.[13]

---

13 It is really difficult to underscore the collective brainpower shown in this picture. There are 17 Nobel Prize winners featured. You can find out more about this remarkable photo and the gathering it is from on Wikipedia (*https://oreil.ly/DyFbF*).

Figure 15-6. Invoking an MTCNN model on a famous image

Invoking complex functionality from a REST API is not inherently earth-shattering. But being able to deploy the code that you want to run safely in a portable, high-performance sandboxed environment is. The fact that you can also run the same behavior locally in Node.js or some other form is equally useful from a testing perspective.

In addition to basic WASI support, WasmEdge supports several of the proposals discussed in Chapter 12 and even a WASI socket extension for adding network support. WasmEdge also has an API similar to the ones we have seen from Wasmer and Wasmtime for embedding WebAssembly behavior in arbitrary other applications.

If you visit the Second State website, you will find other examples of running WasmEdge in uses for blockchain, automotive infrastructure, and a variety of other scenarios. We will touch upon some of that in Chapter 16, but for now we will focus on our final WebAssembly application infrastructure runtime.

wasmCloud

The wasmCloud project (*https://wasmcloud.dev*) is a sophisticated and evolving collection of technologies known previously as waSCC (which stood for WebAssembly Secure Capabilities Connector). It has recently been selected as an official CNCF application runtime project and promises to help developers build actor-based models on orchestrated capabilities across the entire spectrum of locations we have discussed throughout this chapter. I want to focus on it because I think it effectively addresses the various engineering decisions that go into solving the mysteries of the final column of Figure 15-1. It certainly is not the only project that is likely to, but for now it is the most robust and comprehensive distillation of that vision.

wasmCloud provides a comprehensive abstraction from cloud-based infrastructure. The use of actors allows developers to produce business functionality that is based upon message handling and the use of capabilities provided by the infrastructure. *Capabilities* is just a term for nonfunctional requirements needed for actors to have their expectations met by an application runtime. The clean separation allows reuse across different environments as well as hot-swapping of underlying implementations within the same one.

The tools and frameworks associated with wasmCloud are intended to solve the complexities of deploying multilingual code libraries to an increasingly diverse set of platforms, as outlined in Liam Randall's talk that we mentioned earlier. They are focused on only adding the pieces they need, which is why they leverage WebAssembly and WASI. The team made a recent decision around a migration toward the Elixir and OTP platform instead of hand-rolling the concurrency solutions in this ecosystem. They long ago decided to base their connective infrastructure on the NATS toolchains and frameworks for adaptive edge and distributed communication.[14]

What you end up with is a technology stack tracking the evolution of our industry and ready to meet the needs of various runtime configurations and scenarios. Let's quickly walk through the layers involved.

At the base of the stack is WebAssembly and WASI. From here we have a portable and secure architecture that will run in a wide number of runtimes and environments of varying capabilities and resources. Unlike previous sandboxed environments, this gives us the freedom of language choice and the benefit of high-performance results. This base level is shown in Figure 15-7.

---

14 NATS (*https://nats.io*) is also an official CNCF incubating project.

Figure 15-7. The WebAssembly base of the wasmCloud stack

wasmCloud extends the WebAssembly base with signed packages, reduced boiler-plate code, the composable actor model, and horizontal and vertical scalability. It supports multitenant stateless and isolated execution of deployed business functionality. This level is highlighted in Figure 15-8.

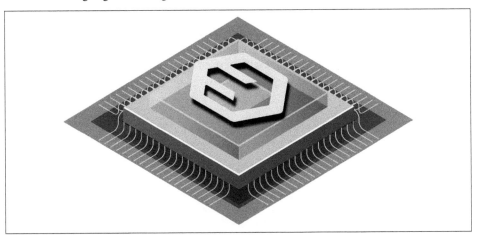

Figure 15-8. The wasmCloud cloud layer extends the WebAssembly base

The capabilities piece on top of the wasmCloud base is the hot-swappable non-functional dependencies an actor needs to fulfill its execution model. wasmCloud includes a wide range of predefined capabilities such as data storage, serving up web resources, message queues, and more. These are visualized in Figure 15-9.

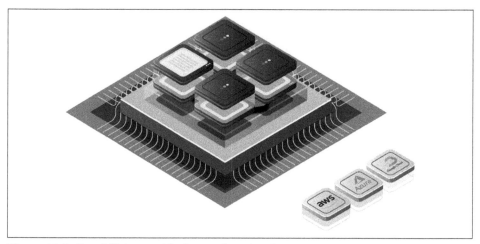

Figure 15-9. Capabilities provide the nonfunctional requirements to actors

Developers will build upon these capabilities and supply their own providers as required for specialized needs. The actors that exist on top of this tier will exist in isolation or composed business functionality that can grow vertically in richer tiers. The underlying distribution model (WebAssembly-based actors) remains fairly lightweight and can take advantage of similarly configured capabilities by constraint-suitable stacks in other environments. Unlike the tight coupling between Kubernetes and containers, this gives organizations more options for reuse. We demonstrate the layer where developers spend the majority of their time in Figure 15-10.

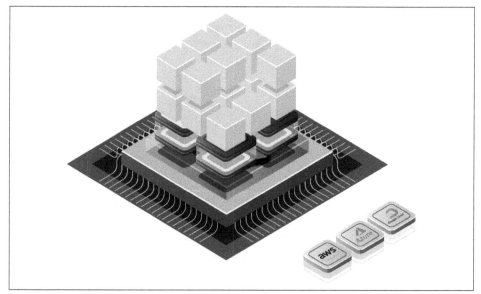

Figure 15-10. Developers spend most of their time creating and composing actors

Finally, all of this is attached to a mesh lattice network that is self-forming and healing. It uses global discovery mechanisms, tunable topologies, and support for offline and online execution modes across various cloud providers. This final flexibility is shown off in Figure 15-11.

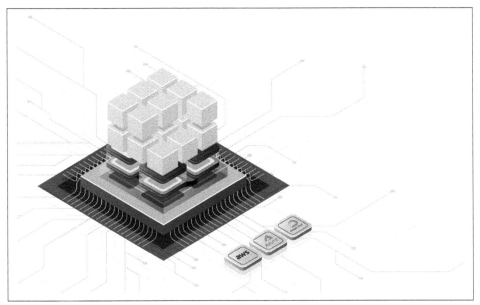

Figure 15-11. The lattice network infrastructure is flexible, self-forming, and healing

The aggregate effect of these design choices is a remarkable ecosystem able to meet the needs of the 21st century. As a final example, the fine folks from Red Badger have published their recent experiments in deploying a wasmCloud cluster across multiple cloud providers. It uses Krustlet and wasmCloud and is detailed on GitHub (*https://oreil.ly/lexpH*). It is a compelling vision of one possible fulfillment of the evolution shown in Figure 15-1.

I fully anticipate that we will see alternative implementations of similar technology structures. I expect great things from the other projects we have mentioned in this chapter, as well as new projects we have not even heard of yet. The trade-offs and technical evolution will remain coherent in other initiatives. Developers will increasingly have less to worry about with respect to the infrastructure they employ, so they can focus on the business value they are primarily paid to develop. Given the heterogeneity of the modern world of software development, I am not sure how else it might be.

Next we will take a final architectural detour into the world of decentralized systems and see what our WebAssembly family of related technologies can do for us there.

## CHAPTER 16

Applied WebAssembly: Decentralized Applications

It's true that contemporary technology permits decentralization, it also permits centralization. It depends on how you use the technology.
  —Noam Chomsky

The software we write takes on a role depending on where and how it is deployed. Legacy systems were often single applications that took in input, did some processing, and produced output. Unix commands are often tools to coordinate together into scripted workflows. In this book, we have largely been discussing WebAssembly's strengths in client-side user interfaces with the occasional foray into server-side technology. These days, our software plays many other parts in the cloud, through microservices architectures, in embedded systems and mobile devices, and through serverless functions.

These different roles often serve an architectural purpose in an attempt to manage change, allow for independent technology choices, meet scale demands, or facilitate reuse and avoid silos. There is an underlying tension to how the disparate elements are organized and coordinated. Most conventional systems are centrally managed, but we are seeing an increased aptitude in developers being able to wrangle widely deployed, decentralized systems into productive use. Let's start by discussing some of the trade-offs.

Centralization Versus Decentralization

Our industry has long vacillated between centralization and decentralization. Neither arrangement is ideal; both have their benefits and negative side effects. Centralization is easy to control, index, optimize, and provide a common experience.

Decentralization can be stable, empowering, and censorship resistant. Mainframes, hosted services, and siloed social media sites are examples of centralization. PCs, mobile devices, and file-sharing systems are examples of types of decentralization.

It is easy to deny people access to centralized resources. They are often fragile if not maintained. Many governments attempt to control access to certain kinds of thinking by controlling access to information. Decentralized systems are difficult to make usable and efficient, and often suffer from market pressures that will encourage recentralization at some point.

The web strikes a pretty nice balance between the two forces in general. On the one hand, anyone can invent a new protocol and listen for clients that speak it on a port. There is no required centralization until we bring naming into it. The DNS has a central orientation. There is an authority even though it is spread out hierarchically for speed and convenience. Once you have a domain name, however, you are able to create as many resources in that domain as you want. You may share them freely and give access to whomever you choose. But, DNS can also be controlled, as people who have gotten on WiFi in coffee shops, airplanes, or countries with oppressive regimes have sadly discovered.

Part of the issue is the use of location-based identity. It is super useful that the names we wish to connect with via the HTTP protocol are the things we will interact with. That said, if we decide to stop hosting these resources, they go away. In my previous book on resource-oriented architecture patterns,[1] I identified the curated URI pattern as a way of bringing stability to the interaction. But as anyone who has ever run into a broken link can attest, the practice is not widely practiced.

One of the benefits of the web is that content producers and content consumers can largely make their own technology choices. By using standards, we can exchange declarative structures defining layouts and styling choices that work well across a range of targets. JavaScript has long been part of that story and now, as you have seen, WebAssembly is too.

Decentralization benefits from consistent use of standards, protocols, and engineering practices that allow arbitrary participants to exchange content. Having the ability to exchange executable content portably, safely, and performantly is going to widen what is possible.

When we built our distributed computing system at Parabon, we had to rely on the Java language and platform in order to get the safety and portability guarantees we needed. We were ultimately a centrally controlled platform, but in a modern setting, it would be fairly straightforward to build a similar decentralized system with

---

1 *Resource-Oriented Architecture Patterns for Webs of Data* (Morgan & Claypool).

WebAssembly, WASI, and the various runtimes we have discussed. In the previous chapter, we saw how this is helping evolve our computational landscape. As Chomsky said, we can support either approach; it is up to us what we do with it.

We will now discuss a handful of decentralized platforms including:

- Bitcoin and legacy Ethereum
- ewasm
- The Polkadot network
- The InterPlanetary File System (IPFS)

From Bitcoin to Ethereum

One of the poster children for decentralized systems is Bitcoin in particular and cryptocurrencies in general.[2] For all the excessive hype and negative naysaying, what Satoshi Nakamoto designed into the system is rather remarkable from a technical and social perspective. There are plenty of unaccounted for externalities that need to be considered when discussing the totality of a technology, but I want to focus on the parts that are relevant to the topic at hand.

Beyond the obvious concept of currency, the Bitcoin system is filled with economic levers that can drive stakeholder behavior. One of its main achievements is the development of a consensus mechanism that allows participants to agree on the rules and their enforcement without a requirement for real identities or weak notions of trust. By now, most people are aware of how it works, but in the interest of clarity, I will summarize it briefly as the basis for modern blockchain thinking. We will connect it back to WebAssembly when we discuss Ethereum as a follow-on platform.

Bitcoin has a maximum currency base that will be released. It uses computationally difficult problems to control the steady release of decreasing amounts of the currency over time. Roughly every 10 minutes or so, a little bit more is added to the ecosystem, but it is tapering off over time. Miners validate all of the transactions that are executing on the platform. That is their main purpose. But, as reward for their effort, they can participate in a recurring puzzle to find the solution to a hash problem. As more miners participate there is more power to attack the problem, so it gets harder over time. In its current form, it would take several hundred thousand years for a single computer to solve a round on its own.

Nobody has that kind of time, so the miners work together in parallel through mining pools to find it in a matter of minutes. The node that finds it announces its solution to the rest of the miners, who verify the outcome. Once everyone comes to a

---

2 *Crypto* means cryptography.

consensus on the result, this entitles that node to award itself the coinbase transaction,[3] which it will share with its pool peers. The winning node must also decide which other transactions will end up in the current block and then link it back to previous blocks. This is where the name *blockchain* comes from.

What actually runs on the nodes is fairly constrained. It is ludicrous numbers of hash transactions, the communication protocols, and the verification of the transactions that involves executing a small, Forth-like (*https://oreil.ly/Sem8J*) language called Script. This mostly just verifies that the account sending Bitcoin to another account is in control of the private keys associated with the account. There really is not a whole lot to it and not much else you can do with it. There is some wiggle room, but it is an intentionally constrained language and therefore easy to support across multiple platforms.

One way that I explain what Parabon was doing is that it was like the SETI@home project (*https://oreil.ly/RYhzc*), except it was a preemptive Java-based general-purpose programming solution. This latter distinction is because SETI@home only did one thing initially.[4] It just chunked through data. As a consequence, the SETI@home researchers could be substantially more comfortable using other people's computers because there was only a fixed number of tasks that it did.

As I indicated in Chapter 15, we were effectively constrained to a particular type of problem in terms of what made sense to run on the platform, but the actual code could be anything we allowed (i.e., no disk or network access). We did prime searches, gene sequence comparisons that scaled linearly, machine learning, thermospheric simulations, and more. As I was the first engineer at the company, one of the questions I was asked was, "How would you control a runaway process?" We were using other people's computers but we were considering allowing clients to run arbitrary code. This is the same dilemma we face with the safety of code we install on our computers, phones, tablets, and watches.

The Bitcoin core developers wanted to keep what could happen on the mining nodes constrained, more like SETI@home. Vitalik Buterin and others wanted to expand what could run on the platform. When it became obvious that it was not going to be possible, the Ethereum project emerged as a result. One of the main differences between the two projects was the nature of what would run on the nodes. The Ethereum developers wanted a Turing-complete language.[5] Without going into a ton of theory, this gets back to the problem of runaway tasks. So, let's take a quick side trip to talk about that.

---

3 The coinbase transaction is how Bitcoin is minted at a controlled pace.

4 They eventually expanded what they did to a more general framework called BOINC (*https://oreil.ly/CDhJj*).

5 I am not going to turn this into a Finite Automata class. If you want to dig into the larger implications (careful, it's a deep rabbit hole), check out this Wikipedia article (*https://oreil.ly/5vQnJ*).

How Do You Solve a Problem Like the Halting Problem?

If we want to run arbitrary tasks on a computational platform, there are two ways to determine if the code will eventually stop. One is to reason about it and the other is to try it out with the unfortunate side effect of potentially waiting for the Heat Death of the Universe to happen before we answer the question. One of those is perhaps harder than the other, and, as it turns out, it isn't trying and waiting (although that is still not recommended).

In computability theory, this is known as an undecidable problem (*https://oreil.ly/Pz9TF*), and it is part of the reason the Bitcoin developers were not enthused by the idea of running a Turing-complete language. If you are compensating people for the time you are using their computer, it would be nice to know if the program will ever finish.[6]

All is not lost, however. Mining nodes on the Ethereum platform must run the arbitrary contract code. The more resources you use computationally (storage, CPU time, etc.), the more you have to pay. It would be really annoying to start executing a contract and lett it run for a few millennia before realizing you would never get paid for that work. The Ethereum team came up with a good solution called "gas." The idea is that if you want to drive across the country, you better have enough money for gas. Otherwise, somewhere in the middle you will run out and you might get stuck. An Ethereum contract is evaluated with a quick heuristic to determine roughly how expensive it will be to run, and the client launching the contract has to cough up that much or more. As the contract executes, it consumes gas and can run out. If it does, the nodes get compensated for effort and you may be left with nothing. It is a reasonable compromise to an otherwise intractable problem. It also simultaneously forces contract developers to exercise caution and test their code locally.

The Ethereum project also intended to run on a variety of hardware and software platforms, so the code that gets executed made sense to be virtualized. The designers created a handful of contract languages, but the one that caught on initially was called Solidity. It has an LLVM-based compiler, but it emits a bytecode that can run on their custom virtual machine. As you can imagine, this was a nontrivial engine to write, so as WebAssembly emerged, there became a lot of interest in migrating to a new virtual machine that they would not have to maintain.

The concept of gas is still important, however. As WebAssembly is being imagined as the engine for several blockchain-based projects, it is unsurprising that the idea has begun to show up in the platforms we are discussing as well.

---

6 Alan Turing demonstrated in 1936 that this was not always possible.

In Example 16-1, you can see a simple implementation that calculates Fibonacci numbers directly in Wat taken from the Wasmtime GitHub repository. If you need a refresher on the algorithm, check out our example in Chapter 4.

Example 16-1. Wat implementation of Fibonacci numbers

```
(module
  (func $fibonacci (param $n i32) (result i32)
    (if
      (i32.lt_s (local.get $n) (i32.const 2))
      (return (local.get $n))
    )
    (i32.add
      (call $fibonacci (i32.sub (local.get $n) (i32.const 1)))
      (call $fibonacci (i32.sub (local.get $n) (i32.const 2)))
    )
  )
  (export "fibonacci" (func $fibonacci))
)
```

Notice there is no concept of time or cost in this calculation. It is recursive but it will just do what you ask it to do. While this is not an excessively hungry calculation, you could keep a node busy calculating a large number of Fibonacci numbers. What we would like is a concept like gas that allows us to do what we want to do, but to measure the cost and to cut it off if it exceeds that cost.

The code in Example 16-2 is able to do this because Wasmtime supports the concept of "fuel." Remember that Store instances are keepers of the runtime instance details, so we allocate 10,000 fuel units in the store. We instantiate a compiled version of our *.wat* file as a module so we can invoke the fibonacci() function.

Example 16-2. Rust Wasmtime example with fuel

```
use anyhow::Result;
use wasmtime::*;

fn main() -> Result<()> {
  let mut config = Config::new();
  config.consume_fuel(true);
  let engine = Engine::new(&config)?;
  let mut store = Store::new(&engine, ());
  store.add_fuel(10_000)?;
  let module = Module::from_file(store.engine(), "examples/fuel.wat")?;
  let instance = Instance::new(&mut store, &module, &[])?;

  // Invoke `fibonacci` export with higher and higher numbers until we
  // exhaust our fuel.
  let fibonacci
```

```
    = instance.get_typed_func::<i32, i32, _>(&mut store, "fibonacci")?;

  for n in 1.. {
    let fuel_before = store.fuel_consumed().unwrap();
    let output = match fibonacci.call(&mut store, n) {
        Ok(v) => v,
        Err(_) => {
          println!("Exhausted fuel computing fib({})", n);
          break;
        }
    };
    let fuel_consumed = store.fuel_consumed().unwrap() - fuel_before;
    println!("fib({}) = {} [consumed {} fuel]", n, output, fuel_consumed);
    store.add_fuel(fuel_consumed)?;
  }
  Ok(())
}
```

Once we have the instance, we start an unbounded loop of n from 1 to infinity. Clearly, we do not want to wait for this code to complete on its own. So, we are going to leverage fuel. Individual instructions are calibrated as having a cost, so we keep track of how much we spend in each iteration and subtract it from our available fuel deposit. Once we run out, our attempt to invoke the function will fail and break out of the loop.

So, we have a general capability that can be built into various runtimes to allow us to run arbitrary code safely without concern about whether it will spin out of control or not. Building a generic blockchain engine out of this capability is clearly one potential use.

ewasm

The legacy Ethereum Virtual Machine is referred to as EVM1. The new version is known as ewasm. The documentation and design process (*https://oreil.ly/Oi6Yn*) are available online. This is a work in progress and there have been many changes along the way, but the goal is still to create a new virtual machine on a WebAssembly base for all of the reasons that should be obvious by now. One consequence that may not be obvious is that this will likely open up contract languages to a much wider variety, given the ease with which LLVM-based compilers can be reused.

The devlopers did not come to this decision lightly. As can be seen in the "Comparison with Other Architectures" section of the ewasm documentation, they considered all manner of intermediate representations and bytecode formats as the possible basis for this new virtual machine.

The main arguments for heading down this path are obviously speed, efficiency, and security. We are talking about a standards-based instruction set that will be curated and extended over time by the W3C. The Ethereum community will benefit from this work and will not have to make all of the design decisions themselves. The widespread and growing toolchain support for a wider number of languages is going to create a natural path for using languages that developers are already familiar with, such as C/C++, Rust, Go, AssemblyScript, and more (including some new ones we will discuss in the final chapter!).

WebAssembly is intrinsically portable, which will also reduce the burden on the Ethereum developer community to target an increasing number of hardware platforms as they become available. This portability and the performance gains will also allow more of the Ethereum platform itself to be expressed in Wasm instructions, which keeps the size of the codebase down when supporting multiple platforms. This is useful from the perspective of both level of effort and code analysis for security auditing.

The developers do not want to design themselves into a corner, however, so they are introducing some new ideas. The first is the Ewasm Contract Interface (ECI), which defines the structure of a contract module. Modules are communicated in the Wasm binary format. Contracts will be allowed to import symbols defined to be part of the Ethereum Environment Interface (EEI). This exposes the core Ethereum API to the ewasm enviroments. You can think of it a little like the relationship between WASI and WASI-host environments. Contracts are expected to export a `main()` function to initiate the contract and a `Memory` instance for sharing data between contracts and their host environments. Again, these should make sense to you by now.

I am not able to give you a proper tutorial for this new platform here, but the basic idea is that contracts will need to be able to fetch and store data, call functionality in other contracts, be deployed at knowable addresses, etc. The concept remains that the more burden a contract puts on the platform, the more cost it will incur. Gas still remains, and so there will be an intricate metering capability similar to what we saw in the previous section but with more nuance.

Because different instructions might cost more or less on different platforms, they are assigning each Wasm opcode to one or more IA-32 (x86) instructions having a fixed cycle count. This is expected to represent an average CPU used to host Ethereum nodes running at approximately 2.2 GHz. One second of CPU use is configured to cost 10 million gas. These numbers are not going to be fixed in time and will be periodically adjusted based upon observation and the evolution of hardware systems.

The cost of an instruction is equivalent to a cycle count × the gas per cycle equivalence for the instruction type. For example, the `get_local` instruction costs 3 cycles and is expected to cost 0.0135 gas. Loading things into and out of memory will have similar costs. Accessing constant values (e.g., `i32.const`) does not require any transfer of data, calculation, or storage, so it is essentially a 0 gas operation.

As there is so much compiled EVM1 bytecode in existence, there are also plans to have a transcompiler to convert EVM1 bytecode into ewasm bytecode for backward compatibility. There are some differences, including that EVM1 uses 256-bit integers by default and ewasm will use 64-bit integers, but there will be compensating actions to make it all work and price the work accordingly in the new environment.

Finally, there will also be predefined contracts for functionality that will be needed as part of the behavior of the Ethereum environment to function properly. This includes a sentinel contract for validation and metering injection, the transcompilation of EVM1 to ewasm, various hashing algorithms (e.g., SHA2-256, RIPEMD160, KECCAK256), and more.

This remains an adventurous work in progress, but the design motivation makes sense and the selection criteria align with many of the reasons we have highlighted for being excited about WebAssembly in general. Decentralized systems have a lot of innate complexity in them. Whatever they can do to standardize, secure, optimize, and expand the range of contract language options available to cryptocurrency smart contract developers is likely to strengthen the Ethereum platform overall.

Polkadot

While Bitcoin is the overall market leader in the cryptocurrency space, Ethereum has emerged as a close second. With its support for multiple languages and arbitrary contracts in a widening collection of languages, if you needed to target a specific, non-Bitcoin platform, Ethereum would be a defensible choice even with some of the growing pains it has experienced over the years. But what if you did not want to tie yourself to a single platform such as Ethereum? This is where Polkadot comes in. It is a new blockchain project designed from the ground up with blockchain interoperability in mind.

Polkadot (*https://polkadot.network*) was founded by Dr. Gavin Wood, author of the Ethereum Yellow Paper,[7] with an eye toward upgradeable, extensible, and interoperable blockchain capabilities. It is one of the cornerstones of the Web3 Foundation.[8]

One of the projects funded by the Web3 Foundation was to bring an ewasm virtual machine into the Polkadot ecosystem. The contract was awarded to Second State, makers of the WasmEdge platform that we introduced in the previous chapter. The project is called Substrate (*https://substrate.dev*), and you can find the project on GitHub (*https://oreil.ly/9ID4I*). With support for the ewasm contract interface and

---

7 The Yellow Paper (*https://oreil.ly/Rj0kP*) famously describes many of the design motivations on the Ethereum platform. If you are interested in blockchain technologies more generally, it would be worth your time to read.

8 The Web3 Foundation (*https://web3.foundation*) funds research into projects that can contribute to the overall success of this decentralized vision.

execution environment, this opens the door for Ethereum contracts to be transparently deployed to Polkadot-based blockchains. Not only does this avoid lock-in, but it also increases the transfer of ideas, contracts, and capabilities into an ever-richer collection of blockchain-based stakeholders. Other projects based upon the Second State ewasm engine include Oasis Ethereum (*https://www.oasiseth.org*) and Parastate (*https://www.parastate.io*).

These are simply a couple of examples of the intersection of WebAssembly and blockchain-flavored decentralization. I anticipate there will be many, many more, but for now I want to wrap up the chapter with a quick introduction of another one of my favorite decentralization projects that is also a star of the Web3 world. It too will benefit from WebAssembly.

InterPlanetary File System (IPFS)

I have to admit, I fell in love with this project initially just for its name. Granted, I have come to respect it and honestly be in awe of what the community has been able to produce since then, but the name still rules. The thing is, it is not just a clever name. It is simultaneously a historical reference and an aspirational nod to a future that is closer than most of us are anticipating.[9] Humans will soon be going back to the moon and making early forays to Mars. The network latencies involved with communicating with bases on these planets are going to be problematic. One aspect of the design criteria for IPFS is to help solve some of these issues. I will not bother explaining how they plan to do this, but perhaps that will pique your curiosity to investigate. The project produces an overwhelming amount of code, documentation, videos, and tutorials, but the main website (*https://ipfs.io*) is a good starting point.

One of the coolest aspects of IPFS is that its developers are designing their layers around the idea of reuse across projects. You do not have to buy into their entire stack, elegant as it is. Instead, you can pick and choose the pieces that your project might benefit from and go from there. Examples of useful (and reusable) projects from this community include Multiformats,[10] libp2p,[11] and IPLD.[12]

While there are many ways WebAssembly is showing up in this community, I want to highlight a simple one. I am not going to describe how IPFS works in detail, but there

---

9 J. C. R. Licklider referred to early versions of the emerging ARPANET (which became the internet) as the Intergalactic Computer Network (*https://oreil.ly/QPNPn*).

10 Multiformats (*https://multiformats.io*) allow you to express hashes, network addresses, and other useful values in a self-describing, flexible state.

11 libp2p (*https://libp2p.io*) is a remarkable, pluggable, extensive networking stack that allows for swapping transports, multiplexing channels, handling high-latency environments, and so much more.

12 IPLD (*https://ipld.io*) is a linked data format for decentralized systems.

are some core ideas. The whole thing is based upon Merkle DAGs (*https://oreil.ly/ iKVSk*). A directed acyclic graph (DAG) is a graph structure that has identifiers based upon hashes of the node's contents. Merkle DAGs are similar to Merkle trees (*https:// oreil.ly/IjrlA*), which are useful for detecting changes of content-based addressable blocks.

The net effect of these decisions is that files can be broken down into dependencies between blocks that are identified by content identifiers (CIDs) driven by the actual content of the blocks. As files change, the only portions that need to be updated are the affected blocks. Doing so does not invalidate the existing immutable Merkle DAG, so multiple versions of files can coexist simultaneously.

If you do not have a background in these kinds of decentralized systems, there are a lot of behind-the-scenes details that we do not need to focus on to make my larger point. To hide those details, I am going to use the Go-based command-line tools from the IPFS project. You can find how to install these in the Appendix if you are interested in trying them. There are libraries in many other languages. Many of these do not require you to install and run things locally if you do not want to. As you will see shortly, there are HTTP gateways for bridging the web as you know it and the IPFS network.

To use the tools, you need to generate an identity. This does not involve your name or anything, it is just an RSA keypair that can be used to digitally sign documents and communicate with the large network. Creating a node identity is easy:

```
brian@tweezer ~> ipfs init
initializing IPFS node at /Users/brian/.ipfs
generating 2048-bit RSA keypair...done
peer identity: QmZoRwJ7YYayf5eNWDweN5GCGJjuRnKGJA3susZqjV8Jcb
to get started, enter:
    ipfs cat /ipfs/QmS4ustL54uo8FzR9455qaxZwuMiUhyvMcX9Ba8nUH4uVv/readme
```

The long CID that starts with QmZoRwJ refers to the node I created. There are no services running yet; we simply have tools that allow us to communicate with the IPFS network. That includes the ability to request files. Files have similar CIDs to the node, as do blocks. If you dig into the IPLD model mentioned previously, you will see that it is just a big interlinked collection of named, immutable nodes. The comment at the end of what was produced in the previous example indicates that we can find out more by issuing that command. As you will soon see, you do not need to have these tools involved, but at this point something needs to know how to communicate with the network. The ipfs command-line tool takes multiple arguments. One of them makes it act like the Unix cat command to show the contents of a file. In this case, it is a file called *readme* referenced as a subelement of the directory it lives in. This convenience is a bit like a fragment identifier on a Web URL to avoid multiple round trips. We can ask for it in one go. The results should look something like what you see in Figure 16-1.

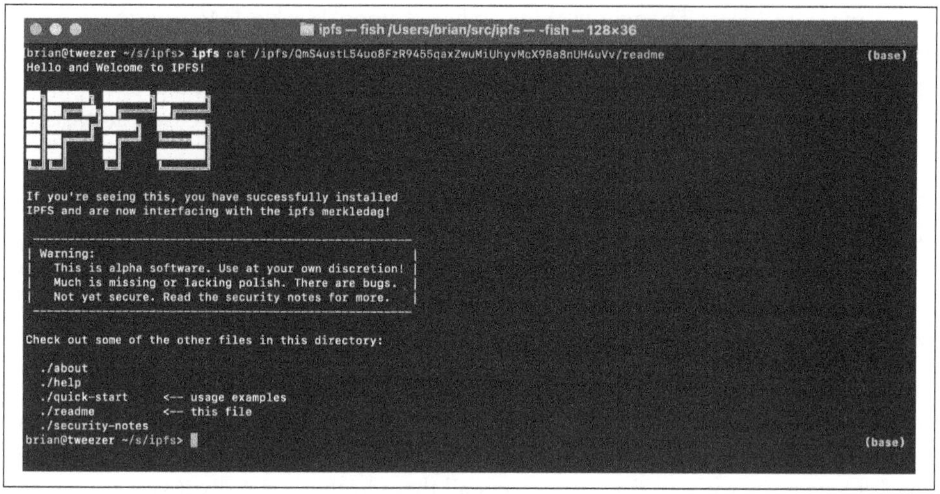

Figure 16-1. Requesting files from IPFS

Note that there are other files in that directory, so you could ask for them as well. If you did not know what files were available, you could simply ask IPFS. Notice that here I am using the directory name on its own. As you can see, each file in the directory has its own CID:

```
brian@tweezer ~/s/ipfs> ipfs ls ↵
    /ipfs/QmS4ustL54uo8FzR9455qaxZwuMiUhyvMcX9Ba8nUH4uVv
QmZTR5bcpQD7cFgTorqxZDYaew1Wqgfbd2ud9QqGPAkK2V 1677 about
QmYCvbfNbCwFR45HiNP45rwJgvatpiW38D961L5qAhUM5Y 189  contact
QmY5heUM5qgRubMDD1og9fhCPA6QdkMp3QCwd4s7gJsyE7 311  help
QmejvEPop4D7YUadeGqYWmZxHhLc4JBUCzJJHWMzdcMe2y 4    ping
QmXgqKTbzdh83pQtKFb19SpMCpDDcKR2ujqk3pKph9aCNF 1681 quick-start
QmPZ9gcCEpqKTo6aq61g2nXGUhM4iCL3ewB6LDXZCtioEB 1091 readme
QmQ5vhrL7uv6tuoN9KeVBwd4PwfQkXdVVmDLUZuTNxqgvm 1162 security-notes
```

Adding files to IPFS is easy. I am going to take the example from Chapter 6 where we rendered a Windows bitmap file from C++ in the browser. As a reminder, this is what is in that directory:

```
brian@tweezer ~/s/i/bitmap> ls -alF
total 1800
drwxr-xr-x  11 brian  staff     352 Aug 18 12:27 ./
drwxr-xr-x   3 brian  staff      96 Aug 18 12:26 ../
-rw-r--r--@  1 brian  staff     893 Aug 18 12:26 Makefile
-rw-r--r--@  1 brian  staff     948 Aug 18 12:26 Makefile.lib
-rw-r--r--@  1 brian  staff     776 Aug 18 12:26 Makefile.orig
-rw-r--r--@  1 brian  staff  247721 Aug 18 12:26 bitmap_image.hpp
-rw-r--r--@  1 brian  staff   21026 Aug 18 12:26 bitmap_test.cpp
-rw-r--r--   1 brian  staff  249496 Aug 18 12:26 bitmap_test.js
-rwxr-xr-x   1 brian  staff  257924 Aug 18 12:26 bitmap_test.wasm*
```

```
-rw-r--r--@ 1 brian  staff  120054 Aug 18 12:26 image.bmp
-rw-r--r--  1 brian  staff    3127 Aug 18 12:26 index.html
```

To add the files, we just go into that directory and issue the following:

```
brian@tweezer ~/s/i/bitmap> ipfs add -r .
added QmUViZoR2ZnnpGXyNxRyVp4kpG64kCYgHLp7w3SdmUsRcf bitmap/Makefile
added QmTPTTSvSdwgjGciTH5EgoPdujcrfXvqqSXDUB83uoFhR5 bitmap/Makefile.lib
added QmWFi2rEqobqnz9RZbWrtjNRcftkbRUNmKSoxZxDuMzhDT bitmap/Makefile.orig
added QmZbBUguGknW7wWAkJoZ2XXiDXAsa1zDQgLSuKn7JX7edy bitmap/bitmap_image.hpp
added QmNffnsKcGhNveuEXUuwmLYUqMEW33ZpmY3Xke1oK7Y7Uh bitmap/bitmap_test.cpp
added QmWcuK2svP5qyDaDksvtWanNqDGDoj3CfuqsJXkrKY3MNo bitmap/bitmap_test.js
added QmRwyDerSuwq1VrP56gy28JsXTXyYhPyHxFWH1zctHHe5m bitmap/bitmap_test.wasm
added QmQDwr7R6WxMJgiV4PWkLMJxpzAV8pXhafwfr5omoD93xp bitmap/image.bmp
added Qmdn3WDNXNm94c5FFBPUDq7kdfoeRP8JfgyjAd1BroQFni bitmap/index.html
added QmZcJdVbvZKz9jB8ymAie6nqPLr6iBGQheEUC8bYraFFpB bitmap
 880.83 KiB / 880.83 KiB [===============================================] 100.00%
```

At this point, the directory has an identifier, as do all of the files. Nobody else in the world can see these yet even if they were able to guess the node identity.[13] In order to publish, you need to start an instance of the IPFS Daemon, a background server that communicates with peers and responds to requests from other nodes. It takes a while for everything to start to get synced up, but the result of running the daemon looks something like the following:

```
brian@tweezer ~> ipfs daemon
Initializing daemon...
go-ipfs version: 0.9.1-dc2715af6
Repo version: 11
System version: amd64/darwin
Golang version: go1.16.6
Swarm listening on /ip4/127.0.0.1/tcp/4001
Swarm listening on /ip4/127.0.0.1/udp/4001/quic
Swarm listening on /ip4/169.254.245.235/tcp/4001
Swarm listening on /ip4/169.254.245.235/udp/4001/quic
Swarm listening on /ip4/192.168.1.169/tcp/4001
Swarm listening on /ip4/192.168.1.169/udp/4001/quic
Swarm listening on /ip6/::1/tcp/4001
Swarm listening on /ip6/::1/udp/4001/quic
Swarm listening on /ip6/fd4b:2552:d54e:3:1444:3cef:8a9b:25f3/tcp/4001
Swarm listening on /ip6/fd4b:2552:d54e:3:1444:3cef:8a9b:25f3/udp/4001/quic
Swarm listening on /ip6/fde3:9366:f229:3:18e0:193e:c7d2:8aaa/tcp/4001
Swarm listening on /ip6/fde3:9366:f229:3:18e0:193e:c7d2:8aaa/udp/4001/quic
Swarm listening on /p2p-circuit
Swarm announcing /ip4/127.0.0.1/tcp/4001
Swarm announcing /ip4/127.0.0.1/udp/4001/quic
Swarm announcing /ip4/192.168.1.169/tcp/4001
Swarm announcing /ip4/192.168.1.169/udp/4001/quic
Swarm announcing /ip6/::1/tcp/4001
```

---

13 I would bet against that.

```
Swarm announcing /ip6/::1/udp/4001/quic
API server listening on /ip4/127.0.0.1/tcp/5001
WebUI: http://127.0.0.1:5001/webui
Gateway (readonly) server listening on /ip4/127.0.0.1/tcp/8000
Daemon is ready
```

The strange-looking identifiers show you the power of the Multiformats I mentioned earlier. These are self-describing network references. We have the various ports and protocols that our daemon is listening on to communicate with its peers. We have the ports it is listening on, the IP addresses it is binding to (e.g., localhost or other interface), what network type it is (i.e., ip4 versus ip6), as well as the preferred transport to use to talk to our node. Notice the distinction between TCP and QUIC over UDP. This is an extremely powerful idea that supports resilience, simple interaction models, and extensibility all throughout the technology stack.

The daemon goes out and looks up bootstrap nodes via DNS. It can use Multicast DNS (mDNS) to find other nodes on the same network. There are many ways for it to communicate with the outside world. But, after a few moments, you can find out who it is talking to as follows. I have elided a ton of results, but we see Multiformat network references for the peers, including their node identities and the preferred means to talk to them:

```
brian@tweezer ~/s/ipfs> ipfs swarm peers
/ip4/1.170.45.218/tcp/44262/p2p/QmbsXKVDhxFDgZW6zxrGfgPjXopvhNmGFqqqazv1kyZLkv
/ip4/1.254.1.205/tcp/45622/p2p/QmRePjhxRLWJoAXan79JzvxeUwqW5DyeZbHfxi3y1bSke7
/ip4/101.18.52.217/udp/38214/quic/p2p/12D3KooWBjaFGCZ1heSh4HBy6tsj3i348hDeGZhBnR
/ip4/101.70.141.179/udp/7962/quic/p2p/12D3KooWAwcdxRJbDXcYh4FxrNkarnT1BGmqYTedc1
/ip4/104.131.131.82/udp/4001/quic/p2p/QmaCpDMGvV2BGHeYERUEnRQAwe3N8SzbUtfsmvsqQL
/ip4/104.207.140.198/udp/4001/quic/p2p/12D3KooWFgmp9SgKqGvcE5zEs19iGq16gpMqeV5CY
/ip4/104.236.47.160/tcp/4001/p2p/QmXhDHnhAr1PAE6pK1GbxN1Ez5zmkJHqvSN1GHSgPiuLWP
/ip4/104.238.220.184/tcp/4001/p2p/QmRi2tR7Uf33VmKhGBUNZvFEuCnFwaLLf2FsdYNcLCm4gu
/ip4/104.248.69.187/tcp/4001/p2p/12D3KooWHoqCWMkMuDrauyD6wuJUrPoQfZGPULj99hX94eu
/ip4/107.173.84.101/tcp/4001/p2p/12D3KooWNKQGwEMJXqta2uV2xBSsVrN1jZKd78CF4QossGg
/ip4/107.184.158.170/udp/35299/quic/p2p/12D3KooWQMeiAvzKWGM7V83ENkNqtgJJhdQeQ2xL
/ip4/109.153.171.191/tcp/4001/p2p/12D3KooWK2mqKoGUtZeiJpKCJc3XWLwyk2oC9isNPzvW6f
/ip4/109.194.47.83/tcp/4001/p2p/QmQmfPz9Xn4cNE6vfWcfrozeNDCx9BJFCdRMM3Cnmx2226
/ip4/109.206.48.199/tcp/35317/p2p/QmaY9GdxBY2ovzD1HNhcyBhawTda7gu6QU8rHv6w4pTfqv
/ip4/111.229.166.178/tcp/4001/p2p/12D3KooWAjVr5JL7VgfoNqT8zro2bp9fMKUamF2WAYE4sy
/ip4/111.92.180.99/tcp/53353/p2p/QmYNmBBbzV7AVytNHmVgoHAKd9CvFRWDj32qvHDyjCgJMe
...
```

The daemon does not start publishing files until someone asks for them, but it also starts up a couple of local services. The first is a read-only HTTP gateway on listening on *ip4/127.0.0.1/tcp/8000*. We have been using the IPFS Go command-line tools, but anyone else on our localhost can access this service without regard to those.

As an example, there is a famous picture of a cat in IPFS. You can ask for its details using the command-line tools:

```
brian@tweezer ~/s/ipfs> ipfs ls ↵
    /ipfs/bafybeidsg6t7ici2osxjkukisd5inixiunqdpq2q5jy4a2ruzdf6ewsqk4/cat.jpg
QmPEKipMh6LsXzvtLxunSPP7ZsBM8y9xQ2SQQwBXy5UY6e 262144
QmT8onRUfPgvkoPMdMvCHPYxh98iKCfFkBYM1ufYpnkHJn 181086
```

What you are seeing are the two blocks that are associated with the file. You can also use the local HTTP gateway from the daemon as demonstrated in Figure 16-2. The URL is obscured but there is nothing fancy; the browser is simply requesting a file over HTTP.

Figure 16-2. Requesting files from IPFS via HTTP gateways

The local HTTP gateway is only one. There is also one run by the IPFS project at *https://ipfs.io/ipfs/<CID>* and one run by CloudFlare at *https://cloudflare-ipfs.com/ ipfs/<CID>*. Just replace the CID with the cat image node name and the file name and you should see it there too.

What I just showed you is way cooler than you may realize, as both of those are TLS-terminated endpoints. This means you can request files out of IPFS without anyone knowing what you are asking for by sniffing packets. IPFS is quite successful at routing around censorship. Any attempt to squash one gateway is likely to initiate several more.

Another service the daemon starts is a web application for browsing the node's details and interacting with the platform more naturally. It is listed as the WebUI in the daemon output above and it is located at *http://127.0.0.1:5001/webui*. As bound, only users on the same machine can hit it, but you could configure it to bind to an IP address so any other local network machines could request files without installing any IPFS tools. This application is shown in Figure 16-3.

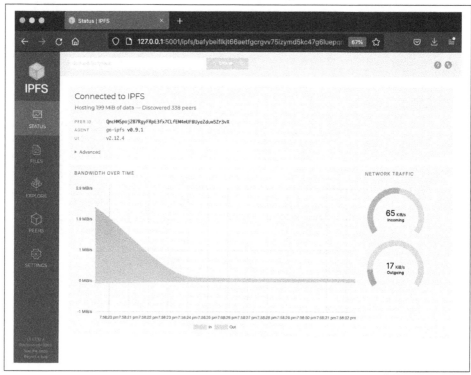

Figure 16-3. Interacting with IPFS via a WebUI

There are a lot of other cool things you can do within the WebUI, but to bring it back to the topic at hand, look closely at the address bar in this window. Port 5001 is serving up a web application...from IPFS:

```
brian@tweezer ~/s/ipfs> ipfs ls ↵
    /ipfs/bafybeiflkjt66aetfgcrgvv75izymd5kc47g6luepqmfq6zsf5w6ueth6y
bafkreigqagdyzmirtqln7dc4qfz5sb7tkdexbzmhwoxzbkma3ka 5324  asset-manifest.json
bafkreihc7efnl2prri6j6krcopelxms3xsh7undpsjqbfsasm7i 34494 favicon.ico
bafkreihmzivzfdhagatgqinzy6u4mfopfldebcc4mvim5rzrdpi 4530  index.html
bafkreicayih3vhhjugxshbar5ylocvcqz4xixuqk6cflyxpnuxf 24008 ipfs-logo-512-ice.png
bafybeiadadzwwymj72nnlyoy6bza4lhps6sofmgmyf6ew5klzwd -     locales/
bafkreicplcott4fe3nnwvz3bidothdtqdvpr5wygbxzoyfozm7t 298   manifest.json
bafybeierqn364ton5lp5ogcu4l22gukzprwieaau7lvcan555n3 -     static/
```

The browser requests the root CID for the directory that the web application is in. *index.html*, as always, is the default file. If you `ipfs cat` that file, you will see that it references the static resources, stylesheets, etc. Somewhere, someone has published this application. It is not being hosted in a conventional sense at a cloud hosting site or anything. I have no direct knowledge of where it originates, but it is being served up locally via an HTTP gateway to my browser.

What about the directory I published earlier with the C++-rendered bitmap files? Because my daemon has been up for a while, other nodes can now ask for that. Check out Figure 16-4 for the gobsmacking result of my application being fronted over TLS by CloudFlare.

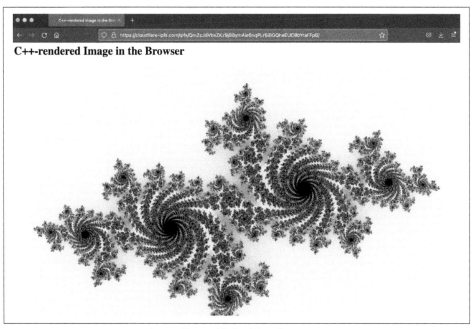

Figure 16-4. Interacting with my files published locally via IPFS HTTP gateways

I am not going to go into any more details, but I want to highlight what else this means. Keep in mind that Merkle DAGs are immutable. If I change my application by modifying one or two files, those are the only things that need to be republished. Remember, publishing is simply adding files to IPFS. Their edits will result in different hashes for their blocks, which means different hashes for the files, which means different hashes for the directory. There is a new top-level CID. But the old one still works. There are games you can play with DNS, but I will leave that for you to discover with the IPFS documentation and tutorials.

What does this have to do with WebAssembly? It is really the intersection of platform benefits that I am highlighting and the implications it will have as another use case. I just demonstrated a web application being served up via a CDN with its geographic distribution without any other hosting needs. It is being served up locally and the results can be cached along the way. This includes C++ code compiled to WebAssembly running in a sandbox on whatever browser or platform you happen to be using. Multiple versions can be supported simultaneously and users can decide when they want to upgrade.

You can serve applications without paying for hosting to arbitrary clients anywhere in the world. You can use whatever language you want to achieve high-performance, interactive systems on whatever platform your users prefer. Customers are comfortable running your applications because of the security protections, and no central authority can easily shut you down.

Tell me that isn't cool.

## CHAPTER 17

WebAssembly and Other Languages

If you talk to a man in a language he understands, that goes to his head. If you talk to him in his own language, that goes to his heart.
—Nelson Mandela

We are getting to the end of our story, at least for now. We have seen a wide range of use cases, language and platform integrations, hosting environments, and more where WebAssembly is shining already. There are quite a few choices for developers to make to be productive and effective with this exciting new platform. There are also concrete reasons why some languages and their associated runtimes work well with WebAssembly and others do not. The lack of garbage collection and good thread support everywhere are among the obstacles that have existed since the early days of the MVP, but both are well on their way to being resolved.

As we saw in Chapter 12, these and other limitations are well understood and increasingly available in various host and runtime environments. The future is bright for much wider support of just about any language developers might like to use. So, please, if your favorite language is not yet supported, keep your chin up. I do not think it will be long before it might be.

That being said, there are incremental efforts, partial solutions, and works in progress for many other popular and even emerging-but-still-somewhat-niche languages that we will address in this chapter. I do not suggest that these are drop-in replacements for the more well-supported languages, but perhaps cracks to let the light in to a brighter polyglot WebAssembly future. As Mandela says in the opening quotation, we can understand many languages, but we love when our own languages are used.

TinyGo

As I mentioned in Chapter 10, I was originally drawn to Go as a systems language to replace C and C++ due to its clean syntax, ties to Unix and Plan 9, and the involvement of Rob Pike and Ken Thompson. When it trailed Rust on support for WebAssembly, my attention waned, but I have always looked forward to the day when that gap would close. We are not there yet, but we are getting much closer thanks to a new variant called TinyGo (*https://tinygo.org*). This project is not specific to WebAssembly, but it is based on a new Go compiler built on the LLVM infrastructure that opens up WebAssembly as a backend.

From the TinyGo FAQ (*https://oreil.ly/SdsjD*), we see that it is a parser based upon the standard library (and thus portable and well supported by various WebAssembly tools such as Emscripten and wasi-sdk) and LLVM for its reusable optimization support. Beyond that, the FAQ indicates that it also includes compiler intrinsics (rules to assist with optimization), a memory allocator, a scheduler, reimplemented common packages, and support for string manipulation.

The "Tiny" portion of TinyGo is a desire to target microcontrollers that are not supported by the conventional Go compiler. Absent the layered architecture of LLVM, adding that kind of support on the backend would be more trouble than it's worth to many developers. LLVM changes the level of effort and therefore opens up all sorts of new possibilities. The other aspect of the regular Go toolchain is that it produces large binaries that are also unsuitable for embedded systems and microcontrollers. The combination of addressing these issues happens to work well in supporting a Go-to-WebAssembly path that is likely to continue to bear fruit and allow Go to be usable in this way.

Given that Rust and Go land in the same space in many people's heads and Rust is also interested in targeting embedded systems with its LLVM-based toolchain, the FAQ goes on to present Go as an option, as it has an admittedly shallower learning curve. It also has thread implementation independent concurrency support via goroutines and channels, and a rich standard library. In Rust, some of those features are supported by dependent Cargo packages. They acknowledge that Rust has its own strengths and advantages, but the larger point is that there is enough demand in the marketplace of ideas to support both languages, so the effort was worth it.

In Figure 17-1, we see the TinyGo Playground in a browser. Hopefully the sneak peek into the runtime `importObject` resonates now that you have learned about WASI and other ways of sharing behavior with WebAssembly runtimes.

Figure 17-1. TinyGo Playground in the browser

If you clone the TinyGo repo (*https://oreil.ly/Nwpag*), there are some examples that highlight interactions that should seem structurally familiar now even if you do not know Go.

If you install the compiler as detailed in the Appendix, you can run the examples. In Example 17-1, you can see the *main.go* file from *examples/wasm/main*.

Example 17-1. Basic TinyGo example

```
package main

func main() {
  println("Hello world!")
}
```

To run the example, you have to execute the following. It builds the named example (e.g., `main`) and then copies the necessary files into an *html* directory. To serve up the contents of that directory, you can run the Go HTTP server:

```
brian@tweezer ~/g/t/s/e/wasm> make main
rm -rf ./html
mkdir ./html
cp ../../../targets/wasm_exec.js ./html/
tinygo build -o ./html/wasm.wasm -target wasm -no-debug ./main/main.go
cp ./main/index.html ./html/
```

```
brian@tweezer ~/g/t/s/e/wasm> go run server.go
2021/08/14 13:49:42 Serving ./html on http://localhost:8080
```

Figure 17-2 demonstrates the unsurprising output from this example.

Figure 17-2. TinyGo main example in the browser

I am not going to replicate the file here, but given what you have seen elsewhere in this book, a perusal of the *wasm_exec.js* file might be of interest to you. The authors of TinyGo have created a common API for invoking Go consistently in browsers, Node.js, Electron applications, and Parcel. You saw a snippet of this file in Figure 17-1.

A more interesting Go example can be found in Example 17-2. Not only do we see more of the Go language in action, we also see the mechanism that they have put in place to interact with the JavaScript environment.

Example 17-2. More interesting Go example

```go
package main

import (
  "strings"
  "syscall/js"
)

func splitter(this js.Value, args []js.Value) interface{} {
  values := strings.Split(args[0].String(), ",")

  result := make([]interface{}, 0)
  for _, each := range values {
    result = append(result, each)
  }

  return js.ValueOf(result)
```

```
}

func main() {
  wait := make(chan struct{}, 0)
  js.Global().Set("splitter", js.FuncOf(splitter))
  <-wait
}
```

The main() method creates a global JavaScript function based on the splitter()
function expressed in the previous example. Running the following invokes the compiler and copies JavaScript files into the *html* directory so this program runs:

```
brian@tweezer ~/g/t/s/e/wasm> make slices
rm -rf ./html
mkdir ./html
cp ../../../targets/wasm_exec.js ./html/
tinygo build -o ./html/wasm.wasm -target wasm -no-debug ./slices/wasm.go
cp ./slices/wasm.js ./html/
cp ./slices/index.html ./html/
```

The copied files include the reusable API in *wasm_exec.js* as before. The *index.html* is
mostly unremarkable, but I show it in Example 17-3 so you can see the input and div
elements.

Example 17-3. Simple HTML file for Go slices example

```
<!DOCTYPE html>

<html>
  <head>
    <meta charset="utf-8"/>
    <title>Go WebAssembly</title>
    <meta name="viewport" content="width=device-width, initial-scale=1"/>
    <script src="wasm_exec.js" defer></script>
    <script src="wasm.js" defer></script>
  </head>
  <body>
    <h1>WebAssembly</h1>
    <p>type values separated by comma, using WebAssembly:</p>
    <input type="text" id="a" value=""/>==<div id="b"></div>
  </body>
</html>
```

As I said, there is not much to this HTML file other than loading the common Go
API I mentioned and the application-specific JavaScript in *wasm.js*. This is shown in
Example 17-4.

Example 17-4. Application-specific JavaScript for the Go slices example

```
'use strict';

const WASM_URL = 'wasm.wasm';

var wasm;

function update() {
  const value = document.getElementById("a").value;
  document.getElementById("b").innerHTML
    = JSON.stringify(window.splitter(value));
}

function init() {
  document.querySelector('#a').oninput = update;

  const go = new Go();
  if ('instantiateStreaming' in WebAssembly) {
    WebAssembly.instantiateStreaming(fetch(WASM_URL),
        go.importObject).then(function (obj) {
          wasm = obj.instance;
          go.run(wasm);
      })
  } else {
    fetch(WASM_URL).then(resp =>
      resp.arrayBuffer()
    ).then(bytes =>
      WebAssembly.instantiate(bytes, go.importObject).then(function (obj) {
        wasm = obj.instance;
        go.run(wasm);
      })
    )
  }
}

init();
```

Other than selecting the streaming or nonstreaming methods of instantiating WebAssembly modules depending on what the environment provides, this code establishes an update() function to invoke when the input field called a changes. The value is sent into the global JavaScript function splitter() on the window instance, which was added from the Go main method. This string will be split on comma-separated boundaries and then sent back to display in the HTML via JavaScript, as shown in Figure 17-3.

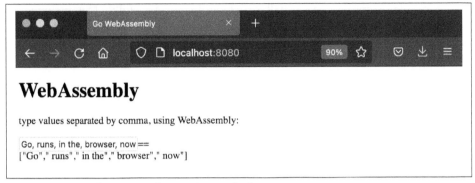

Figure 17-3. Go slices example running in the browser

Obviously, it would be silly to write a WebAssembly module in Go just to split strings like this, but this demo is trying to show you the mechanics of the interaction. I do not think we have seen the final form of Go support for WebAssembly yet, but I am pleased that TinyGo brings this language along as far as it does.

Artichoke

I have long been a fan of the Ruby language. It has a clean syntax and powerful meta-programming capability. It is hard to describe why one language resonates versus another, but Ruby's aesthetic has always appealed to me. Despite this appreciation, I have never really done much with it beyond the occasional Rails project. I remember the excitement everyone felt when Rails first caught the developer community's attention. For a variety of reasons, despite being extremely productive and a well-loved project, performance issues and the need to support another runtime have hampered its world domination. Charles Nutter and the JRuby community (*https://www.jruby.org*) have done a yeoman's job getting Ruby to run on the JVM, but we are now seeing another option emerge in the Artichoke project (*https://artichokeruby.org*).

Artichoke is a Rust-based Ruby runtime environment that is designed to be compatible with Matz's Ruby Interpreter (MRI) (*https://oreil.ly/MOQcO*). It is early days, so I do not want to spend much time on this project, but it seems to be moving quickly and they are looking for contributors, so I wanted to mention it in case you were interested. I would love to see this evolve into a full-throttle way of getting Ruby more fully into WebAssembly environments, as it also supports running untrusted code in a sandboxed environment.

I have detailed some ways to install Artichoke in the Appendix. This includes the Artichoke Ruby interpreter and an irb[1] replacement called airb. For now the easiest way to experiment with this Ruby-to-WebAssembly toolchain is probably through the Playground (*https://artichoke.run*), which can be seen in Figure 17-4.

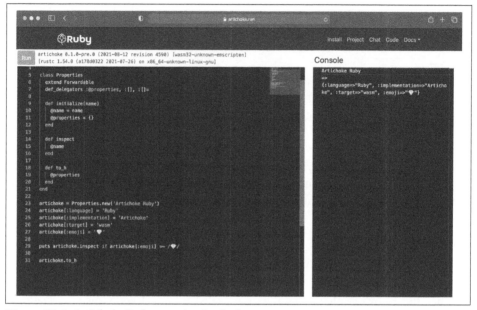

Figure 17-4. Artichoke Ruby running in the browser

As with TinyGo, I do not think this is the end game for Ruby and WebAssembly, but it is real enough that it should give Ruby enthusiasts confidence that at some point in the near future they will be able to participate more fully in the WebAssembly ecosystem.

Swift

The Swift programming language continues to surprise me with its ever widening reach. What seemed initially to be a nice, modern replacement for Objective-C in the macOS and iOS programming world has expanded to be open source, available for server-side development, and a well-supported language for machine learning in the TensorFlow space. It would not be appropriate to classify Swift as officially supporting WebAssembly yet, but, as you will see, it is not far off and I think we will see it in the main toolchain before long.

---

1 The irb (*https://oreil.ly/aCazg*) is an interactive Ruby REPL environment.

Part of the reason it is a natural transition to WebAssembly is because Swift is based upon LLVM like Rust, clang, TinyGo, and many other projects we have discussed. Beyond that, there is a vibrant community interested in seeing these two technologies become more directly compatible.

As per usual, the easiest way to get started playing around at the intersection of Swift and WebAssembly is in the browser. The SwiftWasm webpage (*https://swiftwasm.org*) provides just such an opportunity, as shown in Figure 17-5.

Figure 17-5. SwiftWasm running in the browser

Not only is it possible to execute regular Swift code in the browser, through projects like Tokamak (*https://oreil.ly/4sbDP*), but it is possible to run an increasing number of SwiftUI programs in the browser as well. There is an example of this shown in Figure 17-6.

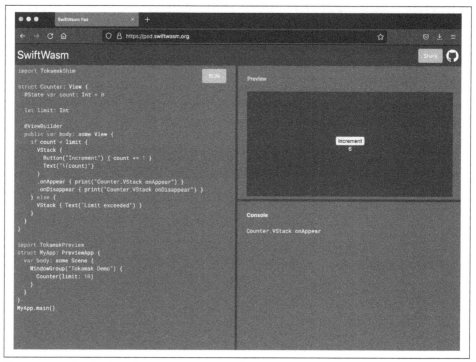

Figure 17-6. SwiftUI application running in the browser

There are many other projects involving Swift and WebAssembly, but one more I wanted to highlight was the Swift, Wasm, and Algorithms project shown in Figure 17-7. This represents an interactive version of the algorithms Apple has added support for at the Swift Algorithms repo (*https://oreil.ly/jKVJg*). This open source package of algorithms focuses on generating sequences, combinations, permutations, and more from collections classes.

The page shown in Figure 17-7 allows users to interactively experiment with the inputs and configurations for these algorithms, which is a great way to learn how they work. By being able to use the Swift code directly, developers can see exactly how it will behave under different circumstances, which is more useful than approximating the libraries by rewriting them in JavaScript.

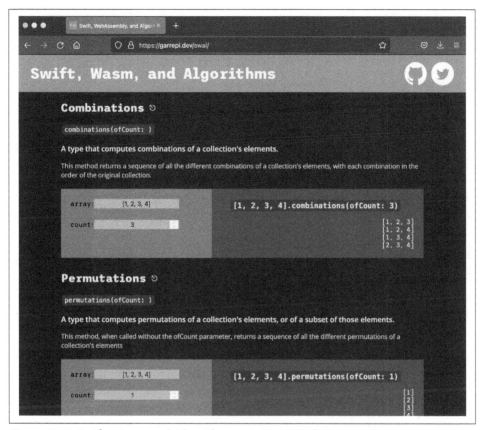

Figure 17-7. Swift, Wasm, and Algorithms as interactive documentation

While the browser-based demos are fun and easy to show off, it will be more interesting to try our hand at more conventional programming. If you install the SwiftWasm toolchain as described in the Appendix, you should be able to run the following commands on macOS or Linux to verify that you have the WebAssembly-aware version of the Swift compiler installed:

```
brian@tweezer ~> swift --version
SwiftWasm Swift version 5.3 (swiftlang-5.3.1)
Target: x86_64-apple-darwin20.6.0
```

In Example 17-5, we have our usual introductory program expressed in Swift.

Example 17-5. "Hello, world!" in Swift

```
print("Hello, world!")
```

We can generate a WASI-targeted version of the program as follows and notably run it in both Wasmer and Wasmtime, which highlights how good the support is already:

```
brian@tweezer ~/s/swift> swiftc -target wasm32-unknown-wasi hello.swift ↵
  -o hello.wasm
brian@tweezer ~/s/swift> wasmer hello.wasm
Hello, world!
brian@tweezer ~/s/swift> wasmtime hello.wasm
Hello, world!
```

There are limitations to what is possible with this integration at the moment. Much of the functionality that the Swift standard library depends upon is not yet available because standard threading support in WebAssembly is still a moving target. Hopefully you can see that we are well on our way to having proper Swift support for WebAssembly, though, both in and outside the browser.

Java

It seems inconceivable that Java is on this list of undersupported languages and runtimes, but alas, it is true. Java's reliance on garbage collection and threads are among the biggest reasons this is still the case. As these proposals advance, things will obviously change, but for now we have a limited number of options.

The first option allows us to embed WebAssembly in Java with Wasmer as we have seen for other languages. That is clearly not the same thing as compiling Java to run on a WebAssembly platform, but it is a start. It depends on the Wasmer library and Java Native Interface (JNI) to load, but it is straightforward enough overall. The basic structure is shown in Example 17-6.

Example 17-6. Our howOld function being called from Java via Wasmer

```
import org.wasmer.Instance;

import java.io.IOException;
import java.nio.file.Files;
import java.nio.file.Paths;

class HowOldExample {
  public static void main(String[] args) throws IOException {
    byte[] bytes = Files.readAllBytes(Paths.get("howold.wasm"));
    Instance instance = new Instance(bytes);

    Function howOld = instance.exports.getFunction("howOld");
    Integer result = (Integer) howOld.apply(2021, 2000)[0];

    System.out.println("Result: " + result);

    instance.close();
```

```
    }
}
```

There is nothing substantially different from what we have seen so far with respect to the Wasmer API. We instantiate an instance of a WebAssembly module, retrieve a Function instance, and invoke it with our parameters. In the *wasmer-java/examples* directory (*https://oreil.ly/RT0RY*), there are additional demonstrations on how to interact with exported Memory instances.

The Bytecode Alliance does not presently maintain Java APIs for interacting with the Wasmtime runtime, but there are community-supported versions available on Git-Hub from Yuto Kawamura (*https://oreil.ly/drnQ9*) and Benjamin Fry (*https://oreil.ly/HH3Xs*). They behave much like the Wasmtime APIs we saw in Rust and .NET in previous chapters.

Another similar option is to use GraalVM, a high-performance JDK distribution that provides support for polyglot development and near-native performance to the Java world. With additional support it is possible to run Python, Ruby, R, JavaScript, WebAssembly, and LLVM-based languages through the LLVM JIT engine. Not only is it possible to write these languages, but it is also possible to have them interoperate. There is a similar API from the GraalVM community for instantiating WebAssembly modules and invoking them from Java, which is substantively equivalent to what we just did. Given the polyglot interoperability, I would concede that it is a step closer to supporting Java and WebAssembly more fully, but it is still not a full solution. Until there is proper, standardized garbage collection and thread support in the WebAssembly ecosystem, it is not going to be straightforward to run Java in this way.

Once this does happen, and we see additional improvements in the WebAssembly runtimes from a performance and optimization perspective, then we will start to see organizations question the need for a JVM and a WebAssembly engine in production. Java itself will not go away, but I can see a scenario in the future where people are fine with a single runtime of comingled software whether it is using GraalVM or a WebAssembly engine.

While Java is not a fully supported language yet, it does not mean there is not a strategy toward adoption. The company Leaning Technologies has a commercial offering called CheerpJ (*https://oreil.ly/nWfY2*) that has some impressive results. The solution is a combination of ahead-of-time compilation, a WebAssembly and JavaScript runtime, and the ability to do dynamic compilation on the fly. I will let you investigate its offering on your own, but you can see the remarkable achievement of running the SwingSet3 demo in the browser in Figure 17-8. This will not represent the ultimate integration strategy from Java and WebAssembly, but if you have a need now to support legacy systems in the browser, it might be an option.

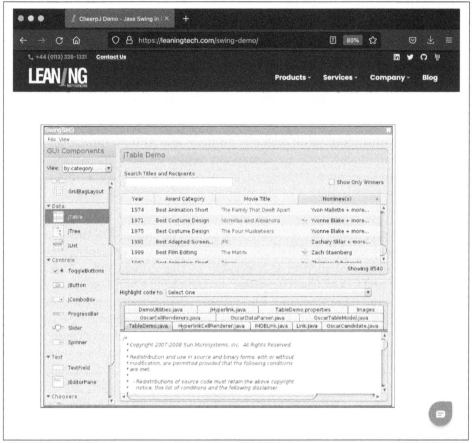

Figure 17-8. The SwingSet3 demo running in a browser via CheerpJ

Kotlin

Kotlin reminds me of the old *Saturday Night Live* ad parody for Shimmer, the combination floor wax and dessert topping.[2] As a language and a runtime, there are so many things it can be, it feels like it falls into multiple categories simultaneously. It can be used to target applications on the JVM, it transpiles to JavaScript to run in the browser, it has a scripting side to its list of identities, and it can generate native applications on iOS and Android via an LLVM compiler.

What it is, undoubtedly, is popular. Different organizations use it for different reasons, but it combines many different language features to create a concise and safe

---

2 NBC is protecting the video, but you can listen to the skit on YouTube (*https://oreil.ly/T76sT*).

industrial-strength object-oriented programming language. It has been adopted as the preferred language for developing Android applications as well as a fully supported language for superstar open source projects such as Spring and Gradle.

Along the way, its developers experimented with generating WebAssembly through its LLVM compiler. As of now, they are deprecating that approach for a more fully supported backend to handle Kotlin to WebAssembly directly. This is definitely a work in progress as they were forming a new team to manage this and trying to staff it up in May 2021.

You can still use the kotlinc-native wasm32 backend to experiment if you like, but that is not going to be a long-term strategy. So, while there are great things in the plans for the pairing between these languages, we must take a wait-and-see approach for the time being.

Zig

It will not surprise me to hear that you might have never heard of Zig, or if you have, only in passing. My favorite anecdote about it is that Jakub Konka, a well-respected software and researcher into algorithms and compiler theory, learned Zig while waiting for a Rust compile to finish.[3] It is a funny story that gets to poke fun at the notoriously slow Rust compiler while also giving you a suggestive hint about what Zig brings to the table.[4]

First of all, as indicated by the story, Zig is a simple language. The website (*https:// ziglang.org*) suggests that your time is better spent debugging your applications rather than your knowledge of programming languages. Complex programming languages are hard to learn and hard to be effective with until you have mastered them over years. Zig has no hidden control flow, no hidden memory allocations, and neither a preprocessor nor a macro system. Its entire syntax is captured in a 500-line parsing expression grammar file.

The functional design aesthetic is captured in the main documentation webpage. It is precisely that: a single page. It is a long, easily searchable file that also functions nicely offline.

Do not confuse Zig's avoidance of flimflammery with a restricted feature set. Zig is a fast, portable language that supports cross-compilation for targeting multiple platforms, a wide range of safety and optimization options, direct support for SIMD vectorization, and much, much more.

---

3 Jakub's hands have been all over WASI, witx, Wasmtime, and more (*http://www.jakubkonka.com*).

4 Although to be fair, it is because Rust is doing so much and has gotten much better over time.

What I am hoping to stress here is not that you need to learn Zig, although it is high on my list of new languages to master. Instead, I want you to think more about the fact that languages bring some amount of value to the table while runtimes bring other types of value. We have imagined a variety of use cases throughout the book that involve anything from reusing legacy libraries to writing safe, modern code that eliminates some runtime errors by turning them into compile time errors. We have a range of options in choosing a language in which to express our application and systems functionality. And, increasingly, we do not need to worry that our niche little language can never be used because it lacks a well-supported runtime platform. I indicated earlier that I thought it was the Ruby runtime that cast a shadow over the developer love affair with Ruby's productivity. These kinds of choices no longer seem to be the showstoppers that they might have been in the past.

Through various API styles, we can connect clients written in one language to services written in another. By adopting loose coupling in the responses (e.g., hypermedia, JSON-LD, etc.), we have the freedom to vary one or the other without impacting either in many cases. Architectural approaches like microservices allow for even more decentralized governance in technology choice as long as it does not put a burden on our operational runtimes and deployment strategies. As WebAssembly modules can officially be consumed as ES6 modules in the near future, there will be even less concern about the language that a software artifact is built in.

I think it is important to highlight that WebAssembly helps manage many of these trade-offs by turning them into not-trade-offs. When you have the freedom to pick a language you love, that is a good match to the problem, that leverages existing developer training and experience, or that allows for longer-term business value capture and reuse, then so many of the big problems we have faced in the past simply evaporate moving forward.

This is not to say that there are not issues in supporting a polyglot language environment. You will want to exercise some amount of oversight in technology choice so that errant developers do not thrust their weird preferences on their peers and then quit. But, if they do, you have the freedom to continue to use their code as long as it works until you have the chance to swap it out.

Whether it is avoiding calcified legacy technology lock-in, insufficient reuse, or roadblocks toward modernization, WebAssembly is well poised to add business value widely and deeply in technology infrastructures. If that means developing business applications in C# and .NET or writing sophisticated modern algorithms in a language like Zig, all of these use cases are on the table. That is worth highlighting more than once because it cuts to the core of the point of this book.

While we certainly are not going to motivate the strengths of Zig in our well-trodden example, it will at least highlight the mechanics to experiment on your own should you get the Zig bug. You will find a Zig version of our howOld() function in

Example 17-7. It does not look substantially different from what we have seen before, but how hard is subtracting one integer from another, really?

Example 17-7. Our howOld function written in Zig

```
export fn howOld(now: i32, then: i32) i32 {
  return now - then;
}
```

Building our example as a "freestanding" WebAssembly module (as opposed to, say, a WASI-targeting one) looks like the following. Do not blink or you might miss the compilation step:

```
brian@tweezer ~/g/w/s/c/zig> zig build-lib howOld.zig ↵
  -target wasm32-freestanding -dynamic
```

We can invoke our new module in a variety of ways, but for something different, let's use the Node.js code in Example 17-8.

Example 17-8. Calling our Zig module from Node.js

```
const fs = require('fs');
const source = fs.readFileSync("./howOld.wasm");
const typedArray = new Uint8Array(source);

WebAssembly.instantiate(typedArray).then(result => {
  const howOld = result.instance.exports.howOld;
  let age = howOld(2021, 2000);
  console.log('You are: ' + age);
});
```

Running this gives the following:

```
brian@tweezer ~/g/w/s/c/zig> node main.js
You are: 21
```

A more interesting example is shown in Example 17-9, which is taken from the Zig website and highlights its WASI support. In this case, we demonstrate the use of capabilities-based security and controlled access to the command line and filesystem by printing out which directories our code has access to as a list of preopens to the runtime.

Example 17-9. A WASI-targeted Zig application using console and potentially filesystem access

```
const std = @import("std");
const PreopenList = std.fs.wasi.PreopenList;

pub fn main() !void {
```

```
var general_purpose_allocator = std.heap.GeneralPurposeAllocator(.{}){};
const gpa = &general_purpose_allocator.allocator;

var preopens = PreopenList.init(gpa);
defer preopens.deinit();

try preopens.populate();

for (preopens.asSlice()) |preopen, i| {
  std.debug.print("{}: {}\n", .{ i, preopen });
  }
}
```

I am not going to go through the Zig-specific details, but basically we are simply printing out what directories we have preopen access to based upon capabilities awarded us by our host environment. Building this application requires a different back-end target. Rather than the "freestanding" WebAssembly module, we will produce a WASI-based one.

The first line in this next example obviously builds the WASI-module. The second one executes it in Wasmtime without giving it access to any directories. Consequently, there is no output. The third line reexecutes Wasmtime with permission to the current directory, which the application is now able to acknowledge:

```
brian@tweezer ~/g/w/s/c/zig> zig build-exe preopens.zig -target wasm32-wasi
brian@tweezer ~/g/w/s/c/zig> wasmtime preopens.wasm
brian@tweezer ~/g/w/s/c/zig> wasmtime --dir=. preopens.wasm
0: Preopen{ .fd = 3, .type = PreopenType{ .Dir = '@"."' } }
```

I am not trying to sell you on Zig.[5] Instead, I am trying to reinforce one of the major themes of this book. WebAssembly is a remarkably value-amplifying technology. Being able to pick a language because it is legacy and therefore useful to reuse or because it is new, exciting, and adds new benefits while being able to target the full menagerie of runtimes we have discussed is quite the achievement.

If you would like to have a little more fun with Zig, check out this implementation of the popular video game *Tetris* written in Zig and using WebGL (*https://oreil.ly/9tzBP*).

Grain

The final language I am going to cover is certainly not the final language that can generate WebAssembly. There are many others we have not had an opportunity to pursue. Instead, I picked a language that is unique from all of the others we have discussed in that it was designed to emit WebAssembly while also being a vehicle for popularizing exciting and exotic new academic language features.

---

5 Although if I have piqued your interest, "Sorry, not sorry."

The Grain language (*https://grain-lang.org*) is young but promising and merges functional benefits, strong-typing, and language accessibility. Many functional programming languages are tremendously powerful, but they also seem arcane and not intended for typical developers. It is nice to see these features show up in developer-friendly languages such as Java (post–JDK 8), Rust, and now Grain. Despite this adoption of the functional style, it is not unnecessarily pure, however, and also supports mutable variables. Balancing type inferencing with a rich standard library of composite structures, direct support for WebAssembly primitives, and the pattern-matching capabilities of Rust are among its chief charms.

The website has great documentation about setting up VS Code with a Grain extension for an all-around positive developer experience. My purpose here is not necessarily to teach you Grain. I will let the online resources and Grain community do that. Instead, I just wanted to end with the idea that language innovation does not have to occur in a vacuum. It is entirely likely that other new programming languages will be designed with WebAssembly in mind. Having a path forward with continuous innovation that is easy to adopt is yet another reminder that we are not dealing with the technology choices of the past.

We can build a future where language and runtime and hardware platform and API style and data model and storage system choices can be unified into a comprehensive vision of technical and business value.

But that, my friends, is probably my next book.

And Then?

There you have it. We have covered tremendous ground in this book, from the basics of the MVP with its low-level details, to the transition out of the browser into WASI-based environments. We have seen remarkably large and sophisticated software projects compiled to WebAssembly, sometimes using shims and shortcuts to deal with the platform limitations. We have also seen the active pace of the new proposals that seek to extend WebAssembly into just about every nook and cranny of our complex, heterogeneous, and ever-changing world of modern software.

And now, we have concluded with a quick survey of how support for WebAssembly is being added nearly across the board to our favorite programming languages in one form or another. It is also being adopted by and driving the features of exciting new languages. It seems like it is becoming an expectation that all of these languages will want to emit WebAssembly output to lay claim to their portion of the future.

Some of the inertia so far has been awareness, but there is now a growing consensus that WebAssembly will have far-reaching impacts at making our software safe, fast, and portable. Where there are limitations and omissions, these are generally being overcome and closed quickly both by extending the platform and by developing tool-chains that protect us from annoying minutiae.

I started talking about WebAssembly professionally on the No Fluff Just Stuff tour (*https://nofluffjuststuff.com*) in early 2017, just after the MVP had been finalized and browser support was becoming ubiquitous. That was clearly well before most people were ready to take advantage of this emerging platform, but I wanted to start painting a picture of what was coming so software developers could be prepared.

I have never become less excited about what this platform has in store for us; my interest has only grown. As you evaluate the various tools, technologies, and use cases we have alighted upon in this book, I hope you have caught at least some of that excitement. Things will continue to change on a weekly basis, but I hope that the majority of what I have written about is stable and worthy of your time.

I thank you for your attention and I cannot wait to see what you do with what you have learned.

Installing WebAssembly Tools

Technology is nothing. What's important is that you have a faith in people, that they're basically good and smart, and if you give them tools, they'll do wonderful things with them.
—Steve Jobs

It is unsurprising, given all of the languages, tools, and frameworks that we discuss in this book, that there is a fair amount to install. This appendix will not be comprehensive, but will try to point you in the right direction to getting everything going. Some of the tools are easier to install on Linux or macOS, but most should work on Windows too.

Installing WebAssembly Binary Toolkit (WABT)

The WebAssembly Binary Toolkit (WABT) provides a suite of tools for converting things to and from the various formats we have discussed as well as several others. It includes tools for dumping out details about the modules, validating their structures, and more.

There are quite good instructions on the GitHub repo for building on all three major operating systems, so there is no point in replicating that here. The repo is located here: *https://github.com/WebAssembly/wabt*

One thing I did want to point out was that some of the tools are also available online. It shouldn't be too surprising that WebAssembly tools might also run in the browser. If you want to try converting formats without installing the tools, you can try them out here: *https://webassembly.github.io/wabt/demo*

Additionally, there is a spin-off project called Wabt.js that allows you to use much of the functionality from the toolkit in the browser. Its GitHub repository is here: *https://github.com/AssemblyScript/wabt.js*

Installing LLVM

LLVM looks like it would stand for something, but it doesn't. It's just the name for an exceptionally cool modular compiler architecture that serves as the basis for languages such as Rust, Swift, Julia, and many more.

LLVM is able to emit platform-specific codes even for different platforms if you install the correct tooling. It is also useful for experimenting with optimizations, running the intermediate form in a virtual machine, and producing WebAssembly.

I highly recommend you install LLVM through one of the installers rather than building it from scratch, as it takes forever and consumes an obscene amount of disk space. Depending on your OS, you may already have a version installed. The macOS toolchain is LLVM-based, but that version does not yet interoperate with WebAssembly.

The main website is here: *https://llvm.org*

There are installers for most major operating systems, so you should not have difficulty finding one that will work.

Installing Emscripten

The Emscripten toolchain is a set of tools that wrap the LLVM tools. Originally it emitted asm.js, but now it supports WebAssembly directly. In addition to assisting with compiling existing C and C++ code, it has drop-in replacements for other command-line tools for building software such as Make and configure.

With its macros and compiler directives, it is fairly straightforward to simplify communicating between JavaScript host environments in the browser or Node.js. It has support for widely used dependencies like the standard library and OpenGL.

The Getting Started guide has good instructions for multiple operating systems, so your best bet will be to investigate this site: *https://emscripten.org/docs/getting_started/index.html*

Installing Wasm3

Wasm3 bills itself as "the fastest WebAssembly interpreter, and the most universal runtime." The GitHub repo is here: *https://github.com/wasm3/wasm3*

Given the variety of platforms it runs on and languages it works with, I am not going to challenge them on that. It currently runs on:

- Linux, Windows, macOS, FreeBSD, Android, iOS
- OpenWrt, Yocto, Buildroot (network equipment)

- Raspberry Pi and other single-board computers
- A variety of microcontrollers
- Most modern browsers

It is also doing a good job of tracking the various new proposals.

It is easy enough to build from source, but there are several installers documented here: *https://github.com/wasm3/wasm3/blob/main/docs/Installation.md*

I also encourage you to check out the helpful cookbook here: *https://github.com/wasm3/wasm3/blob/main/docs/Cookbook.md*

Installing Wasmtime

Wasmtime was originally a Mozilla project but is maintained by the Bytecode Alliance these days, which refers to it as "a standalone wasm-only optimizing runtime for WebAssembly and WASI."

It is one of the most up-to-date runtimes for the various proposals and has an extensive set of programmatic libraries, as you have seen throughout the book.

There is quite extensive documentation here: *https://docs.wasmtime.dev*

You can find installation instructions here: *https://docs.wasmtime.dev/cli-install.html*

Installing Wasmer

Wasmer was one of the first nonbrowser and non-Node.js WebAssembly runtimes I encountered. It predated WASI but quickly added support.

The main website for Wasmer is: *https://wasmer.io*

In addition to being a standalone runtime, it has integration support for:

- Rust
- C and C++
- JavaScript
- Go
- Python
- PHP
- Ruby

It also maintains the WebAssembly Package Manager (WAPM), WebAssembly.sh, and the Wasienv toolkit.

A great place for getting started and installing the runtime is the excellent documentation here: *https://docs.wasmer.io/ecosystem/wasmer/getting-started*

Installing Rust Tools

Rust clearly has a big place in the WebAssembly ecosystem, but it has a lot to speak of on its own as a safe, fast programming language that is rapidly growing in adoption.

The main website is: *https://rust-lang.org*

You will generally want to use the rustup tool for managing your Rust toolchain. It supports nightly, beta, and stable versions. Based upon your own level of comfort or a desire for the latest and greatest features, you can quickly and easily switch between the various channels that are installed. It is easy to install multiple channels whenever you want. It is also possible to install backends for other architectures if you are interested in cross-compiling.

Start by installing the rustup toolchain documented here: *https://www.rust-lang.org/tools/install*

To generate WebAssembly directly, you will have to install the backend. You can pick whichever channel you want, but to install the nightly WebAssembly backend, you would do this:

```
~/s/r/wasm> rustup target add wasm32-unknown-unknown --toolchain nightly
```

To use the backend when compiling Rust, you would do something like this if you did not make it the default toolchain:

```
~/s/r/wasm> rustc +nightly --target wasm32-unknown-unknown ↵
    -O --crate-type=cdylib add.rs -o add.wasm
```

To generate WASI code, you will want the WASI backend installed:

```
~/s/r/wasm> rustup target add wasm32-wasi --toolchain nightly
```

To use it if it is not the default toolchain:

```
~/s/r/wasm> rustc hello.rs --target wasm32-wasi
```

Notice that the regular Rust native backend, regular WebAssembly, and WASI backends are distinct depending on what you want to target.

If you want to interact seamlessly between Rust and JavaScript, you will probably want to install wasm-bindgen.

An excellent introduction to the tool is here: *https://rustwasm.github.io/wasm-bindgen*

With the Rust tools installed, you should be able to install it with:

```
~/s/rust> cargo install -f wasm-bindgen-cli
```

Installing .NET Tools

As you have seen in the book, .NET has become a robust WebAssembly environment, particularly now that it is cross-platform.

The good news is that it is a piece of cake to install. The instructions for the major operating systems are located here: *https://dotnet.microsoft.com/download*

Once those are installed, you should be able to run the command-line examples we featured in the book.

Installing AssemblyScript

AssemblyScript is emerging as a strong player in the WebAssembly world. It strikes a nice balance between the past and the future. You do not have to learn C or C++ code and can stay in a somewhat familiar language space while still producing higher-performance software.

The main website is here: *https://www.assemblyscript.org*

Installation instructions are here: *https://www.assemblyscript.org/quick-start.html*

Installing IPFS

The InterPlanetary File System (IPFS) is not directly related to WebAssembly, but as a key player in the decentralized space there are several places they intersect. I highlighted one example in the book.

If you would like to find out more about the project, the website is here: *https://ipfs.io*

You have some choices for installation, which are detailed here: *https://ipfs.io/#install*

Installing TinyGo

As I indicated in the last chapter, TinyGo is emerging as a nice starting point for the integration between Go and WebAssembly in addition to its support for microcontrollers and other embedded systems.

The main website is here: *https://tinygo.org*

Instructions for installing on various operating systems or Docker are available here: *https://tinygo.org/getting-started/install*

Installing Artichoke

Artichoke is a compelling beginning of getting Ruby to the WebAssembly party. It is still early days but, as I mentioned, they are looking for contributors.

You can find installation instructions here: *https://www.artichokeruby.org/install*

Installing SwiftWasm

SwiftWasm is also in early stages but shows a lot of promise for this increasingly interesting language that has escaped its macOS origins. There are a variety of installation options available here: *https://book.swiftwasm.org/getting-started/setup.html*

Installing Zig and Grain

Zig and Grain are both compelling new languages that I am very interested in digging into. While they are not widely used by any stretch of the imagination, interest in them is growing. The fact that they have strong emerging WebAssembly strategies is likely to amplify their impact quickly since you will not need new runtime tooling in many circumstances.

Even though they are separate and unrelated, I have bundled them together because I think they serve similar roles and are at similar places.

I encourage you to dig in further to both.

Zig is available here: *https://ziglang.org/download*

Grain is available here: *https://grain-lang.org/docs/getting_grain*

Index

Istio, 184

J

K

L

About the Author

Brian Sletten is a liberal arts–educated software engineer with a focus on forward-leaning technologies. His experience has spanned many industries including retail, banking, online games, defense, finance, hospitality, and health care. He has a BS in computer science from the College of William and Mary and lives in Auburn, CA. He focuses on web architecture, resource-oriented computing, social networking, the Semantic Web, data science, 3D graphics, visualization, scalable systems, security consulting, and other technologies of the late 20th and early 21st centuries. He is also a rabid reader, devoted foodie, and has excellent taste in music. If pressed, he might tell you about his international pop recording career.

Colophon

The animal on the cover of *WebAssembly: The Definitive Guide* is a Norwich terrier. These fearless, active, and affectionate litte dogs were popular among students at Cambridge University in the 1870s, who kept them as pets and dorm-room ratters. In the US, the Norwich found success hunting both vermin and foxes as their small size allowed them to follow the creatures into their dens where foxhounds couldn't.

The Norwich terrier was first recognized as a breed by the American Kennel Club in 1936. Their stocky bodies stand only 10 inches tall at the shoulders and weigh about 12 pounds, making them one of the smallest terrier breeds. They are described as having a "slightly foxy expression" with small, dark eyes and prick ears with pointed tips. The Norwich's wiry topcoat can be any shade of red, grizzle (black or red hairs mixed with white), wheaten, or black and tan, with a soft, downy undercoat for insulation. Norwich terriers are closely related to the Norfolk terrier, which was considered the drop-ear version of the Norwich for many years—they were only recognized as a separate breed by the AKC in 1979.

The Norwich typically lives 10 to 14 years and, like most terriers, they are high-energy dogs that require daily exercise or tasks to keep them happy. While they are much more social than other working terrier breeds and get along well with other dogs, they do have a strong prey drive and may chase cats, other small pets, or anything they perceive as "prey." As a result, Norwich terriers should always be kept on-leash when outside the home or in an unfenced area. They can be loyal family pets, but need early socialization and careful supervision around small children.

Many of the animals on O'Reilly covers are endangered; all of them are important to the world.

The cover illustration is by Karen Montgomery. The cover fonts are Gilroy Semibold and Guardian Sans. The text font is Adobe Minion Pro; the heading font is Adobe Myriad Condensed; and the code font is Dalton Maag's Ubuntu Mono.

O'REILLY®

There's much more
where this came from.

Experience books, videos, live online
training courses, and more from O'Reilly
and our 200+ partners—all in one place.

Learn more at oreilly.com/online-learning